❧ Literature for Listening

AN ORAL INTERPRETER'S ANTHOLOGY

◄ Literature for Listening

AN ORAL INTERPRETER'S ANTHOLOGY

Letters - Short Stories - Poetry - Drama - Essays

KEITH BROOKS
Dept. of Speech, The Ohio State University

EUGENE BAHN
Dept. of Speech, Wayne State University

L. LaMONT OKEY
Dept. of Speech, The University of Michigan

ALLYN AND BACON, INC.   BOSTON

To those who follow
With every hope for renewed inspiration . . .

CRAIG WILLIAM and TODD RANDALL
NAN, LINTON, MARGARET, DAVID and MARTEL
CYNTHIA ANE and PER LaMONT

Printed in the United States of America.

Library of Congress catalog card number: 68-26730

✥ Preface

LITERATURE FOR LISTENING is an anthology of letters, short stories, poetry, drama, and essays for sharing aloud. It is predicated on the firm belief that activating a literary experience through the social and behavioral interaction of an oral interpreter and a listener insures the richest and most lasting involvement in our literary heritage.

It should be recognized that literature is action-oriented and that the function of the oral interpreter is to *discover* and *share* this action. This process—the communicative act of oral interpretation—is accomplished only as there is a union among the component parts: the literature, the interpreter, and the listener. Without this union, the act of sharing and your understanding and appreciation of literature are incomplete.

As an oral interpreter of literature you are an uncommon literary critic. You are unique. You are the only literary critic whose analysis is but a means to an end—that end being a synthesis through vocal and physical suggestion. Furthermore, your uniqueness as a literary critic includes a social responsibility—an obligation to involve your listener in your judgments of the intent of the literature.

LITERATURE FOR LISTENING challenges you to *share* the great thoughts of the great writers. May this anthology be but a beginning!

K.B.
E.B.
L.L.O.

❧ Contents

LETTERS

SHORT STORIES

POETRY

DRAMA

ESSAYS

❧ Literature for Listening

AN ORAL INTERPRETER'S ANTHOLOGY

Letters

PLINY THE YOUNGER

Pliny the Younger, born about 61 A.D., poet and critic, is one of the well-known letter writers of ancient Rome. This letter gives a graphic description of the eruption of Mount Vesuvius.

TO CORNELIUS TACITUS

The letter which, in compliance with your request, I wrote to you concerning the death of my uncle, has raised, you say, your curiosity to know not only what terrors, but what calamities I endured when left behind at Misenum (for there I broke off my narrative).

"Though my shock'd soul recoils, my tongue shall tell."

My uncle having set out, I gave the rest of the day to study—the object which had kept me at home. After which I bathed, dined, and retired to short and broken slumbers. There had been for several days before some shocks of earthquake, which the less alarmed us as they are frequent in Campania; but that night they became so violent that one might think that the world was not being merely shaken, but turned topsy-turvy. My mother flew to my chamber; I was just rising, meaning on my part to awaken her, if she was asleep. We sat down in the forecourt of the house, which separated it by a short space from the sea. I know not whether I should call it courage or inexperience—I was not quite eighteen—but I called for a volume of Livy, and began to read, and even went on with the extracts I was making from it, as if nothing were the matter. Lo and behold, a friend of my uncle's, who was just come to him from Spain, appears on the scene; observing my mother and me seated, and that I have actually a book in my hand, he sharply censures her patience and my indifference; nevertheless I still went on intently with my author.

It was now six o'clock in the morning, the light still ambiguous and faint. The buildings around us already tottered, and though we stood upon open ground, yet as the place was narrow and confined, there was certain and formidable danger from their collapsing. It was not till then we resolved to quit the town. The common people follow us in the utmost consternation, preferring the judgement of others to their own (wherein the extreme of fear resembles prudence), and impel us onwards by pressing in a crowd upon our rear. Being got outside the houses, we halt in the midst of a most strange and dreadful scene. The coaches which we had ordered out, though upon the most level ground, were sliding to and fro, and could not be kept steady even when stones were put against the wheels. Then we

3

beheld the sea sucked back, and as it were repulsed by the convulsive motion of the earth; it is certain at least the shore was considerably enlarged, and now held many sea-animals captive on the dry sand. On the other side, a black and dreadful cloud bursting out in gusts of igneous serpentine vapour now and again yawned open to reveal long fantastic flames, resembling flashes of lightning but much larger.

Our Spanish friend already mentioned now spoke with more warmth and instancy: "If your brother—if your uncle," said he, "is yet alive, he wishes you both may be saved; if he has perished, it was his desire that you might survive him. Why therefore do you delay your escape?" We could never think of our own safety, we said, while we were uncertain of his. Without more ado our friend hurried off, and took himself out of danger at the top of his speed.

Soon afterwards, the cloud I have described began to descend upon the earth, and cover the sea. It had already begirt the hidden Capreae, and blotted from sight the promontory of Misenum. My mother now began to beseech, exhort, and command me to escape as best I might; a young man could do it; she, burdened with age and corpulency, would die easy if only she had not caused my death. I replied, I would not be saved without her, and taking her by the hand, I hurried her on. She complies reluctantly and not without reproaching herself for retarding me. Ashes now fall upon us, though as yet in no great quantity. I looked behind me; gross darkness pressed upon our rear, and came rolling over the land after us like a torrent. I proposed while we yet could see, to turn aside, lest we should be knocked down in the road by the crowd that followed us and trampled to death in the dark. We had scarce sat down, when darkness overspread us, not like that of a moonless or cloudy night, but of a room when it is shut up, and the lamp put out. You could hear the shrieks of women, the crying of children, and the shouts of men; some were seeking their children, others their parents, others their wives or husbands, and only distinguishing them by their voices; one lamenting his own fate, another that of his family; some praying to die, from the very fear of dying; many lifting their hands to the gods; but the greater part imagining that there were no gods left anywhere, and that the last and eternal night was come upon the world.

There were even some who augmented the real perils by imaginary terrors. Newcomers reported that such or such a building at Misenum had collapsed or taken fire—falsely, but they were credited. By degrees it grew lighter; which we imagined to be rather the warning of approaching fire (as in truth it was) than the return of day: however, the fire stayed at a distance from us: then again came darkness, and a heavy shower of ashes; we were obliged every now and then to rise and shake them off, otherwise we should have been buried and even crushed under their weight. I might have boasted that amidst dangers so appalling, not a sigh or expression of fear escaped from me, had not my support been founded in that miserable, though strong consolation, that all mankind were involved in the same calamity, and that I was perishing with the world itself.

At last this dreadful darkness was attenuated by degrees to a kind of cloud or smoke, and passed away; presently the real day returned, and even the sun appeared, though lurid as when an eclipse is in progress. Every object that presented itself to our yet affrighted gaze was changed, cover'd over with a drift of ashes, as with snow. We returned to Misenum, where we refreshed ourselves as well as we could, and passed an anxious night between hope and fear; though indeed with a much larger share of the latter, for the earthquake still continued, and several enthusiastic people were giving a grotesque turn to their own and their neighbours' calamities by terrible predictions. Even then, however, my mother and I, notwithstanding the danger we had passed, and that which still threatened us, had no thoughts of leaving the place, till we should receive some tidings of my uncle.

And now, you will read this narrative, so far beneath the dignity of a history, without any view of transferring it to your own; and indeed you must impute it to your own request, if it shall appear scarce worthy of a letter. FAREWELL.

QUEEN ELIZABETH I*

This series of letters written by Queen Elizabeth I of England (1533–1603) shows her indomitable will, her direct attack on problems of state, her sense of humor and her shrewdness. These letters touch upon her life from her youth to her death.

XV. TO QUEEN MARY

Elizabeth wrote this letter when she learned that she was to be sent to the Tower.

March 16, 1554.

If any ever did try this old saying, 'that a king's word was more than another man's oath,'[1] I most humbly beseech your Majesty to verify it to me, and to remember your last promise and my last demand, that I be not condemned without answer and due proof, which it seems that I now am; for without cause proved, I am by your Council from you commanded to go to the Tower, a place more wanted for a false traitor than a true subject, which though I know I desire it not, yet in the face of all this realm it appears proved. I pray to God I may die the shamefullest death that any ever died, if I may mean any such thing; and to this present hour I protest before God (Who shall judge my truth, whatsoever malice shall devise), that I never practised, counselled, nor consented to anything that might be prejudicial to your person anyway, or dangerous to the state by any means. And therefore I humbly beseech your Majesty to let me answer afore yourself, and not suffer me to trust to your Councillors, yea, and that afore I go to the Tower, if it be possible; if not, before I be further condemned. Howbeit, I trust assuredly your Highness will give me leave to do it afore I go, that thus shamefully I may not be cried out on, as I now shall be; yea, and that without cause. Let conscience move your Highness to pardon this my boldness, which innocency procures me to do, together with hope of your natural kindness, which I trust will not see me cast away without desert, which what it is I would desire no more of God but that you truly knew, but which thing I think and believe you shall never by report know, unless by yourself you hear. I have heard of many in my time cast away for

---

* From G. B. Harrison, *The Letters of Queen Elizabeth*, published by Cassell & Co. Ltd., London.
[1] Said by King John of France when he returned to his captivity in England.

want of coming to the presence of their Prince; and in late days I heard my Lord of Somerset say that if his brother had been suffered to speak with him he had never suffered; but persuasions were made to him so great that he was brought in belief that he could not live safely if the Admiral lived, and that made him give consent to his death. Though these persons are not to be compared to your Majesty, yet I pray God the like evil persuasions persuade not one sister against the other, and all for that they have heard false report, and the truth not known. Therefore, once again, kneeling with humbleness of heart, because I am not suffered to bow the knees of my body, I humbly crave to speak with your Highness, which I would not be so bold as to desire if I knew not myself most clear, as I know myself most true. And as for the traitor Wyatt, he might peradventure write me a letter, but on my faith I never received any from him. And as for the copy of the letter sent to the French King, I pray God confound me eternally if ever I sent him word, message, token, or letter, by any means, and to this truth I will stand in till my death.

Your Highness's most faithful subject, that hath been from the beginning, and will be to my end,

ELIZABETH.

I humbly crave but only one word of answer from yourself.

III. TO MARY, QUEEN OF SCOTS

Here Elizabeth replies to Mary, Queen of Scots, for her "uncomely, passionate, ireful and vindictive speeches."

Westminster, February 1, 1572.

MADAME,

Of late time I have received divers letters from you, to the which you may well guess by the accidents of the time why I have not made any answer, but especially because I saw no matter in them that required any such answer as could have contented you; and to have discontented you had been but an increase of your impatience, which I thought time would have mitigated as it commonly does when the cause thereof is not truly grounded, and that it be so understood. But now finding by your last letter of the 27th of the last an increase of your impatience, tending also to uncomely, passionate, ireful and vindictive speeches, I thought to change my former opinion, and by patient and advised words to move you to stay or qualify your passions, and to consider that it is not the manner to obtain good things with evil speeches, nor benefits with injurious challenges, nor to conclude, all in one word, good to yourself, with doing evil to myself. Yet to avoid the fault which I note that you have committed in filling a long letter with multitude of sharp and injurious words, I will not by way of letter write any more of the matter, but have rather chosen to commit to my cousin, the Earl of Shrewsbury, the things which I have thought meet, upon the reading of your letter, to be imparted to you, as he hath in a memorial in writing to show to you; wherewith, I think, if reason may be admitted to be with you at the reading, you will follow hereafter the course of the last part of your letter rather than the first (the latter being written in a calm, and the former in a storm), wishing to you the same grace of God that we wish to ourself, and that He may direct you to desire and attain to that is meet for you as well in honour as in all other quietness.

XXXVII. TO WILLIAM CECIL, LORD BURGHLEY

Burghley, disheartened by the constant worries of the last months and conscious that he was disliked by some of his powerful colleagues in the Council, wished to resign his office.

May 8, 1583.

SIR SPIRIT,

I doubt I do nickname you for those of your kind, they say, have no sense. But I have lately seen an *ecce signum*, that if an ass kick you, you feel it too soon. I will recant you from being spirit, if ever I perceive that you disdain not such a feeling. Serve God, fear the King, and be a good fellow to the rest. Let never care appear in you for such a rumour, but let them well know that you desire the righting of such wrong by making known their error, than you to be so silly a soul as to forshow what you ought to do, or not freely deliver what you think meetest, and pass of no man so much, as not to regard her trust who putteth it in you.

God bless you, and long may you last,

Omnino E. R.

XL. TO CATHERINE DE MEDICI, QUEEN MOTHER OF FRANCE

When Queen Elizabeth learned of the death of the Duke of Anjou, younger brother of the French King and prospective husband for herself, she wrote this letter to Catherine de Medici, Queen Mother of France.

(Translated from the French)

c. July 1584.

MADAM,

If the extremity of my misfortune had not equalled my grief for his sake, and had not rendered me unequal to touch with a pen the wound that my heart suffered, it would not be possible that I had so greatly forgotten to visit you with the fellowship of regret that I afford you, which I assure myself cannot exceed mine; for, although you were his mother, yet there remain to you several other children. But for myself, I find no consolation if it be not death, which I hope will make us soon to meet. Madam, if you could see the image of my heart you would there see the picture of a body without a soul; but I will not trouble you more with my plaints, having too many of your own. It remains at this present that I vow and swear to you that I will turn a great part of my love for him to the King, my good brother, and you, assuring you that you will find me the faithfullest daughter and sister that ever Princes had; and for this principal cause that he, to whom I had altogether dedicated myself, belonged to you so near; from whom, if he had had the divine favour of longer life, you would have known it further. Madam, I pray you give [   ] credit to this gentleman who will more amply tell you on my behalf my thoughts in your case, and believe that I will accomplish them faithfully as if I were your natural daughter. [? As] God please, Whom I pray to give you long life and all consolation.

Your very affectionate sister and cousin,

ELIZABETH.

II. TO ROBERT DUDLEY, EARL OF LEICESTER

The Queen wrote this sharp letter to Leicester when she learned that he was taking too much authority upon himself in Flushing. The Queen regarded this as an encroachment upon her own power.

February 10, 1586.

How contemptuously we conceive ourself to have been used by you, you shall by this bearer understand, whom we have expressly sent unto you to charge you withal. We could never have imagined had we not seen it fall out in experience that a man raised up by ourself and extraordinarily favoured by us above any other subject of this land, would have in so contemptible a sort broken our commandment, in a cause that so greatly toucheth us in honour; whereof, although you have showed yourself to make but little accompt, in most undutiful a sort, you may not therefore think that we have so little care of the reparation thereof as we mind to pass so great a wrong in silence unredressed: and, therefore, our express pleasure and commandment is, that all delays and excuses laid apart, you do presently, upon the duty of your allegiance, obey and fulfil whatsoever the bearer hereof shall direct you to do in our name: whereof fail you not, as you will answer the contrary at your uttermost peril.

VIII. TO MARY, QUEEN OF SCOTS

At the beginning of the trial of Mary, Queen of Scots, at Fotheringhay on 12th October, 1586, she received this letter from Queen Elizabeth.

(Translated from the French)

October 1586.

You have in various ways and manners attempted to take my life and to bring my kingdom to destruction by bloodshed. I have never proceeded so harshly against you, but have, on the contrary, protected and maintained you like myself. These treasons will be proved to you and all made manifest.

Yet it is my will, that you answer the nobles and peers of the kingdom as if I were myself·present. I therefore require, charge, and command that you make answer for I have been well informed of your arrogance.

Act plainly without reserve, and you will sooner be able to obtain favour of me.

ELIZABETH.

X. TO HENRY III, KING OF FRANCE

In January, 1587, the French Ambassador pleaded on behalf of Mary, Queen of Scots, before Queen Elizabeth. His threatening words resulted in this strong letter from the Queen.

January 1587.

SIR, MY GOOD BROTHER,

The old ground, on which I have often based my letters, appears to me so changed at present, that I am compelled to alter the style, and instead of returning thanks, to use complaints. My God! how could you be so unreasonable as to reproach the injured party, and to compass the death of an innocent one by allowing her to become the prey of a murderess? But, without reference to my rank, which is nowise inferior to your own, nor to my friendship to you, most sincere, for I have wellnigh forfeited all reputation among the Princes of my own religion, by neglecting them in order to prevent disturbances in your dominions; exposed to dangers such as scarcely any Prince ever was before; expecting, at least, some ostensible reasons and offers for security against the daily danger, for the epilogue of this whole negotiation: you are, in spite of all this, so blinded by the words of those who I pray may not ruin you, that instead of a thousand thanks, which I had merited for such singular services, Monsieur de Bellievre has addressed language to my ears, which, in truth, I know not well how to interpret. For, that you should be angry at my saving my own life, seems to me the threat of an enemy, which, I assure you, will never put me in fear, but is the shortest way to make me dispatch the cause of so much mischief. Let me, I pray you, understand in what sense I am to take these words; for I will not live an hour to endure that any Prince whatsoever should boast that he had humbled me into drinking such a cup as that. Monsieur de Bellievre has, indeed, somewhat softened his language, by adding that you in nowise wish any danger to accrue to me, and still less to cause me any. I therefore write you these few words, and if it please you to act accordingly, you shall never find a truer friend; but if otherwise, I neither am in so low a place, nor govern realms so inconsiderable, that I should in right and honour, yield to any living Prince who would injure me, and I doubt not, by the grace of God, to make my cause good for my own security.

I beseech you to think rather of the means of maintaining than of diminishing my friendship. Your Realm, my good brother, cannot abide many enemies. Give not the rein in God's name to wild horses, lest they should shake you from your saddle. I say this to you out of a true and upright heart, and implore the Creator to grant you long and happy life.

ELIZABETH.

XI. TO JAMES THE SIXTH, KING OF SCOTLAND

The condemnation of Mary, Queen of Scots, aroused great feeling in Scotland, and James dispatched commissioners to intercede for his mother and to discuss his own rights of succession to the English throne. Whilst Mary's fate was still uncertain a new conspiracy was reported to the Council by William Stafford, brother to Sir Edward Stafford, Ambassador in France, who declared that Chasteauneuf, the French Ambassador in London, had tried to persuade him to have the Queen murdered. Chasteauneuf retorted that the true story was that Stafford had made the proposal to him and that he had forborn to send him bound to the Queen out of love for his family. Whatever may be the truth of the story, it so greatly increased the clamour for Mary's death that the Queen was persuaded to sign the warrant for her execution on 1st February.

January 1587.

I find myself so troubled lest sinister tales might delude you, my good brother, that I have willingly found out this messenger, whom I know most sincere to you and a true subject to me, to carry unto you my most sincere meaning toward you, and to request this just desire, that you never doubt my entire goodwill in your behalf; and do protest, that, if you knew, even since the arrival of your Commissioners (which if they liest, they may tell you), the extreme danger my life was in, by an Ambassador's honest silence, if not invention, and such good complices as have themselves, by God's permission, unfolded the whole conspiracy, and have avouched it before his face, though it be the peril of their own lives, yet voluntarily, one of them never being suspected brake it with a Councillor to make me acquainted therewith. You may see whither I keep the serpent that poisons me, when they confess to have reward. By saving of her life they would have had mine. Do I not make myself, trow ye, a goodly prey for every wretch to devour? Transfigure yourself into my state, and suppose what you ought to do, and thereafter weigh my life, and reject the care of murder, and shun all baits that may untie our amities, and let all men know, that Princes know best their own laws, and misjudge not that you know not. For my part, I will not live to wrong the meanest. And so I conclude you with your own words, you will prosecute or mislike as much those that seek my ruin as if they sought your heart blood, and would I had none in mine if I would not do the like; as God knoweth, to Whom I make my humble prayers to inspire you with best desires.

Your most affectionate sister and cousin,

ELIZABETH R.

I am sending you a gentleman forthwith, the other being fallen sick, who I trust shall yield you good reason of my actions.

XIII. TO JAMES THE SIXTH, KING OF SCOTLAND

Queen Elizabeth wrote this letter when she received the report that Mary, Queen of Scots, had been executed. Historians differ as to Elizabeth's true feelings in hearing of this act; some believe that this letter reveals her true feelings, while others doubt the sincerity of her statements.

February 14, 1587.

My dear Brother, I would you knew (though not felt) the extreme dolor that overwhelms my mind, for that miserable accident which (far contrary to my meaning) hath befallen. I have now sent this kinsman of mine, whom ere now it hath pleased you to favour, to instruct you truly of that which is too irksome for my pen to tell you. I beseech you that as God and many more know, how innocent I am in this case: so you will believe me, that if I had bid aught I would have bid by it. I am not so base minded that fear of any living creature or Prince should make me afraid to do that were just; or done, to deny the same. I am not of so base a lineage, nor carry so vile a mind. But, as not to disguise, fits not a King, so will I never dissemble my actions, but cause them show even as I meant them. Thus assuring yourself of me, that as I know this was deserved, yet if I had meant it I would never lay it on others' shoulders; no more will I not damnify myself that thought it not.

The circumstance it may please you to have of this bearer. And for your part, think you have not in the world a more loving kinswoman, nor a more dear friend than myself; nor any that will watch more carefully to preserve you and your estate. And who shall otherwise persuade you, judge them more partial to others than you. And thus in haste I leave to trouble you: beseeching God to send you a long reign. The 14th of February, 1586.

Your most assured loving sister and cousin,

ELIZAB. R.

SIR JOHN HARINGTON*

Sir John Harington (1561[?]–1612) wrote this letter to his wife the year before the Queen died. It shows the love he had for his wife as well as his confidence in her, as he reveals his sensitive reactions to the ageing Queen.

TO LADY MARY HARINGTON

December 27, 1602.

Sweet Mall,

I herewith send thee, what I woud God none did know, some ill bodings of the realme and its welfare. Oure deare Queene, my royale godmother, and this state's natural mother, dothe now bear shew of human infirmitie, too faste for that evil which we shall get by her dethe, and too slowe for that good which shee shall get by her releasement from pains and miserye.

Deare Mall, how shall I speake what I have seen, or what I have felt?— Thy good silence in these matters emboldens my pen. For, thanks to the swete god of silence! thy lips do not wanton out of discretion's path, like the many gossipping dames we coud name, who lose their husband's fast hold in good friends, rather than hold fast their own tongues. Nowe I will truste thee with greate assurance, and whilst thou doste broode over thy young ones in the chamber, thou shalte read the doinges of thy greiving mate in the cowrte.

I finde some lesse mindfull of whate they are soone to lose, than of what they may perchance hereafter get. Nowe, on my owne parte, I cannot blote from my memorie's table, the goodnesse of our Sovereigne Ladie to me, even (I will saie) before borne; her affectione to my mother who waited in privie chamber, her betterring the state of my father's fortune (which I have, alass! so much worsted,) her watchings over my youthe, her likinge to my free speech, and admiration of my little learning and poesy, which I did so muche cultivate on her commande, have rootede such love, suche dutyfull remembraunce of her princelie virtues, that to turne askante from her condition withe tearless eyes, would staine and foule the springe and founte of gratitude.

It was not mainie daies since I was bidden to her presence. I bleste the happy momente; and founde her in moste pitiable state. She bade the archbishope aske me if I had seene Tyrone? I replied, with reverence, that

---

* From *The Letters and Epigrams of Sir John Harington,* edited by Norman Egbert McClure. Published by University of Pennsylvania Press. Copyright 1930 and reprinted with the permission of the publisher.

"I had seene him withe the Lord Deputie." She lookede up, with much choler and greife in her countenance and saide, "Oh, nowe it mindeth me that you was *one* who sawe this manne *elsewhere:*—and hereat, she droppede a teare, and smote her bosome. She helde in her hande a goldene cuppe, whiche she often put to her lippes; but, in soothe, her hearte seemethe too fulle to lacke more fillinge. This sighte movede me to thinke on whate paste in Irelande; and I truste she did not lesse thinke on *some* who were busier there than myselfe. She gave me a message to the Lord Deputie, and bade me come to the chamber at seven o clocke. Hereat some who were aboute her did marvel, as I do not holde so highe place as those she did not chuse to do her commandes. Deare Mall, if I gette no profitte, I shall gette some envie, and this businesse maye turne to some accounte withe the Lord Deputie. Her Majestie enquirede of some matters whiche I had written; and as she was pleasede to note my fancifulle braine, I was not unheedfull to feede her humoure, and reade some verses, whereat she smilede once, and was pleasede to saie;—"When thou doste feele creepinge tyme at thye gate, these fooleries will please thee lesse; I am paste my relishe for suche matters: thou seeste my bodilie meate dothe not suite me well; I have eaten but one ill tastede cake since yesternighte." She rated moste grievouslie, at noone, at some who minded not to bringe uppe certaine matters of accounte. Several menne have been sente to, and when readie at hande, her Highnesse hathe dismissede in anger; but who, dearest Mall, shall saye, that *"youre Highnesse hathe forgotten."* . . .

Nexte monthe I will see thie swete face, and kiss my boys and maids, which I praie thee not to omitte on my accounte. Send me up, by my manne Combe, my Petrarche. Adeiu, swete Mall.

I am thine ever lovinge
John Harington.

MADAME DE SÉVIGNÉ*

Madame de Sévigné (1626–1696), French noblewoman, wrote well over a thousand letters, most of them to her daughter. Horace Walpole says of her:

Madame de Sévigné shines both in grief and gayety. There is too much of sorrow for her daughter's absence; yet it is always expressed by new terms, by new images, and often by wit, whose tenderness has a melancholy air. When she forgets her concern, and returns to her natural disposition,—gayety,—every paragraph has novelty; her allusions, her applications, are the happiest possible. She has the art of making you acquainted with all her acquaintance, and attaches you even to the spots she inhabited. Her language is correct, though unstudied; and when her mind is full of any great event, she interests you with the warmth of a dramatic writer, not with the chilling impartiality of an historian.

LETTER XVII. TO M. DE COULANGES

Paris, Monday, December 15, 1670.

I am going to tell you a thing the most astonishing, the most surprising, the most marvellous, the most miraculous, the most magnificent, the most confounding, the most unheard of, the most singular, the most extraordinary, the most incredible, the most unforeseen, the greatest, the least, the rarest, the most common, the most public, the most private till to-day, the most brilliant, the most enviable; in short, a thing of which there is but one example in past ages, and that not an exact one neither; a thing that we cannot believe at Paris; how then will it gain credit at Lyons? a thing which makes everybody cry, "Lord, have mercy on us!" a thing which causes the greatest joy to Madame de Rohan and Madame de Hauterive; a thing, in fine, which is to happen on Sunday next, when those who are present will doubt the evidence of their senses; a thing which, though it is to be done on Sunday, yet perhaps will not be finished on Monday. I cannot bring myself to tell it you: guess what it is. I give you three times to do it in. What, not a word to throw at a dog? Well then, I find I must tell you. Monsieur de Lauzun is to be married next Sunday at the Louvre, to ——, pray guess to whom! I give you four times to do it in, I give you six, I give you a hundred. Says Madame de Coulanges, "It is really very hard to guess: perhaps it is Madame de la Vallière." Indeed, Madam, it is not. "It is Mademoiselle de Retz, then." No, nor she neither; you are extremely provincial. "Lord, bless me," say you, "what stupid wretches we are! it is Mademoiselle de Colbert all the while." Nay, now you are still farther from the mark. "Why then it must certainly be Mademoiselle de Créqui." You have it not yet. Well, I find I must tell you at last. He is to be married next Sunday, at the Louvre, with the King's leave, to Mademoiselle, Mademoiselle de—Mademoiselle—guess, pray guess her name: he is to be married to

* From *Letters of Madame de Sévigné*, Vols. I and II. Selected with an Introductory Essay by Richard Aldington. Copyright 1927–1928 Bretano's.

Mademoiselle, the great Mademoiselle; Mademoiselle, daughter to the late Monsieur; Mademoiselle, granddaughter of Henry the Fourth; Mademoiselle d'Eu, Mademoiselle de Dombes, Mademoiselle de Montpensier, Mademoiselle d'Orléans, Mademoiselle, the King's cousin-german, Mademoiselle, destined to the Throne, Mademoiselle, the only match in France that was worthy of Monsieur. What glorious matter for talk! If you should burst forth like a bedlamite, say we have told you a lie, that it is false, that we are making a jest of you, and that a pretty jest it is without wit or invention; in short, if you abuse us, we shall think you quite in the right; for we have done just the same things ourselves. Farewell, you will find by the letters you receive this post, whether we tell you truth or not.

LETTER XXIII. TO MME. DE GRIGNAN

Friday, February 20, 1671.

I cannot express how desirous I am to hear from you. Consider, my dear, I have not had a letter since that from La Palice: I know nothing of the rest of my journey to Lyons, nor of your route to Provence. I am very certain that there are letters for me; but then I want them, and they do not come. I have nothing left to comfort and amuse me but writing to you.

You must know that Wednesday night last, after I came from M. de Coulanges where we had been making up our packets for the post, I began to think of going to bed. That is nothing very extraordinary, you will say; but what follows is so. About three o'clock in the morning I was awakened with a cry of Thieves! Fire! and it seemed so near, and grew so loud, that I had not the least doubt of its being in the house; I even fancied I heard them talking of my little granddaughter. I imagined she was burned to death, and in that apprehension got up without a light, trembling in such a manner that I could scarcely stand. I ran directly to her room, which is the room that was yours, and found everything quiet; but I saw Guitant's house all in flames, and the fire spreading to Madame de Vauvineux's. The flames cast a light over our court-yard and that of Guitant, that made them look shocking. All was outcry, hurry, and confusion, and the beams and joists falling down made a dreadful noise. I immediately ordered our doors to be opened, and my people to give assistance. Monsieur de Guitant sent me a casket of valuables, which I secured in my cabinet, and then went into the street, to gape like the rest. There I found Monsieur and Madame Guitant in a manner naked; Madame de Vauvineux, the Venetian Ambassador, and all his people, with little Vauvineux, whom they were carrying fast asleep to the Ambassador's house, with a great deal of movables and plate. Madame de Vauvineux had removed all her goods. As for our house, I knew it was as

safe as if it had been on an island, but I was greatly concerned for my poor
neighbours. Madame Guêton and her brother gave some excellent directions, but we were all in consternation; the fire was so fierce that there was
no approaching it, and no one supposed it would cease till it had burnt poor
Guitant's house entirely down. Guitant himself was a melancholy object; he
was for flying to save his mother, who was in the midst of the flames, as he
supposed, in the upper part of the house; but his wife clung about him, and
held him as tightly as she could. He was in the greatest distress between the
grief of not being able to save his mother, and the fear of injuring his wife,
who was nearly five months with child. At last he begged me to lay hold of
her, which I did, and he went in search of his mother, who, he found, had
passed through the flames and was safe. He then endeavoured to save some
papers, but found it impossible to get near the place where they were. At
length he came back to the spot where he had left us, and where I had
prevailed on his wife to sit down. Some charitable Capuchins worked so
well, and so skilfully, that they cut off the communication of the fire. Water
was thrown upon the rest that was burning, and at last the battle ceased for
want of combatants, but not till several of the best apartments were entirely
consumed. It was looked upon as fortunate that any part of the house was
saved; though as it is poor Guitant will lose at least ten thousand crowns:
for they propose to rebuild the room that was painted and gilded. There
were several fine pictures of M. Le Blanc's lost, whose house it was, besides
tables, looking-glasses, tapestry, and other valuable pieces of furniture. They
are greatly concerned about some letters, which I imagine to be those of the
Prince. By this it was near five o'clock in the morning, and time to think of
getting Madame de Guitant to rest; I offered her my bed, but Madame
Guêton put her into hers, as she had several apartments in her house
unoccupied. We wished her to be bled, and sent for Boucher, who is
apprehensive of a miscarriage from the violence of the fright. She is still at
Madame Guêton's, where everybody goes to see her. You will naturally ask,
how the fire happened; but that no one can tell. There was not a spark in
the room where it first broke out. Could anyone have thought of diverting
himself at so melancholy a time, what pictures might he not have drawn of
us in the situation we were then in! Guitant was naked, except his shirt and
drawers; his wife was without stockings, and had lost one of her slippers;
Madame de Vauvineux was in a short underpetticoat, without a night-
gown; all the footmen and neighbours were in their night-caps. The
Ambassador, in his night-gown and long peruke, maintained very well the
importance of a serenissimo; but his secretary was a most admirable figure.
You talk of the breast of Hercules; this was quite another thing; we had a
full view of it: it was white, fat, plump, and perfectly exposed, for the
string that should have tied his shirt had been lost in the engagement. So
much for the melancholy news of one quarter. Let me beg of Deville that
he would take his rounds every night, after the family is in bed, to see that
the fire is out everywhere, for we cannot be too careful to prevent accidents
of this kind. I hope the water was favourable to you in your passage; in a

word, I wish you every happiness, and implore the God of heaven to preserve you from every evil.

Monsieur de Ventadour was to have been married on Thursday, that is yesterday, but is ill of a fever. The Marshal de la Motte has lost as good as five hundred crown's worth of fish. The other day while we were at table at M. du Man's, Courcelles told us he had two such great bumps on his head, that he could not get his wig on. This silly speech made us all rise from table before we had done with the fruit, for fear of laughing in his face. Presently after in came d'Olonne, upon which M. de la Rochefoucauld whispers me, "Madame, these two can never stay in a room together": and so it proved; for shortly after Courcelles went away.

Here are a number of trifles for you, my dear child; for to be continually telling you that I love you, that I think of nothing but you, that I employ myself about nothing but what concerns you, that you are the delight of my life, and that no one was ever so tenderly beloved, must certainly be a tiresome repetition.

LETTER CLXXVIII. TO MME. DE GRIGNAN

Paris, Monday, January 10, 1689.

We often stumble upon the same ideas, my dear child; I even think that I wrote to you from the Rocks what you say in your last letter respecting time. I now consent that it should fly; the days have no longer anything so dear and precious for me as I found them to contain when you were at the Hôtel de Carnavalet. I enjoyed, I made the most of, every hour; I treasured it as a miser does his gold; but in absence, the case is different; time cannot fly fast enough till the wished-for period arrives; we hurry it along, and would willingly dispose of all the intermediate space in favour of the days to which we aspire; it is a piece of tapestry which we are eager to finish; we are lavish of hours, and bestow them on anyone. But, I own, that when I reflect on the point to which this profusion of hours and days leads me, I tremble. I am no longer certain of any, and reason presents me with the image of what I am certain to find in my way. My child, I will put an end to these reflections with you, and endeavour to turn them to my own advantage.

The Abbé Têtu is in an alarming way for want of sleep. The physicians would not answer for his intellect; he is sensible of his situation, which is an additional calamity: he is kept alive merely by opium; he seeks for diversion and amusement, and accordingly frequents public places. We want him to go to Versailles to see the King and Queen of England, and the Prince of

Wales. Can there be a grander spectacle, or one more capable of affording the highest interest? It appears that the Prince of Orange favoured the King's flight. The king was sent to Exeter, where it was his intention to go; the front of his house was well guarded and all the back doors left open. The Prince was not inclined to sacrifice his father-in-law; he remains in London in the place of the King, without taking upon himself the title, being only desirous of restoring what he thinks the true religion, and supporting the laws of the country, without spilling a drop of blood: this is precisely the reverse of what we thought of him; we see him in a very different point of view. Our King, however, acts in a manner almost divine with respect to their Britannic Majesties, for is it not being the representative of the Almighty, to support a King banished, betrayed, and abandoned? The noble ambition of our sovereign is gratified by acting this part; he went to meet the Queen, with all his household, and a hundred coaches and six. When he perceived the Prince of Wales's carriage, he alighted and affectionately embraced him; he then ran to the Queen, who was by this time alighted; he saluted her, talked with her some time, placed her at his right hand in his carriage, and presented the Dauphin and Monsieur to her, who were also in the carriage, and conducted her to St. Germain, where she found everything prepared for her like a Queen, all sorts of apparel, and a rich casket containing six thousand louis-d'ors. The King of England was expected the next day at St. Germain, where the King waited for him; he arrived late: His Majesty went to the end of the guard-room to meet him; the King of England made an inclination, as if to embrace his knees, but the King prevented him, and embraced him three or four times very cordially. They talked together in a low voice for nearly a quarter of an hour; the King presented the Dauphin and Monsieur to him, the Princes of the blood, and Cardinal de Bonzi. He conducted him to the Queen's apartment, who could scarcely refrain from tears; after a conversation of a few minutes His Majesty led them to the apartment of the Prince of Wales, where they again conversed for some time, and he then withdrew, not choosing to be attended back, saying to the King, "This is your house; when I come you will do the honours of it, and I will do the honours of mine when you come to Versailles." The next day, which was yesterday, the Dauphiness went there with all the Court. I know not how they regulated the chairs, for they had those belonging to the Queen of Spain; and the Queenmother of England was treated as a daughter of France; I shall hereafter send you these particulars. His Majesty sent the King of England ten thousand louis-d'ors; the latter looks old and fatigued; the Queen is thin, with fine black eyes swelled with weeping; a fine complexion, but rather pale; a large mouth, beautiful teeth, a fine figure, and a great share of sense; no wonder if with all these she pleases every one who beholds her. Here is matter for general conversation, that will not soon be exhausted.

The poor Chevalier can neither write nor go to Versailles, which grieves us sadly, as he has a thousand things to do there; but he is not ill: on Saturday he supped with Madame de Coulanges, Madame de Vauvineux, M.

de Duras, and your son, at the Lieutenant's, where the healths of the first and second were drank, that is to say, Madame de la Fayette's and yours, for you have yielded to the date of friendship. Yesterday Madame de Coulanges gave a very pretty supper to the gouty gentlemen, the Abbé de Marsillac, the Chevalier de Grignan, and M. de Lamoignon, whose nephritic complaints stood him in stead of the gout: his wife and the *divinities* were admitted in consequence of colds which they are never without; I in consideration of the rheumatism I had twelve years ago, and Coulanges, for deserving to have the gout. There was no scarcity of conversation; the little man sang, and gave the Abbé de Marsillac great pleasure, which he expressed by his admiration, and by imitating the tones and manners, which reminded me so strongly of his father that I could not help being affected. Your son was at the Mesdemoiselles de Castelnau's; there is a younger sister, very pretty, and very agreeable, who is quite to your son's taste, and he leaves the squint-eyed girl to Sanzei: he took a hautboy with him, and they danced till midnight. This society is very pleasant to the Marquis, as he meets Saint Hérem, Janin, Choiseul, and Ninon there; so that he is not in a foreign country. The Chevalier does not seem to be in haste to marry him, nor does M. de Lamoignon seem very desirous of marrying his daughter. We can say nothing with respect to the marriage of M. de Mirepoix, this is the work of M. de Montfort: people seem to be infatuated, or else their heads are turned, for they do not think as they used to do; in short, this man seems impelled by his destiny, and what can be done in such a case?

M. de Lauzun is not gone back to England: he has an apartment at Versailles, and is perfectly satisfied; he has written to Mademoiselle to have the honour of seeing her, which has given her great offence. I have performed a masterpiece; I have been to visit Madame de Ricouart, who is lately returned, very well pleased at being a widow. You have nothing to do but appoint me to complete your acknowledgments, like your romances, do you recollect? I thank the amiable Paulina for her letter, I am confident her person would please me: so she could then find no appellation for me but that of *Madam?* this is being very serious. Adieu, my dear child; preserve your health, in other words, your beauty, which I so much admire.

HORACE WALPOLE

Horace Walpole (1717-1797), an author, was a friend of Thomas Gray, the poet, and printed Gray's Odes. Walpole's letters give a good picture of eighteenth century England and the reign of the Georges. He wrote the novel The Castle of Otranto (1764).

GEORGE III., THE NEW KING.—FUNERAL OF GEORGE II.

To George Montague, Esq.

ARLINGTON STREET, *Nov.* 13, 1760.

Even the honeymoon of a new reign don't produce events every day. There is nothing but the common saying of addresses and kissing hands. . . .

Do you know, I had the curiosity to go to the burying t'other night; I had never seen a royal funeral,—nay, I walked as a rag of quality, which I found would be, and so it was, the easiest way of seeing it. It is absolutely a noble sight. The Prince's chamber, hung with purple, and a quantity of silver lamps, the coffin under a canopy of purple velvet, and six vast chandeliers of silver on high stands, had a very good effect. The Ambassador from Tripoli and his son were carried to see that chamber. The procession, through a line of footguards, every seventh man bearing a torch, the horseguards lining the outside, their officers with drawn sabres and crape sashes on horseback, the drums muffled, the fifes, bells tolling, and minute-guns,—all this was very solemn. But the charm was the entrance of the Abbey, where we were received by the Dean and Chapter in rich robes, the choir and almsmen bearing torches; the whole Abbey so illuminated that one saw it to greater advantage than by day,—the tombs, long aisles, and fretted roof, all appearing distinctly, and with the happiest *chiaroscuro*. There wanted nothing but incense, and little chapels here and there, with priests saying mass for the repose of the defunct; yet one could not complain of its not being catholic enough. I had been in dread of being coupled with some boy of ten years old; but the heralds were not very accurate, and I walked with George Grenville, taller and older, to keep me in countenance. When we came to the chapel of Henry the Seventh, all solemnity and decorum ceased; no order was observed, people sat or stood where they could or would; the yeomen of the guard were crying out for help, oppressed by the immense weight of the coffin; the Bishop read sadly, and blundered in the prayers; the fine chapter, "Man that is born of a woman," was chanted, not read; and the anthem, besides being immeasurably tedious, would have served as well for a nuptial. The real serious part was the figure of the Duke of Cumberland, heightened by a thousand melancholy circumstances. He had a dark brown adonis, and a cloak of black cloth, with a train of five yards. Attending the funeral of a father could not be pleasant,—his leg extremely bad, yet forced to stand upon it near two hours; his face bloated and distorted with his late paralytic stroke, which has affected, too, one of his eyes, and placed over the mouth of the vault, into which, in all probability, he must himself so soon descend: think how unpleasant a situation! He bore it all with a firm and unaffected countenance. This grave scene was fully contrasted by the burlesque Duke of Newcastle. He fell into a fit of crying the moment he came into the chapel, and flung himself back in a stall, the Archbishop hovering over him with a smelling-bottle; but in two minutes his curiosity got the better of his hypocrisy, and he ran about the chapel with his glass to spy who was or was not there, spying with one hand, and mopping his eyes with the other. Then returned the fear of catching cold; and the Duke of Cumberland, who was sinking with heat, felt himself weighed down, and turning round, found it was the Duke of Newcastle standing upon his train, to avoid the chill of the marble. It was very theatric to look down into the vault, where the coffin lay, attended by mourners with lights. Clavering, the groom of the bedchamber, refused to sit up with the body, and was dismissed by the King's order.

I have nothing more to tell you, but a trifle, a very trifle. The King of Prussia has totally defeated Marshal Daun. This, which would have been prodigious news a month ago, is nothing to-day; it only takes its turn among the questions, "Who is to be groom of the bedchamber? what is Sir T. Robinson to have?" I have been to Leicester-fields to-day; the crowd was immoderate. I don't believe it will continue so. Good night. Yours ever.

SAMUEL JOHNSON

Samuel Johnson (1709–1784) was one of the most important literary figures of his time. He wrote verses, criticism, published an edition of Shakespeare, compiled his famous A Dictionary of the English Language *and wrote essays, some of which appeared in* The Rambler. *Included here is a letter which presumably appeared in that publication.*

NUMB. 191. TUESDAY, JANUARY 14, 1752.

Cereus in vitium flecti, monitoribus asper.	HOR.

The youth——
Yielding like wax, th' impressive folly bears;
Rough to reproof, and slow to future cares.   FRANCIS.

TO THE RAMBLER.

Dear Mr. Rambler,

I have been four days confined to my chamber by a cold, which has already kept me from three plays, nine sales, five shows, and six card-tables, and put me seventeen visits behind-hand; and the doctor tells my mamma, that if I fret and cry, it will settle in my head, and I shall not be fit to be seen these six weeks. But, dear Mr. Rambler, how can I help it? At this very time Melissa is dancing with the prettiest gentleman;—she will breakfast with him to-morrow, and then run to two auctions, and hear compliments, and have presents; then she will be drest, and visit, and get a ticket to the play; then go to cards and win, and come home with two flambeaux before her chair. Dear Mr. Rambler, who can bear it?

My aunt has just brought me a bundle of your papers for my amusement. She says, you are a philosopher, and will teach me to moderate my desires, and look upon the world with indifference. But, dear sir, I do not wish, nor intend to moderate my desires, nor can I think it proper to look upon the world with indifference, till the world looks with indifference on me. I have been forced, however, to sit this morning a whole quarter of an hour with your paper before my face; but just as my aunt came in, Phyllida had brought me a litter from Mr. Trip, which I put within the leaves; and read about *absence* and *inconsolableness*, and *ardour*, and *irresistible passion*, and *eternal constancy*, while my aunt imagined that I was puzzling myself with your philosophy, and often cried out, when she saw me look confused, "If there is any word that you do not understand, child, I will explain it."

Dear soul! how old people that think themselves wise may be imposed upon! But it is fit that they should take their turn, for I am sure, while they

25

can keep poor girls close in the nursery, they tyrannize over us in a very shameful manner, and fill our imaginations with tales of terrour, only to make us live in quiet subjection, and fancy that we can never be safe but by their protection.

I have a mamma and two aunts, who have all been formerly celebrated for wit and beauty, and are still generally admired by those that value themselves upon their understanding, and love to talk of vice and virtue, nature and simplicity, and beauty and propriety; but if there was not some hope of meeting me, scarcely a creature would come near them that wears a fashionable coat. These ladies, Mr. Rambler, have had me under their government fifteen years and a half, and have all that time been endeavouring to deceive me by such representations of life as I now find not to be true; but I know not whether I ought to impute them to ignorance or malice, as it is possible the world may be much changed since they mingled in general conversation.

Being desirous that I should love books, they told me, that nothing but knowledge could make me an agreeable companion to men of sense, or qualify me to distinguish the superficial glitter of vanity from the solid merit of understanding; and that a habit of reading would enable me to fill up the vacuities of life without the help of silly or dangerous amusements, and preserve me from the snares of idleness and the inroads of temptation.

But their principal intention was to make me afraid of men; in which they succeeded so well for a time, that I durst not look in their faces, or be left alone with them in a parlour; for they made me fancy, that no man ever spoke but to deceive, or looked but to allure; that the girl who suffered him that had once squeezed her hand, to approach her a second time, was on the brink of ruin; and that she who answered a billet, without consulting her relations, gave love such power over her, that she would certainly become either poor or infamous.

From the time that my leading-strings were taken off, I scarce heard any mention of my beauty but from the milliner, the mantua-maker, and my own maid; for my mamma never said more, when she heard me commended, but "the girl is very well," and then endeavoured to divert my attention by some inquiry after my needle, or my book.

It is now three months since I have been suffered to pay and receive visits, to dance at publick assemblies, to have a place kept for me in the boxes, and to play at lady Racket's rout; and you may easily imagine what I think of those who have so long cheated me with false expectations, disturbed me with fictitious terrors, and concealed from me all that I have found to make the happiness of woman.

I am so far from perceiving the usefulness or necessity of books, that if I had not dropped all pretensions to learning, I should have lost Mr. Trip, whom I once frighted into another box, by retailing some of Dryden's remarks upon a tragedy; for Mr. Trip declares, that he hates nothing like hard words, and I am sure, there is not a better partner to be found; his very walk is a dance. I have talked once or twice among ladies about principles and ideas, but they put their fans before their faces, and told me I was too wise for them, who for their part never pretended to read any thing but the play-bill, and then asked me the price of my best head.

Those vacancies of time which are to be filled up with books I have never yet obtained; for, consider, Mr. Rambler, I go to bed late, and therefore cannot rise early; as soon as I am up, I dress for the gardens; then walk in the park; then always go to some sale or show, or entertainment at the little theatre; then must be dressed for dinner; then must pay my visits; then walk in the park; then hurry to the play; and from thence to the card-table. This is the general course of the day, when there happens nothing extraordinary; but sometimes I ramble into the country, and come back again to a ball; sometimes I am engaged for a whole day and part of the night. If, at any time, I can gain an hour by not being at home, I have so many things to do, so many orders to give to the milliner, so many alterations to make in my clothes, so many visitants' names to read over, so many invitations to accept or refuse, so many cards to write, and so many fashions to consider, that I am lost in confusion, forced at last to let in company or step into my chair, and leave half my affairs to the direction of my maid.

This is the round of my day; and when shall I either stop my course, or so change it as to want a book? I suppose it cannot be imagined, that any of these diversions will soon be at an end. There will always be gardens, and a park, and auctions, and shows, and playhouses, and cards; visits will always be paid, and clothes always be worn; and how can I have time unemployed upon my hands?

But I am most at a loss to guess for what purpose they related such tragick stories of the cruelty, perfidy, and artifices of men, who, if they ever were so malicious and destructive, have certainly now reformed their manners. I have not, since my entrance into the world, found one who does not profess himself devoted to my service, and ready to live or die as I shall command him. They are so far from intending to hurt me, that their only contention is, who shall be allowed most closely to attend, and most frequently to treat me; when different places of entertainment, or schemes of pleasure are mentioned, I can see the eye sparkle and the cheeks glow of him whose proposals obtain my approbation; he then leads me off in triumph, adores my condescension, and congratulates himself that he has lived to the hour of felicity. Are these, Mr. Rambler, creatures to be feared? Is it likely that an injury will be done me by those who can enjoy life only while I favour them with my presence?

As little reason can I yet find to suspect them of stratagems and fraud. When I play at cards, they never take advantage of my mistakes, nor exact from me a rigorous observation of the game. Even Mr. Shuffle, a grave gentleman, who has daughters older than myself, plays with me so negligently, that I am sometimes inclined to believe he loses his money by design, and yet he is so fond of play, that he says, he will one day take me to his house in the country, that we may try by ourselves who can conquer. I have not yet promised him; but when the town grows a little empty, I shall think upon it, for I want some trinkets, like Letitia's, to my watch. I do not doubt my luck, but must study some means of amusing my relations.

For all these distinctions I find myself indebted to that beauty which I was never suffered to hear praised, and of which, therefore, I did not before know the full value. The concealment was certainly an intentional fraud, for my aunts have eyes like other people, and I am every day told, that nothing but blindness can escape the influence of my charms. Their whole account of that world which they pretend to know so well, has been only one fiction entangled with another; and though the modes of life oblige me to continue some appearances of respect, I cannot think that they, who have been so clearly detected in ignorance or imposture, have any right to the esteem, veneration, or obedience of,

Sir, Yours,

BELLARIA.

WOLFGANG AMADEUS MOZART*

Wolfgang Amadeus Mozart (1756–1791), born in Salzburg, Austria, was a child prodigy. His letters, like his music, reflect his happy and gay nature, his tenderness and his depth of feeling in love and grief. The first letter below he wrote upon the completion of an opera.

48

Milan, Dec. 18, 1772.

I hope, dear sister, that you are well, dear sister. When this letter reaches you, dear sister, my opera will be *in scena*, dear sister. Think of me, dear sister, and try, dear sister, to imagine with all your might that my dear sister sees and hears it also. In truth, it is hard to say, as it is now eleven o'clock at night, but I do believe, and don't at all doubt, that in the daytime it is brighter than at Easter. My dear sister, to-morrow we dine with Herr von Mayer; and do you know why? Guess! Because he invited us. The rehearsal to-morrow is to be in the theatre. The *impresario*, Signor Cassiglioni, has entreated me not to say a word of this to a soul, as all kinds of people would come crowding in, and that we don't wish. So, my child, I beg, my child, that you won't say one syllable to any one on the subject, or too many people would come crowding in, my child. *Approposito*, do you know the history that occurred here? Well, I will relate it to you. We were going home straight from Count Firmiani's, and when we came into our street we opened our door, and what do you think happened? We went in. Good-bye, my pet. Your unworthy brother (frater),

WOLFGANG.

---

* From *The Letters of Wolfgang Amadeus Mozart*, translated by Lady Wallace. Reprinted with the permission of Houghton Mifflin Company.

97

MADEMOISELLE, MA TRÈS-CHÈRE COUSINE,—

You perhaps think or believe that I must be dead? Not at all! I beg you will not think so, for how could I write so beautifully if I were dead? Could such a thing be possible? I do not attempt to make any excuses for my long silence, for you would not believe me if I did. But truth is truth; I have had so much to do that though I have had time to think of my cousin, I have had no time to write to her, so I was obliged to let it alone. But at last I have the honor to inquire how you are, and how you fare? If we soon shall have a talk? If you write with a lump of chalk? If I am sometimes in your mind? If to hang yourself you're inclined? If you're angry with me, poor fool? If your wrath begins to cool?—Oh! you are laughing! *Victoria!* I knew you could not long resist me, and in your favor would enlist me. Yes! yes! I know well how this is, though I'm in ten days off to Paris. If you write to me from pity, do so soon from Augsburg city, so that I may get your letter, which to me would be far better.

Now let us talk of other things. Were you very merry during the Carnival? They are much gayer at Augsburg at that time than here. I only wish I had been there that I might have frolicked about with you. Mamma and I send our love to your father and mother, and to our cousin, and hope they are well and happy; better so, so better! *A propos,* how goes on your French? May I soon write you a French letter? from Paris, I suppose?

Now, before I conclude, which I must soon do because I am in haste, (having just at this moment nothing to do,) and also have no more room, as you see my paper is done, and I am very tired, and my fingers tingling from writing so much, and lastly, even if I had room, I don't know what I could say, except, indeed, a story which I have a great mind to tell you. So listen! It is not long since it happened, and in this very country too, where it made a great sensation, for really it seemed almost incredible, and, indeed, between ourselves, no one yet knows the result of the affair. So, to be brief, about four miles from here—I can't remember the name of the place, but it was either a village or a hamlet, or something of that kind. Well, after all, it don't much signify whether it was called Triebetrill or Burmsquick; there is no doubt that it was some place or other. There a shepherd or herdsman lived, who was pretty well advanced in years, but still looked strong and robust; he was unmarried and well-to-do, and lived happily. But before telling you the story, I must not forget to say that this man had a most astounding voice when he spoke; he terrified people when he spoke! Well! to make my tale as short as possible, you must know that he had a dog called Bellot, a very handsome large dog, white with black spots. Well! this shepherd was going along with his sheep, for he had a flock of eleven thousand under his care, and he had a staff in his hand, with a pretty rose-colored topknot of ribbons, for he never went out without his staff; such was his invariable custom. Now to proceed; being tired, after having gone a couple of miles, he sat down on a bank beside a river to rest. At last he fell asleep, when he dreamt that he had lost all his sheep, and this fear awoke him, but to his great joy he saw his flock close beside him. At length he got up again and went on, but not for long; indeed, half an hour could scarcely have elapsed, when he came to a bridge which was very long, but with a parapet on both sides to prevent any one falling into the river. Well; he looked at his flock, and as he was obliged to cross the bridge, he began to drive over his eleven thousand sheep. Now be so obliging as to wait till the eleven thousand sheep are all safely across, and then I will finish the story. I already told you that the result is not yet known; I hope, however, that by the time I next write to you, all the sheep will have crossed the bridge; but if not, why should I care? So far as I am concerned, they might all have stayed on this side. In the meantime you must accept the story so far as it goes; what I really know to be true I have written, and it is better to stop now than to tell you what is false, for in that case you would probably have discredited the whole, whereas now you will only disbelieve one half.

I must conclude, but don't think me rude; he who begins must cease, or the world would have no peace. My compliments to every friend, welcome to kiss me without end, forever and a day, till good sense comes my way; and a fine kissing that will be, which frightens you as well as me. Adieu, ma chère cousine! I am, I was, I have been, oh! that I were, would to heavens I were! I will or shall be, would, could, or should be—what?—A blockhead!

W. A. M.

106. TO ABBÉ BULLINGER

Paris, July 3, 1778.

My very Dear Friend,—

Mourn with me! This has been the most melancholy day of my life; I am now writing at two o'clock in the morning. I must tell you that my mother, my darling mother, is no more. God has called her to Himself; I clearly see that it was His will to take her from us, and I must learn to submit to the will of God. The Lord giveth, and the Lord taketh away. Only think of all the distress, anxiety, and care I have endured for the last fourteen days. She died quite unconscious, and her life went out like a light. She confessed three days before, took the sacrament, and received extreme unction. The last three days, however, she was constantly delirious, and to-day, at twenty minutes past five o'clock, her features became distorted, and she lost all feeling and perception. I pressed her hand, I spoke to her, but she did not see me, she did not hear me, and all feeling was gone. She lay thus till the moment of her death, five hours after, at twenty minutes past ten at night. There was no one present but myself, Herr Heiner, a kind friend whom my father knows, and the nurse. It is quite impossible for me to describe the whole course of the illness to-day. I am firmly convinced that she must have died, and that God had so ordained it. All I would ask of you at present is to act the part of a true friend, by preparing my father by degrees for this sad intelligence. I have written to him by this post, but only that she is seriously ill; and now I shall wait for your answer and be guided by it. May God give him strength and courage! My dear friend, I am consoled not only now, but have been so for some time past. By the mercy of God I have borne it all with firmness and composure. When the danger became imminent, I prayed to God for only two things—a happy death for my mother, and strength and courage for myself; and our gracious God heard my prayer and conferred these two boons fully on me. I entreat you, therefore, my best friend, to watch over my father for me; try to inspire him with courage, that the blow may not be too hard and heavy on him when he learns the worst. I also, from my heart, implore you to comfort my sister. Pray go straight to them, but do not tell them she is actually dead— only prepare them for the truth. Do what you think best, say what you please; only act so that my mind may be relieved, and that I may not have to dread another misfortune. Support and comfort my dear father and my dear sister. Answer me at once, I entreat. Adieu! Your faithful

W. A. M.

180

Vienna, Dec. 15, 1781.

. . . My very dearest father, you demand an explanation of the words in the closing sentence of my last letter. Oh! how gladly would I long ago have opened my heart to you, but I was deterred by the reproaches I dreaded for even thinking of such a thing at so unseasonable a time, although merely *thinking* can never be unseasonable. My endeavors are directed at present to securing a small but certain income, which, together with what chance may put in my way, may enable me to live and—to marry! You are alarmed at this idea; but I entreat you, my dearest, kindest father, to listen to me. I have been obliged to disclose to you my purpose; you must therefore allow me to disclose to you my reasons also, and very well-grounded reasons they are. My feelings are strong, but I cannot live as many other young men do. In the first place, I have too great a sense of religion, too much love for my neighbor to do so, and too high a feeling of honor to deceive any innocent girl. My disposition has always inclined me more to domestic life than to excitement; I never from my youth upwards have been in the habit of taking any charge of my linen or clothes, &c., and I think nothing is more desirable for me than a wife. I assure you I am forced to spend a good deal owing to the want of proper care of what I possess. I am quite convinced that I should be far better off with a wife, (and the same income I now have,) for how many other superfluous expenses would it save! Others come, to be sure, in their place, but I know what they are, and can regulate accordingly, and, in short, lead an orderly life. An unmarried man, in my opinion, enjoys only half a life. Such are my views, and such they will always remain. I have thought and reflected sufficiently, and I shall ever continue to think the same. But now, who is the object of my love? Do not be startled, I entreat. Not one of the Webers, surely? Yes, one of the Webers,—not Josepha, not Sophie, but the third daughter, Constanze. I never met with such diversity of dispositions in any family. The eldest is idle, coarse, and deceitful—crafty and cunning as a fox; Madame Lange (Aloysia) is false and unprincipled, and a coquette; the youngest is still too childish to have her character defined,—she is merely a good-humored, frivolous girl; may God guard her from temptation! The third, however, namely, my good and beloved Constanze, is the martyr of the family, and probably on this very account the kindest-hearted, the cleverest, and, in short, the best of them all; she takes charge of the whole house, and yet does nothing right in their eyes. Oh! my dear father, I could write you pages were I to describe to you all the scenes that I have witnessed in that house; but if you wish it I will do so in my next letter. Before, however, releasing you from this subject, I must make you better acquainted with the character of my Constanze. She is not plain, but at the same time far from being handsome; her whole beauty consists in a pair of bright black eyes and a pretty figure. She is not witty, but has enough sound good sense to enable her to fulfill her duties as a wife and mother. It is utterly false that she is inclined to be extravagant; on the contrary, she is invariably very plainly dressed, for the little her mother can spend on her children she gives to the two others, but to Constanze nothing. It is true that her dress is always neat and nice, however simple, and she can herself make most of the things requisite for a young lady. She dresses her own hair, understands housekeeping, and has the best heart in the world. I love her with my whole soul, as she does me. Tell me if I could wish for a better wife. I must add that, at the time I gave up my situation, my love had not begun; it first arose (while living with them) from her tender care and attentions. All I now wish is, that I may procure some permanent situation, (and this, thank God, I have good hopes of,) and then I shall never cease entreating your consent to my rescuing this poor girl, and thus making, I may say, all of us quite happy, as well as Constanze and myself; for, if I am happy, you are sure to be so, dearest father, and one half of the proceeds of my situation shall be yours.

I have thus opened my heart to you, and fully explained my words. I in turn beg you to explain those in your last letter: "You do not believe that I was aware of a proposal made to you, but to which you have given no answer?" I don't understand one word of this. I know of no proposal. Pray, have compassion on your son. Ever your dutiful son.

199

Vienna, August 7, 1782.

You are very much mistaken in your son if you can believe him capable of base conduct. My beloved Constanze, now, thank God, at last my wife, knew my circumstances long ago, and heard from me that I had nothing whatever to expect from you;[1] but her attachment and love for me were so great that she gladly and joyfully sacrificed her future life to share my fate. I thank you, with all the tender affection a son must always feel towards a father, for your kind consent and blessing. I felt I could rely on it; and you knew that I was myself only too well aware of all—all that could be said against such a step; but without injury to my conscience and my honor I could not act otherwise, and I knew I could place implicit confidence in your consent. After waiting two posts in vain for your answer, the day of our wedding having been finally settled, (by which time your reply ought to have arrived,) being quite assured of your consent, I was married, by the blessing of God, to my beloved Constanze. Next day I received both your letters at once. Now the event has taken place, and I entreat your forgiveness for my perhaps too hasty trust in your fatherly love. This candid confession gives you a fresh proof of my regard for truth, and my detestation of falsehood. My dear wife will herself by the next post write to her kind father-in-law to entreat his blessing, and to her beloved sister-in-law to solicit the continuance of her valued friendship. No one attended the marriage but Constanze's mother and youngest sister, Herr von Thorwarth

---

[1] The father, when he at last gave his consent to the marriage, desired Wolfgang to observe that he (the father) could no longer expect assistance from his son in his distressed circumstances, caused by his efforts to promote that son's welfare; that Wolfgang, in return, must not hope, either now or hereafter, to receive anything from his father, and that he wished his bride to be told this.

in his capacity of guardian, Herr von Zetto (Landrath) who gave away the bride, arid Gilofsky [of Salzburg] as my best man. When the ceremony was over, both my wife and I shed tears; all present (even the priest) were touched on seeing the emotion of our hearts. Our sole wedding festivities consisted of a supper, which Baroness Waldstädten gave us, and indeed it was more princely than baronial. My darling is now a hundred times more joyful at the idea of going to Salzburg; and I am willing to stake—ay, my very life, that you will rejoice still more in my happiness when you really know her; if, indeed, in your estimation, as in mine, a high-principled, honest, virtuous, and pleasing wife ought to make a man happy.

I send you herewith a short march. I hope that all will arrive in due time, and be to your taste. The first *allegro* must be played with much fire, the last as *prestissimo* as possible. My opera (by Gluck's desire) was given again yesterday. Gluck was very complimentary to me about it. I dine with him to-morrow. You see in what haste I write. My dear wife and I kiss your hands a thousand times.

205. TO BARONESS VON WALDSTÄDTEN

Vienna, Oct. 2, 1782.

Dearest, best and fairest,
Golden, silver, and sugared,
Most perfect, and precious,
highly esteemed
Baroness![1]

I have the honor to send your Ladyship the rondo, the two volumes of plays, and the little book of stories. I committed a great blunder yesterday. I thought I had something particular to say, but it went fairly out of my stupid head;—it was to thank your Ladyship for having taken so much trouble about the handsome dress-coat, and for your goodness in promising me one; but I omitted doing so, which is, indeed, too often the case with me. I may well say that I am both a most fortunate and unfortunate man,—unfortunate from the time when I saw your ladyship so charmingly *frisée* at the ball, for my peace of mind is now gone! I do nothing but sigh and groan. During the remainder of the ball I could dance no more,—I could only skip about. When supper came, I could not eat,—I could only gobble. At night, instead of slumbering softly and sweetly, I slept like a dormouse, and snored like a bear; and (without presumption) I think I may venture to

---

[1] The address is, "à Madame Madame la Baronne de Waldstädten, née de Scheffer, à Leopoldstadt."

lay a wager that with your Ladyship it was pretty much the same *à propor-tion*. You smile? You blush? I am indeed happy; my felicity is secured. But, alas! alas! who taps me on the shoulder? Who glares at my writing? My wife! Well! it is a fact that, having got her at last, I must keep her. What is to be done? I must praise her, and try to imagine that it is all true. My wife, who is an angel of a woman, and I, who am a pattern husband, send you 1000 kind wishes, and remain your Ladyship's faithful vassals,

> MOZART Magnus corpore parvus,
> et
> CONSTANTIA omnium uxorum pulcherrima
> et prudentissima.

Vienna, Oct. 2, 1782.

P. S.—We beg you will *not* give our kind regards to the Aurnhammers.

CHARLES LAMB*

Charles Lamb (1775–1834) and his sister, Mary, wrote Tales from Shakespeare *together. He established himself as a critic and as an essayist. He is famous for his familiar literary style.*

LXXV. TO THOMAS MANNING

Oct. 16th, 1800.

Dear Manning,—Had you written one week before you did, I certainly should have obeyed your injunction; you should have seen me before my letter. I will explain to you my situation. There are six of us in one department. Two of us (within these four days) are confined with severe fevers; and two more, who belong to the Tower Militia, expect to have marching orders on Friday. Now six are absolutely necessary. I have already asked and obtained two young hands to supply the loss of the *feverites*. And, with the other prospect before me, you may believe I cannot decently ask leave of absence for myself. All I can promise (and I do promise, with the sincerity of St Peter, and the contrition of sinner Peter if I fail) that I will come *the very first spare week*, and go nowhere till I have been at Cambridge. No matter if you are in a state of pupilage when I come; for I can employ myself in Cambridge very pleasantly in the mornings. Are there not libraries, halls, colleges, books, pictures, statues? I wish you had made London in your way. There is an exhibition quite uncommon in Europe, which could not have escaped *your genius*,—a live rattlesnake, ten feet in length, and the thickness of a big leg. I went to see it last night by candlelight. We were ushered into a room very little bigger than ours at Pentonville. A man and woman and four boys live in this room, joint tenants with nine snakes, most of them such as no remedy has been discovered for their bite. We walked into the middle, which is formed by a half-moon of wired boxes, all mansions of *snakes*—whip-snakes, thunder-snakes, pig-nose-snakes, American vipers, and *this monster*. He lies curled up in folds. Immediately a stranger entered (for he is used to the family, and sees them play at cards,) he set up a rattle like a watchman's in London, or near as loud, and reared up a head, from the midst of these folds, like a toad, and shook his head, and showed every sign a snake can show of irritation. I had the foolish curiosity to strike the wires with my finger, and the devil flew at me with his

* From *The Works of Charles Lamb—Letters*, Vols. I and II. Edited with Preface by William MacDonald. Published by E. P. Dutton & Co., Inc. Reprinted by permission of the publishers.

toadmouth wide open; the inside of his mouth is quite white. I had got my finger away, nor could he well have bit me with his big mouth, which would have been certain death in five minutes. But it frightened me so much, that I did not recover my voice for a minute's space. I forgot, in my fear, that he was secured. You would have forgot too, for 'tis incredible how such a monster can be confined in small gauzy-looking wires. I dreamed of snakes in the night. I wish to heaven you could see it. He absolutely swelled with passion to the bigness of a large thigh. I could not retreat without infringing on another box; and just behind, a little devil not an inch from my back had got his nose out, with some difficulty and pain, quite through the bars! He was soon taught better manners. All the snakes were curious, and objects of terror: but this monster, like Aaron's serpent, swallowed up the impression of the rest. He opened his cursed mouth, when he made at me, as wide as his head was broad. I hallooed out quite loud, and felt pains all over my body with the fright.

I have had the felicity of hearing George Dyer read out one book of the *Farmer's Boy*. I thought it rather childish. No doubt, there is originality in it, (which, in your self-taught geniuses, is a most rare quality, they generally getting hold of some bad models, in a scarcity of books, and forming their taste on them,) but no *selection*. *All* is described.

Mind, I have only heard read one book.

Yours sincerely,

Philo-Snake,

C. L.

LXXXIV. TO WILLIAM WORDSWORTH

Jan. 30th, 1801.

I ought before this to have replied to your very kind invitation into Cumberland. With you and your sister I could gang anywhere; but I am afraid whether I shall ever be able to afford so desperate a journey. Separate from the pleasure of your company, I don't much care if I never see a mountain in my life. I have passed all my days in London, until I have formed as many and intense local attachments as any of you mountaineers can have done with dead Nature. The lighted shops of the Strand and Fleet Street; the innumerable trades, tradesmen, and customers, coaches, waggons, playhouses; all the bustle and wickedness round about Covent Garden; the very women of the Town; the watchmen, drunken scenes, rattles; life awake, if you awake, at all hours of the night; the impossibility of being dull in Fleet Street; the crowds, the very dirt and mud, the sun shining upon houses and pavements, the print-shops, the old book-stalls, parsons cheapening books, coffee-houses, steams of soups from kitchens, the pantomimes— London itself a pantomime and a masquerade—all these things work themselves into my mind, and feed me, without a power of satiating me. The wonder of these sights impels me into night-walks about her crowded streets, and I often shed tears in the motley Strand from fulness of joy at so much life. All these emotions must be strange to you; so are your rural emotions to me. But consider, what must I have been doing all my life, not to have lent great portions of my heart with usury to such scenes?

My attachments are all local, purely local. I have no passion (or have had none since I was in love, and then it was the spurious engendering of poetry and books,) for groves and valleys. The rooms where I was born, the furniture which has been before my eyes all my life, a book-case which has followed me about like a faithful dog, (only exceeding him in knowledge,) wherever I have moved, old chairs, old tables, streets, squares, where I have sunned myself, my old school,—these are my mistresses. Have I not enough, without your mountains? I do not envy you. I should pity you, did I not know that the mind will make friends of any thing. Your sun, and moon, and skies, and hills, and lakes, affect me no more, or scarcely come to me in more venerable characters, than as a gilded room with tapestry and tapers, where I might live with handsome visible objects. I consider the clouds above me but as a roof beautifully painted, but unable to satisfy the mind: and at last, like the pictures of the apartment of a connoisseur, unable to afford him any longer a pleasure. So fading upon me, from disuse, have been the beauties of Nature, as they have been confinedly called; so ever fresh, and green, and warm are all the inventions of men, and assemblies of men in this great city. I should certainly have laughed with dear Joanna.

Give my kindest love, and my sister's, to D. and yourself; and a kiss from me to little Barbara Lewthwaite. Thank you for liking my play.

C. L.

LORD BYRON

Lord Byron (1788–1824) is best known for his poetry, including The Prisoner of Chillon, Childe Harold's Pilgrimage, Don Juan *and other poems. In these letters we discern something of the dramatic spirit of this romantic adventurer who died while working for Greek independence.*

852.—TO JOHN MURRAY

Ravenna, Dec.r 9th 1820.

DEAR MURRAY,—I intended to have written to you at some length by this post, but as the Military Commandant is now lying dead in my house, on Fletcher's bed, I have other things to think of.

He was shot at 8 o'Clock this evening about two hundred paces from our door. I was putting on my great Coat to pay a visit to the Countess G., when I heard a shot, and on going into the hall, found all my servants on the balcony exclaiming that "a Man was murdered." As it is the custom here to let people fight it through, they wanted to hinder me from going out; but I ran down into the Street: Tita, the bravest of them, followed me; and we made our way to the Commandant, who was lying on his back, with five wounds, of which three in the body—one in the heart. There were about him Diego, his Adjutant, crying like a Child; a priest howling; a Surgeon who dared not touch him; two or three confused and frightened Soldiers; one or two of the boldest of the mob; and the Street dark as pitch, with the people flying in all directions. As Diego could only cry and wring his hands, and the Priest could only pray, and nobody seemed able or willing to do anything except exclaim, shake and stare, I made my Servant and one of the mob take up the body; sent off Diego crying to the Cardinal, the Soldiers for the Guard; and had the Commandant conveyed up Stairs to my own quarters. But he was quite gone. I made the Surgeon examine him, and examined him myself. He had bled inwardly, and very little external blood was apparent. One of the Slugs had gone quite through—all but the Skin: I felt it myself. Two more shots in the body, one in a finger, and another in the arm. His face not at all disfigured: he seems asleep, but is growing livid. The Assassin has not been taken; but the gun was found—a gun filed down to half the barrel.

He said nothing but *O Dio!* and *O Gesu* two or three times.

The house was filled at last with Soldiers, officers, police, and military; but they are clearing away—all but the Sentinels, and the body is to be removed tomorrow. It seems that, if I had not had him taken into my house, he might have lain in the Streets till morning; as here nobody meddles with such things, for fear of the consequences—either of public suspicion, or private revenge on the part of the Slayers. They may do as they please: I shall never be deterred from a duty of humanity . . .

He was a brave officer, but an unpopular man. The whole town is in confusion.

You may judge better of things here by this detail, than by anything which I could add on the Subject: communicate this letter to Hobhouse and Douglas K.ᵈ, and believe me

Yours ever truly,

B.

P.S.—The poor Man's wife is not yet aware of his death: they are to break it to her in the morning.

The Lieutenant, who is watching the body, is smoking with the greatest *Sangfroid:* a strange people.

ABRAHAM LINCOLN (1809–1865)*

John D. Johnston, Lincoln's stepbrother, has asked Lincoln for a loan of eighty dollars. This is Lincoln's reply.

* Letter to John D. Johnston, Lincoln's stepbrother, from *Abraham Lincoln: His Speeches and Writings,* published by The World Publishing Co., Copyright 1946. Reprinted by permission.

Dear Johnston:

Your request for eighty dollars I do not think it best to comply with now. At the various times when I have helped you a little, you have said to me, "We can get along very well now" but in a very short time I find you in the same difficulty again. Now this can only happen by some defect in your *conduct.* What that defect is, I think I know. You are not *lazy,* and still you *are* an *idler.* I doubt whether since I saw you, you have done a good whole day's work, in any one day. You do not very much dislike to work; and still you do not work much, merely because it does not seem to you that you could get much for it. This habit of uselessly wasting time, is the whole difficulty; and it is vastly important to you, and still more so to your children that you should break this habit. It is more important to them, because they have longer to live, and can keep out of an idle habit before they are in it, easier than they can get out after they are in.

You are now in need of some [ready?] money; and what I propose is, that you shall go to work, "tooth and nails" for somebody who will give you money for it. Let father and your boys take charge of things at home—prepare for a crop, and make the crop; and you go to work for the best money wages, or in discharge of any debt you owe, that you can get. And to secure you a fair reward for your labor, I now promise you that for every dollar you will, between this and the first of next May, get for your own labor, either in money, or on your own indebtedness, I will then give you one other dollar. By this, if you hire yourself at ten dolla[rs] a month, from me you will get ten more, making twenty dollars a month for your work. In this, I do not mean you shall go off to St. Louis, or the lead mines, or the gold mines in Calif[ornia,] but I [mean for you to go at it for the best wages you] can get close to home in Coles county. Now if you will do this, you will be soon out of debt, and what is better, you will have a habit that will keep you from getting in debt again. But if I should now clear you out, next year you would be just as deep in as ever. You say you would almost give your place in Heaven for $70 or $80. Then you value your place in Heaven very cheapl[y] for I am sure you can with the offer I make you get the seventy or eighty dollars for four or five months work. You say if I

42

furnish you the money you will deed me the land, and, if you dont pay the money back, you will deliver possession. Nonsense! If you cant now live *with* the land, how will you then live without it? You have always been [kind]to me, and I do not now mean to be unkind to you. On the contrary, if you will but follow my advice, you will find it worth more than eight times eighty dollars to you.

> Affectionately
> Your brother
> A. Lincoln

CHARLES DICKENS

Charles Dickens (1812–1870), the popular nineteenth century English novelist, made two lecture tours in America. In his letters he describes the royal welcome he received on his arrival as well as his successes while he was there.

TO CHARLES DICKENS

PARKER HOUSE, BOSTON, U.S.,
Saturday, Thirtieth November, 1867.

MY DEAR CHARLEY,—You will have heard before now how fortunate I was on my voyage, and how I was not sick for a moment. These screws are tremendous ships for carrying on, and for rolling, and their vibration is rather distressing. But my little cabin, being for'ard of the machinery, was in the best part of the vessel, and I had as much air in it, night and day, as I chose. The saloon being kept absolutely without air, I mostly dined in my own den, in spite of my being allotted the post of honour on the right hand of the captain.

The tickets for the first four readings here (the only readings announced) were all sold immediately. The tickets for the first four readings in New York (the only readings announced there also) were on sale yesterday, and were all sold in a few hours. Engagements of any kind and every kind I steadily refuse, being resolved to take what is to be taken myself. Dolby is nearly worked off his legs; nothing can exceed his energy and good humour, and he is extremely popular everywhere. My great desire is to avoid much travelling, and to try to get the people to come to me, instead of my going to them. If I can effect this to any moderate extent, I shall be saved a great deal of knocking about.

As they don't seem (Americans who have heard me on their travels excepted) to have the least idea here of what the readings are like, and as they are accustomed to mere readings out of a book, I am inclined to think the excitement will increase when I shall have begun. Everybody is very kind and considerate, and I have a number of old friends here, at the Bar and connected with the University. I am now negotiating to bring out the dramatic version of *No Thoroughfare* at New York. It is quite upon the cards that it may turn up trumps.

I was interrupted in that place by a call from my old secretary in the States, Mr. Putnam. It was quite affecting to see his delight in meeting his old master again. And when I told him that Anne was married, and that I had (unacknowledged) grandchildren, he laughed and cried together. I suppose you don't remember Longfellow, though he remembers you in a black velvet frock very well. He is now white-haired and white-bearded, but remarkably handsome. He still lives in his old house, where his beautiful wife was burnt to death. I dined with him the other day, and could not get the terrific scene out of my imagination. She was in a blaze in an instant, rushed into his arms with a wild cry, and never spoke afterwards.

My love to Bessie, and to Mekitty, and all the babbies.—Ever, my dear Charley,

Your affectionate Father.

While he was in Baltimore Dickens had the idea of setting up a walking-match, to take place in Boston. This was to take place between James R. Osgood, an American, and George Dolby, a British citizen. Obviously, Dickens had great fun in promoting this event.

WASHINGTON, *Tuesday, Fourth February,* 1868.

My DEAREST MAMIE,—I began here last night with great success. The audience was a superior one, composed of the foremost public men and their families. At the end of the *Carol* they gave a great break out, and applauded, I really believe, for five minutes. Immense enthusiasm . . .

I dined (against my rules) with Charles Sumner on Sunday, he having been an old friend of mine. Mr. Secretary Staunton (War Minister) was there. He is a man of very remarkable memory, and famous for his acquaintance with the minutest details of my books. Give him any passage anywhere, and he will instantly cap it and go on with the context. He was commander-in-chief of all the Northern forces concentrated here, and never went to sleep at night without first reading something from my books, which were always with him. I put him through a pretty severe examination, but he was better up than I was.

The gas was very defective indeed last night, and I began with a small speech, to the effect that I must trust to the brightness of their faces for the illumination of mine; this was taken greatly. In the *Carol* a most ridiculous incident occurred all of a sudden. I saw a dog look out from among the seats in the central aisle, and look very intently at me. The general attention being fixed on me, I don't think anybody saw the dog; but I felt so sure of his turning up again and barking, that I kept my eye wandering about in search of him. He was a very comic dog, and it was well for me that I was reading a very comic part of the book. But when he bounced out into the centre aisle again, in an entirely new place (still looking intently at me) and tried the effect of a bark upon my proceedings, I was seized with such a

paroxysm of laughter, that it communicated itself to the audience, and we
roared at one another loud and long.

The President has sent to me twice, and I am going to see him to-morrow.
He has a whole row for his family every night. Dolby rejoined his chief
yesterday morning, and will probably remain in the august presence until
Sunday night. He and Osgood, 'training for the match,' are ludicrous
beyond belief. I saw them just now coming up a street, each trying to pass
the other, and immediately fled. Since I have been writing this, they have
burst in at the door and sat down on the floor to blow. Dolby is now
writing at a neighbouring table, with his bald head smoking as if he were on
fire. Kelly (his great adherent) asked me, when he was last away, whether it
was quite fair that I should take Mr. Osgood out for 'breathers' when Mr.
Dolby had no such advantage. I begin to expect that half Boston will turn
out on the twenty-ninth to see the match. In which case it will be unspeakably droll.

ROBERT AND ELIZABETH BARRETT BROWNING*

Robert (1812–1889) and Elizabeth Barrett Browning (1806–1861), both famous for their poetry, were the main characters in the play, The Barretts of Wimpole Street, *by Rudolph Besier. The letters which follow give some of the highlights in their romance.*

R. B. TO E. B. B.

New Cross, Hatcham, Surrey.
[Post-mark, January 10, 1845.]

I love your verses with all my heart, dear Miss Barrett,—and this is no off-hand complimentary letter that I shall write,—whatever else, no prompt matter-of-course recognition of your genius, and there a graceful and natural end of the thing. Since the day last week when I first read your poems, I quite laugh to remember how I have been turning and turning again in my mind what I should be able to tell you of their effect upon me, for in the first flush of delight I thought I would this once get out of my habit of purely passive enjoyment, when I do really enjoy, and thoroughly justify my admiration—perhaps even, as a loyal fellow-craftsman should, try and find fault and do you some little good to be proud of hereafter!— but nothing comes of it all—so into me has it gone, and part of me has it become, this great living poetry of yours, not a flower of which but took root and grew—Oh, how different that is from lying to be dried and pressed flat, and prized highly, and put in a book with a proper account at top and bottom, and shut up and put away . . . and the book called a 'Flora,' besides! After all, I need not give up the thought of doing that, too, in time; because even now, talking with whoever is worthy, I can give a reason for my faith in one and another excellence, the fresh strange music, the affluent language, the exquisite pathos and true new brave thought; but in this addressing myself to you—your own self, and for the first time, my feeling rises altogether. I do, as I say, love these books with all my heart—and I love you too. Do you know I was once not very far from seeing—really seeing you? Mr. Kenyon said to me one morning 'Would you like to see Miss Barrett?' then he went to announce me,—then he returned . . . you were too unwell, and now it is years ago, and I feel as at some untoward passage in my travels, as if I had been close, so close, to some world's-wonder in chapel or crypt, only a screen to push and I might have entered, but there

---

* From The Letters of *Robert Browning and Elizabeth Barrett Barrett*, Vols. I and II. Reprinted by permission of Harper & Row, Publishers.

47

was some slight, so it now seems, slight and just sufficient bar to admission, and the half-opened door shut, and I went home my thousands of miles, and the sight was never to be?

Well, these Poems were to be, and this true thankful joy and pride with which I feel myself,

Yours ever faithfully,
ROBERT BROWNING.

Miss Barrett,
50 Wimpole St.
R. Browning.

E. B. B. TO R. B.

50 Wimpole Street: Jan. 11, 1845.

I thank you, dear Mr. Browning, from the bottom of my heart. You meant to give me pleasure by your letter—and even if the object had not been answered, I ought still to thank you. But it is thoroughly answered. Such a letter from such a hand! Sympathy is dear—very dear to me: but the sympathy of a poet, and of such a poet, is the quintessence of sympathy to me! Will you take back my gratitude for it?—agreeing, too, that of all the commerce done in the world, from Tyre to Carthage, the exchange of sympathy for gratitude is the most princely thing!

For the rest you draw me on with your kindness. It is difficult to get rid of people when you once have given them too much pleasure—*that* is a fact, and we will not stop for the moral of it. What I was going to say—after a little natural hesitation—is, that if ever you emerge without inconvenient effort from your 'passive state,' and will *tell* me of such faults as rise to the surface and strike you as important in my poems, (for of course, I do not think of troubling you with criticism in detail) you will confer a lasting obligation on me, and one which I shall value so much, that I covet it at a distance. I do not pretend to any extraordinary meekness under criticism and it is possible enough that I might not be altogether obedient to yours. But with my high respect for your power in your Art and for your experience as an artist, it would be quite impossible for me to hear a general observation of yours on what appear to you my master-faults, without being the better for it hereafter in some way. I ask for only a sentence or two of general observation—and I do not ask even for *that*, so as to tease you—but in the humble, low voice, which is so excellent a thing in women—particularly when they go a-begging! The most frequent general criticism I receive, is, I think, upon the style, 'if I *would* but change my style'! But *that* is an objection (isn't it?) to the writer bodily? Buffon says, and every sincere writer must feel, that '*Le style c'est l'homme;*' a fact, however, scarcely calculated to lessen the objection with certain critics.

Is it indeed true that I was so near to the pleasure and honour of making your acquaintance? and can it be true that you look back upon the lost opportunity with any regret? *But*—you know—if you had entered the 'crypt,' you might have caught cold, or been tired to death, and *wished* yourself 'a thousand miles off;' which would have been worse than travelling them. It is not my interest, however, to put such thoughts in your head about its being 'all for the best;' and I would rather hope (as I do) that what I lost by one chance I may recover by some future one. Winters shut me up as they do dormouse's eyes; in the spring, *we shall see:* and I am so much better that I seem turning round to the outward world again. And in the meantime I have learnt to know your voice, not merely from the poetry but from the kindness in it. Mr. Kenyon often speaks of you—dear Mr. Kenyon!—who most unspeakably, or only speakably with tears in my eyes,—has been my friend and helper, and my book's friend, and helper! critic and sympathiser, true friend of all hours! You know him well enough, I think, to understand that I must be grateful to him.

I am writing too much,—and notwithstanding that I am writing too much, I will write of one thing more. I will say that I am your debtor, not only for this cordial letter and for all the pleasure which came with it, but in other ways, and those the highest: and I will say that while I live to follow this divine art of poetry, in proportion to my love for it and my devotion to it, I must be a devout admirer and student of your works. This is in my heart to say to you—and I say it.

And, for the rest, I am proud to remain

Your obliged and faithful

ELIZABETH B. BARRETT.

Robert Browning, Esq.
New Cross, Hatcham, Surrey.

R. B. TO E. B. B.

Saturday Morning.
[Post-mark, September 13, 1845.]

. . . I am not what your generous self-forgetting appreciation would sometimes make me out—but it is not since yesterday, nor ten nor twenty years before, that I began to look into my own life, and study its end, and requirements, what would turn to its good or its loss—and I *know*, if one may know anything, that to make that life yours and increase it by union with yours, would render me *supremely happy*, as I said, and say, and feel.

My whole suit to you is, in that sense, *selfish*—not that I am ignorant that *your* nature would most surely attain happiness in being conscious that it made another happy—but *that best, best end of all*, would, like the rest, come from yourself, be a reflection of your own gift.

Dearest, I will end here—words, persuasion, arguments, if they were at my service I would not use them—I believe in you, altogether have faith in you—in you . . . R. B.

R. B. TO E. B. B.

Thursday Morning.
[Post-mark, September 10, 1846.]

What do you expect this letter will be about, my own dearest? Those which I write on the mornings after our days seem naturally to *answer* any strong point brought out in the previous discourse, and not then completely disposed of . . . so they generally run in the vile fashion of a disputatious 'last word'; 'one word yet'—do not they? Ah, but you should remember that never does it feel so intolerable,—the barest fancy of a possibility of losing you—as when I have just seen you and heard you and, alas—left you for a time; on these occasions, it seems so horrible—that if the least recollection of a fear of yours, or a doubt . . . anything which might be nursed, or let grow quietly into a serious obstacle to what we desire—if *that* rises up threateningly,—do you wonder that I begin by attacking *it?* There are always a hundred deepest reasons for gratitude and love which I could write about, but which my after life shall prove I never have forgotten . . . still, that very after-life depends perhaps on the letter of the morning reasoning with you, teazing, contradicting. Dearest Ba, I do not tell you that I am justified in plaguing you thus, at any time . . . only to get your pardon, if I can, on the grounds—the true grounds.

And this pardon, if you grant it, shall be for the past offences, not for any fresh one I mean to commit now. I will not add one word to those spoken yesterday about the extreme perilousness of delay. You *give* me yourself. Hitherto, from the very first till this moment, the giving hand has been advancing steadily—it is not for me to grasp it lest it stop within an inch or two of my forehead with its crown.

I am going to town this morning, and will leave off now.

What a glorious dream; through nearly two years—without a single interval of blankness,—much less, bitter waking!

I may say *that*, I suppose, safely through whatever befalls!

Also I will ever say, God bless you, my dearest dearest,—my perfect angel you have been! While I am only your R.

My mother is deeply gratified at your present.

12 o'clock. On returning I find your note,
'I will do as you wish—understand'—then I understand you are in earnest.
If you *do* go on Monday, our marriage will be impossible for another
year—the misery! You see what we have gained by waiting. We must be
married directly and go to Italy. I will go for a licence to-day and we can
be married on Saturday. I will call to-morrow at 3 and arrange everything
with you. We can leave from Dover &c., *after* that,—but otherwise, impossible! Inclose the ring, or a substitute—I have not a minute to spare for the
post.

Ever your own R.

E. B. B. TO R. B.

[Post-mark, September 18, 1846.]

Dearest, here is the paper of addresses. I cannot remember, I am so
confused, half of them.
Surely you say wrong in the hour for to-morrow. Also there is the
express train. Would it not be better?

Your Ba.

R. B. TO E. B. B.

11½ Friday.
[Post-mark, September 18, 1846.]

My own best Ba. How thankful I am you have seen my blunder—I took
the other company's days for the South Western's changed. What I shall
write now is with the tables before me (of the Railway) and a transcript
from *to-day's* advertisement in the *Times*.
The packet will leave to-morrow evening, from the Royal Pier,

Southampton at *nine*. We leave Nine Elms, Vauxhall, at *five*—to arrive at *eight*. Doors close *five* minutes before. I will be at Hodgson's *from* half-past three to *four precisely* when I shall hope you can be ready. I shall go to Vauxhall, apprise them that luggage is coming (yours) and send *mine* there—so that we both shall be unencumbered and we can take a cab or coach from H's.

Never mind your scanty preparations . . . we can get everything at Leghorn,—and the new boats carry parcels to Leghorn on the 15th of every month, remember—so can bring what you may wish to send for.

I enclose a letter to go with yours. The cards as you choose—they are here—we can write them from Paris or elsewhere. The advertisement, as you advise. All shall be cared for.

God bless and strengthen you, my ever dearest dearest—I will not trust myself to speak of my feelings for you—worship well belongs to such fortitude. One struggle more—if all the kindness on your part brought a strangely insufficient return, is it not possible that this step may produce all you can hope? Write to me one word more. Depend on me. I go to Town about business.

Your own, own R.

E. B. B. TO R. B.

Friday Night.
[Post-mark, September 19, 1846.]

At from half-past three to four, then—four will not, I suppose, be too late. I will not write more—*I cannot*. By to-morrow at this time, I shall have *you* only, to love me—my beloved!

You *only!* As if one said *God only*. And we shall have *Him* beside, I pray of Him.

I shall send to your address at New Cross your Hanmer's poems—and the two dear books you gave me, which I do not like to leave here and am afraid of hurting by taking them with me. Will you ask *our* Sister to put the parcel into a drawer, so as to keep it for us?

Your letters to me I take with me, let the 'ounces' cry out aloud, ever so. I *tried* to leave them, and I could not. That is, they would not be left: it was not my fault—I will not be scolded.

Is this my last letter to you, ever dearest? Oh—if I loved you less . . . a little, little less.

Why I should tell you that our marriage was invalid, or ought to be; and that you should by no means come for me to-morrow. It is dreadful . . .

dreadful . . . to have to give pain here by a voluntary act—for the first time in my life.

Remind your mother and father of me affectionately and gratefully—and your Sister too! Would she think it too bold of me to say *our* Sister, if she had heard it on the last page?

Do you pray for me to-night, Robert? Pray for me, and love me, that I may have courage, feeling both—

Your own

Ba.

The boxes are *safely sent.* Wilson has been perfect to me. And *I* . . . calling her 'timid,' and afraid of her timidity! I begin to think that none are so bold as the timid, when they are fairly roused.

MARK TWAIN*

Mark Twain, born Samuel Langhorne Clemens (1835–1910), probably the best known American humorist, carried into his letters much of the same humor that is characteristic of his stories and essays.

The Clemens apartments at the Métropole became a sort of social clearinghouse of the Viennese art and literary life, much more like an embassy than the home of a mere literary man. Celebrities in every walk of life, persons of social and official rank, writers for the press, assembled there on terms hardly possible in any other home in Vienna. Wherever Mark Twain appeared in public he was a central figure. Now and then he read or spoke to aid some benefit, and these were great gatherings attended by members of the royal family. It was following one such event that the next letter was written.

(Private)

TO REV. J. H. TWICHELL, IN HARTFORD:

HOTEL METROPOLE,
VIENNA, *Feb. 3, '98.*

DEAR JOE,—There's that letter that I began so long ago—you see how it is: can't get time to finish anything. I pile up lots of work, nevertheless. There may be idle people in the world, but I'm not one of them. I say "Private" up there because I've got an adventure to tell, and you mustn't let a breath of it get out. First I thought I would lay it up along with a thousand others that I've laid up for the same purpose—to talk to you about, but—those others have vanished out of my memory; and that must not happen with this.

The other night I lectured for a Vienna charity; and at the end of it Livy and I were introduced to a princess who is aunt to the heir apparent of the imperial throne—a beautiful lady, with a beautiful spirit, and very cordial in her praises of my books and thanks to me for writing them; and glad to meet me face to face and shake me by the hand—just the kind of princess that adorns a fairy tale and makes it the prettiest tale there is.

* From *Mark Twain's Letters*, Vol. II, edited by Albert Bigelow Paine. Copyright 1917 by Mark Twain Company; renewed 1945 by Clara Clemens Samossoud. Reprinted by permission of Harper & Row, Publishers.

Very well, we long ago found that when you are noticed by supremacies, the correct etiquette is to go, within a couple of days, and pay your respects in the quite simple form of writing your name in the Visitors' Book kept in the office of the establishment. That is the end of it, and everything is squared up and ship-shape.

So at noon to-day Livy and I drove to the Archducal palace, and got by the sentries all right, and asked the grandly-uniformed porter for the book and said we wished to write our names in it. And he called a servant in livery and was sending us up stairs; and said her Royal Highness was out but would soon be in. Of course Livy said "No—no—we only want the book;" but he was firm, and said, "You are Americans?"

"Yes."

"Then you are expected, please go up stairs."

"But indeed we are not expected—please let us have the book and—"

"Her Royal Highness will be back in a *very* little while—she commanded me to *tell* you so—and you must wait."

Well, the soldiers were there close by—there was no use trying to resist—so we followed the servant up; but when he tried to beguile us into a drawing-room, Livy drew the line; she wouldn't go in. And she wouldn't stay up there, either. She said the princess might come in at any moment and catch us, and it would be too infernally ridiculous for anything. So we went down stairs again—to my unspeakable regret. For it was too darling a comedy to spoil. I was hoping and praying the princess would come, and catch us up there, and that those other Americans who *were* expected would arrive, and be taken for impostors by the portier, and shot by the sentinels—and then it would all go into the papers, and be cabled all over the world, and make an immense stir and be perfectly lovely. And by that time the princess would discover that *we* were not the right ones, and the Minister of War would be ordered out, and the garrison, and they would come for us, and there would be another prodigious time, and *that* would get cabled too, and—well, Joe, I was in a state of perfect bliss. But happily, oh, so happily, that big portier wouldn't let us out—he was sorry, but he must obey orders—we must go back up stairs and wait. Poor Livy—I couldn't help but enjoy her distress. She said we were in a fix, and how *were* we going to explain, if the princess should arrive before the rightful Americans came? We went up stairs again—laid off our wraps, and were conducted through one drawing room and into another, and left alone there and the door closed upon us.

Livy was in a state of mind! She said it was too theatrically ridiculous; and that I would never be able to keep my mouth shut; that I would be sure to let it out and it would get into the papers—and she tried to make me promise—"Promise *what?*" I said—"to be quiet about this? Indeed I won't—it's the best thing that ever happened; I'll tell it, and add to it; and I wish Joe and Howells were here to make it perfect; I can't make all the rightful blunders myself—it takes all three of us to do justice to an opportunity like this. I would just like to see Howells get down to his work and explain, and lie, and work his futile and inventionless subterfuges when that princess comes raging in here and wanting to *know*." But Livy could not hear fun—it was not a time to be trying to be funny—we were in a most miserable and shameful situation, and if—

Just then the door spread wide and our princess and 4 more, and 3 little princes flowed in! Our princess, and her sister the Archduchess Marie Therese (mother to the imperial Heir and to the young girl Archduchesses present, and aunt to the 3 little princes)—and we shook hands all around and sat down and had a most sociable good time for half an hour—and by and by it turned out that we *were* the right ones, and had been sent for by a messenger who started too late to catch us at the hotel. We were invited for 2 o'clock, but we beat that arrangement by an hour and a half.

Wasn't it a rattling good comedy situation? Seems a kind of pity we were the right ones. It would have been such nuts to see the right ones come, and get fired out, and we chatting along comfortably and nobody suspecting us for impostors.

We send lots and lots of love.

MARK.

TO R. W. GILDER, IN NEW YORK:

VILLA DI QUARTO, FLORENCE,
June 7, '04.

DEAR GILDER FAMILY,—I have been worrying and worrying to know what to do: at last I went to the girls with an idea: to ask the Gilders to get us shelter near their summer home. It was the first time they have not shaken their heads. So to-morrow I will cable to you and shall hope to be in time.

An hour ago the best heart that ever beat for me and mine went silent out of this house, and I am as one who wanders and has lost his way. She who is gone was our head, she was our hands. We are now trying to make plans—*we:* we who have never made a plan before, nor ever needed to. If she could speak to us she would make it all simple and easy with a word, and our perplexities would vanish away. If she had known she was near to death she would have told us where to go and what to do: but she was not suspecting, neither were we. (She had been chatting cheerfully a moment before, and in an instant she was gone from us and we did not know it. We were not alarmed, we did not know anything had happened. It was a blessed death—

she passed away without knowing it.) She was all our riches and she is gone: she was our breath, she was our life and now we are nothing.

We send you our love—and with it the love of you that was in her heart when she died.

S. L. CLEMENS.

JOHN JAY CHAPMAN*

This famous love letter by John Jay Chapman (1862–1933), author, as well as the letter following it, deserves a place in this collection.

TO MINNA TIMMINS CHAPMAN

[In preserving this letter, written on one of Chapman's business visits to the West, his wife endorsed the envelope, 'La miraculosa littera d'amore.']

[Postmarked LITTLETON, COLO. Sept. 21, '92]

I have sealed up each one of these letters thinking I had done—and then a wave of happiness has come over me—remembering you—only you, my Minna—and the joy of life. Where were you, since the beginning of the world? But now you are here, about me in every space, room, sunlight, with your heart and arms and the light of your soul—and the strong vigor your presence. It was not a waste desert in Colorado. It is not a waste time, for you are here and many lives packed into one life, and the green shoot out of the heart of the plant, springing up blossoms in the night, and many old things have put on immortality and lost things have come back knocking within, from before the time I was conceived in the womb, there were you also. And what shall we say of the pain! it was false—and the rending, it was unnecessary. It was the breaking down of the dams that ought not to have been put up—but being up it was the sweeping away of them that the waters might flow together.

This is a love letter, is it not? How long is it since I have written you a love letter, my love, my Minna? Was the spring hidden that now comes bubbling up overflowing curb and coping-stone, washing my feet and my knees and my whole self? How are the waters of the world sweet—if we should die, we have drunk them. If we should sin—or separate—if we should fail or secede—we have tasted of happiness—we must be written in the book of the blessed. We have had what life could give, we have eaten of the tree of knowledge, we have known—we have been the mystery of the universe.

Is love a hand or a foot—is it a picture or a poem or a fireside—is it a compact or a permission or eagles that meet in the clouds—No, no, no, no. It is light and heat and hand and foot and ego. If I take the wings of the

* From *John Jay Chapman and His Letters*, edited by M. A. DeWolfe Howe, published by Houghton Mifflin Company, Copyright 1937. Reprinted by permission of Houghton Mifflin Company.

morning and remain in the uttermost parts of the sea, there are thou also—
He descended into Hell and on the third day rose again—and there art thou
also—in the lust or business—in the stumblings and dry places, in sickness
and health—every sort of sickness there also—what matter is it what else the
world contains—if you only are in it in every part of it? I can find no
corner of it without you—my eyes would not see it. It is empty—I have
seen all that is there and it is nothing, and over creation are your wings.
Have we not lived three years now together—and daily nearer—grafted till
the very sap of existence flows and circulates between us—till I know as I
write this—your thoughts—till I know as a feeling, a hope, a thought, passes
through me—it is yours? Why the agony of those old expressions and
attempts to come by diligent, nervous, steady, fixing of the eye on the
graver's tool, as if the prize depended on drawing it straight, those pounds
of paper and nights of passionate composition—did they indeed so well do
their work that the goal was carried—or was it the silent communion—of
the night—even after days of littleness or quarrel that knitted us together?
It does not matter, love, which it was. It put your soul so into my body that
I don't speak to you to convey meaning. I write only for joy and happiness.
How diligently have we set fact to fact and consideration against consideration during the past years—as if we were playing dominoes for our life.
How cloudy I have been—dragging you down, often nailing useless nails,
cutting up and dissecting, labeling, crucifying small things—and there was
our great love over us, growing, spreading—I wonder we do not shine—or
speak with every gesture and accent giving messages from the infinite—like
a Sibyl of Michael Angelo. I wonder people do not look after us in the
street as if they had seen an angel.

TUO GIOVANNI

TO EVELYN AMES AND FREDERICK HALL

[ON THEIR ENGAGEMENT.]

SYLVANIA
BARRYTOWN-ON-HUDSON
May 18: 1909

MY DEAR EVELYN AND FRED

I congratulate you both and am overjoyed. Elizabeth and I could not help
suspecting something of the kind in January and I have been tempted ever
since to write you to go ahead and plunge and don't fear your fate too
much, etc. I was only restrained by knowing such things must come of their
own force and power. So I am relieved to hear that I may tell you how

much we both liked and believed in Hall and hoped it would come off. As for happiness the less you argue about it and concern yourself with it the better. Any marriage may be unhappy and all marriages contain terrible grinding difficulties of character. Marriage demands the utmost of human virtue. That's why it is valuable. You will suffer immensely and would have suffered immensely no matter who or when you had married. What of it? We cannot escape it—ought not to seek to escape it. Rather we ought to prepare for it as necessary to our and all men's fulfillment. Happy those to whom it is not denied.

Yours affectionately (I mean both of you)

JACK

ROBERT FROST*

So much is known of Robert Frost (1875–1963), the man, and so little of the poet as a child, that the letter "To Sabra Peabody" merits inclusion. The second letter shows his appreciation of the English friendships he made and of the country that first launched him as a poet. He left England the year after World War I started.

4. TO SABRA PEABODY

DEAR SABE,

   I will answer your letter to let you know that I am well and hope you are the same. About me liking Lida [Storer] better than you you are all wrong because I like you twice as much as I do her and always have thought more of you than any other girl I know of. I thought you were going to the entertainment the other night but I didn't see you there. I saw Eva Hattie and your mother there. There is no fun in getting mad every so [often so] lets see if we cant keep friends Im sure I am willing. I know I have not treated you as I ought to sometimes and sometimes I don't know wheather you are mad or not and we have gotten mad and then we would get friends again ever since Westons party when I first came here. There are not many girls I like but when I like them I fall dead in love with them and there are not many I like just because I can have some fun with them like I can Lida but I like you because I cant help myself and when I get mad at you I feel mad at myself to.

From your loveing   Rob

100. TO HAROLD MONRO

[c. 13 February 1915]   [Liverpool]

DEAR MONRO

   This with my best goodbyes. Thanks for everything. I had intended to see you before leaving but at the last moment we go rather precipitously; so

* From *Selected Letters of Robert Frost,* edited by Lawrance Thompson. Copyright © 1964 by Holt, Rinehart and Winston, Inc. Reprinted by permission of the Estate of Robert Frost and Holt, Rinehart and Winston, Inc.

that I am scanting duties. Anyway I don't want too much made of my going or I should feel as if I were never coming back. I shall be back just as soon as I have earned a little more living. England has become half my native land—England the victorious. Good friends I have had here and hope to keep.

Yours ever   Robert Frost

FRANZ KAFKA*

Franz Kafka (1883–1924), German novelist and essayist, is particularly well known for The Trial, The Castle *and* Amerika. *His works frequently combine the dream world and the real world. His* Letters to Milena *reveal his philosophical observations as well as his affection for Milena.*

It's a long time since I wrote to you, Frau Milena, and even today I'm writing only as the result of an incident. Actually, I don't have to apologize for my not writing, you know after all how I hate letters. All the misfortune of my life—I don't wish to complain, but to make a generally instructive remark—derives, one could say, from letters or from the possibility of writing letters. People have hardly ever deceived me, but letters always—and as a matter of fact not only those of other people, but my own. In my case this is a special misfortune of which I won't say more, but at the same time also a general one. The easy possibility of letter-writing must—seen merely theoretically—have brought into the world a terrible disintegration of souls. It is, in fact, an intercourse with ghosts, and not only with the ghost of the recipient but also with one's own ghost which develops between the lines of the letter one is writing and even more so in a series of letters where one letter corroborates the other and can refer to it as a witness. How on earth did anyone get the idea that people can communicate with one another by letter! Of a distant person one can think, and of a person who is near one can catch hold—all else goes beyond human strength. Writing letters, however, means to denude oneself before the ghosts, something for which they greedily wait. Written kisses don't reach their destination, rather they are drunk on the way by the ghosts. It is on this ample nourishment that they multiply so enormously. Humanity senses this and fights against it and in order to eliminate as far as possible the ghostly element between people and to create a natural communication, the peace of souls, it has invented the railway, the motor car, the aeroplane. But it's no longer any good, these are evidently inventions being made at the moment of crashing. The opposing side is so much calmer and stronger; after the postal service it has invented the telegraph, the telephone, the radiograph. The ghosts won't starve, but we will perish.

I'm surprised that you haven't written about this yet, not in order to prevent or achieve something with its publication, for that it is too late, but in order at least to show "them" that they have been recognized.

One can also recognize "them", incidentally, by the exceptions, for sometimes they allow a letter to pass without interfering, and it arrives like a friendly hand, light and kind it lays itself in one's own. Well, this too probably only appears to be so, such cases are perhaps the most dangerous and one should beware more of them than of others. But if it is a deception, then in any case it's a complete one.

Something of this kind happened to me today and this is really why it occurred to me to write to you. Today I received a letter from a friend[1] whom you also know; we hadn't written to each other for a long time, which is most sensible. It follows from the above that letters are a perfect anti-sleep remedy. What a condition they arrive in! Dried out, empty and provocative, a joy of the moment followed by long suffering. While reading them, forgetting oneself, the little sleep that one owns gets up, flies off through the open window and doesn't return for a long time. This is the reason why we don't write to one another. But I think of him often, though too fleetingly. All my thinking is too fleeting. But last night I thought a great deal of him, for hours, spent the night hours in bed (so precious to me because of their hostility) repeating to him again and again with the same words in an imaginary letter several facts which at that moment seemed most important to me. And in the morning a letter from him actually arrived, and contained moreover the remark that the friend had had, for a month—or better, a month ago—the feeling that he ought to come and see me, a remark which strangely coincided with things that I had experienced.

This letter-incident caused me to write a letter and since I had already started, how could I not write to you, too, Frau Milena, to whom I perhaps enjoy writing most (as far as one ever enjoys writing letters, which however is said only for the ghosts who greedily besiege my table).

---

[1] Presumably Milena herself.

ALEXANDER WOOLLCOTT*

Alexander Woollcott (1887–1943), critic and noted wit, wrote essays and reviews in addition to his letters.

TO CAPTAIN THORNTON WILDER

New York City
November 13, 1942

DEAR THORNTON:

I was staying at the White House for a week, living in the Lincoln Room but sleeping in a little ante-chamber because, unlike Edna Ferber (a previous occupant), I felt unequal to the strain of lying in his bed. Walter Lippmann, in order to illustrate a point we had been discussing, had just sent around by messenger the new *Yale Review* anthology and there was a brief New Orleans play of yours which I had never read and which I sat down and read at once. Well, I was going to write you about *that* but—

Then on Monday of this week I was free for a few hours and went around to sup with Dr. Kommer and that ineffably beautiful Paget girl who married Raimund von Hoffmannstahl. En route Kommer had picked up Harry Luce. So there was much talk of your reading Horace at Chefoo and I worked him up into a dither about *The Skin of Our Teeth*. He wanted *Life* to do a photographic blast about it (their photographers are on their way to Washington tonight for the purpose) and for me to write the accompanying text. I said I couldn't do this without seeing the play again and couldn't—physically couldn't—go down to Washington. So in the way of these great typhoons, or whatever you call them, he passed the word along to a chain of underlings with the result that yesterday Dan Longwell wrote me about *my* notion of going to Washington to cover the play for *Life*.

I am dictating this on a train bearing me toward Whitehall and the island where Dorothy Parker will join me tomorrow. I will have four days in which to sort out the books and files that must go with me when the island is closed as it will be, sine die, in another fortnight. On Wednesday I go back to the Peter Bent Brigham Hospital for a week of tinkering. I assured the heart specialist that I will no longer undertake to do the work of ten men. I must ingloriously do the work of only five.

---

* From *The Letters of Alexander Woollcott*, edited by Beatrice Kaufman and Joseph Hennessey. Copyright 1944 by The Viking Press, Inc. Reprinted by permission of The Viking Press, Inc.

Then a lecture to twelve thousand women in St. Paul on a new book, a new play and a new movie. (The book is Hesketh Pearson's G.B.S.) Then two days in Chicago largely with Lloyd Lewis but a little with Bob Hutchins. Then back to New York for quite some time.

A. W.

P.S. In the course of a discussion about my dubious equipment for editing an anthology for service men Felix Frankfurter sends me this anecdote about Holmes:

"I don't suppose in our time there has been anyone more truly well read than the Justice. But it is a fact that some of the most famous among the orthodox classics in literature he did not get around to reading until late in life. Indeed it was a favorite belief of his that the great classics should be read late and not early. It was when he was about eighty that he began to read a lot of books that most people would be ashamed to deny they had not read. He said he was reading for Judgment Day—that when he appeared for examination Mon Dieu might say, 'Holmes, what do you think of the *Odyssey?*' or 'Holmes, what do you think of Thucydides?' And he would feel rather naked to have to reply, 'I am sorry, Sir, but I haven't read them.' So he would ask from time to time about books to read. I remember on one occasion saying to him, 'Mon Dieu might ask you what you think about Moneypenny and Buckles *Life of Disraeli.*' And he said, 'I don't care for biography, and if Mon Dieu is interested in such trivial things then I don't care much for him.' "

A. W.

MARIANNE MOORE (1887–) AND THE FORD MOTOR COMPANY*

DEPARTMENT OF AMPLIFICATION

DEPARTMENT OF ENGLISH,
UNIVERSITY OF MICHIGAN,
MARCH 15, 1957

To the Editors, *The New Yorker,*

DEAR SIRS:

After reading Winthrop Sargeant's recent Profile of Miss Marianne Moore, Brooklyn's celebrated poet, it occurred to me that you (and Mr. Sargeant) might be interested in an exchange of correspondence that took place some time ago between Miss Moore and the Ford Motor Company. The letters were lent to me by an official of the Ford Company as the sort of thing that should interest a university English department.

Sincerely,

CLARENCE BROWN

P.S. The letters speak pretty well for themselves, though two items of exegesis might be useful. First, Miss Moore sent with her second letter a postcard bearing a photograph of a plant called the silversword; on the back was written, in a spidery hand, "This may be kept." Second, the Ford Company's Christmas message was accompanied, I believe, by two dozen roses and the appropriate seasonal greenery. In any case, here are the letters, for which permission to publish has been granted:

OCTOBER 19, 1955

MISS MARIANNE MOORE,
CUMBERLAND STREET,
BROOKLYN 5, NEW YORK

DEAR MISS MOORE:

This is a morning we find ourselves with a problem which, strangely enough, is more in the field of words and the fragile meaning of words than in car-making. And we just wonder whether you might be intrigued with it sufficiently to lend us a hand.

* From *A Marianne Moore Reader* by Marianne Moore. Copyright © 1957 by *The New Yorker*. Originally appeared in *The New Yorker*. Reprinted by permission of The Viking Press, Inc. and Ford Motor Company.

Our dilemma is a name for a rather important new series of cars.
We should like this name to be more than a label. Specifically, we should
like it to have a compelling quality in itself and by itself. To convey,
through association or other conjuration, some visceral feeling of elegance,
fleetness, advanced features and design. A name, in short, that flashes a
dramatically desirable picture in people's minds. (Another "Thunderbird"
would be fine.)

Over the past few weeks this office has confected a list of three hundred-
odd candidates which, it pains me to relate, are characterized by an embarrassing pedestrianism. We are miles short of our ambition. And so we are
seeking the help of one who knows more about this sort of magic than
we.

As to how we might go about this matter, I have no idea. But, in any
event, all would depend on whether you find this overture of some
challenge and interest.

Should we be so fortunate as to have piqued your fancy, we will be
pleased to write more fully. And, of course, it is expected that our relations
will be on a fee basis of an impeccably dignified kind.

Respectfully,
DAVID WALLACE
Special Products Division

OCTOBER 21, 1955

Let me take it under advisement, Mr. Wallace. I am complimented to be
recruited in this high matter.

I have seen and admired "Thunderbird" as a Ford designation. It would
be hard to match; but let me, the coming week, talk with my brother, who
would bring ardor and imagination to bear on the quest.

Sincerely yours,
MARIANNE MOORE

OCTOBER 27, 1955

DEAR MR. WALLACE:

My brother thought most of the names I had considered suggesting to
you for your new series too learned or too labored, but thinks I might ask if
any of the following approximate the requirements:

THE FORD SILVER SWORD

This plant, of which the flower is a silver sword, I believe grows only on
the Hawaiian Island Maui, on Mount Haleakala (House of the Sun); found
at an altitude of from 9,500 to 10,000 feet. (The leaves—silver-white—sur-

rounding the individual blossoms—have a pebbled texture that feels like Italian-twist backstitch allover embroidery.)

My first thought was of a bird series—the swallow species—Hirundo, or, phonetically, Aerundo. Malvina Hoffman is designing a device for the radiator of a made-to-order Cadillac, and said in her opinion the only term surpassing Thunderbird would be hurricane; and I then thought Hurricane Hirundo might be the first of a series such as Hurricane Aquila (eagle), Hurricane Accipiter (hawk), and so on. A species that takes its dinner on the wing ("swifts").

If these suggestions are not in character with the car, perhaps you could give me a sketch of its general appearance, or hint as to some of its exciting potentialities—though my brother reminds me that such information is highly confidential.

Sincerely yours,

MARIANNE MOORE

NOVEMBER 4, 1955

DEAR MISS MOORE:

I'm delighted that your note implies that you are interested in helping us in our naming problem.

This being so, procedures in this rigorous business world dictate that we on this end at least document a formal arrangement with provision for a suitable fee or honorarium before pursuing the problem further.

One way might be for you to suggest a figure which could be considered for mutual acceptance. Once this is squared away, we will look forward to having you join us in the continuation of our fascinating search.

Sincerely,

DAVID WALLACE

Special Products Division

NOVEMBER 7, 1955

DEAR MR. WALLACE:

It is handsome of you to consider remuneration for service merely enlisted. My fancy would be inhibited, however, by acknowledgment in advance of performance. If I could be of specific assistance, we could no doubt agree on some kind of honorarium for the service rendered.

I seem to exact participation; but if you could tell me how the suggestions submitted strayed—if obviously—from the ideal, I could then perhaps proceed more nearly in keeping with the Company's objective.

Sincerely yours,

MARIANNE MOORE

DEAR MISS MOORE:

Our office philodendron has just benefitted from an extra measure of water as, pacing about, I have sought words to respond to your recent generous note. Let me state my quandary thus. It is unspeakably contrary to procedure to accept counsel—even needed counsel—without a firm prior agreement of conditions (and, indeed, to follow the letter of things, without a Purchase Notice in quadruplicate and three Competitive Bids). But then, seldom has the auto business had occasion to indulge in so ethereal a matter as this. So, if you will risk a mutually satisfactory outcome with us, we should like to honor your wish for a fancy unencumbered.

As to wherein your earlier suggestions may have "strayed," as you put it—they did not at all. Shipment No. 1 was fine, and we would like to luxuriate in more of same—even those your brother regarded as overlearned or labored. For us to impose an ideal on your efforts would, I fear, merely defeat our purpose. We have sought your help to get an approach quite different from our own. In short, we should like suggestions that we ourselves would not have arrived at. And, in sober fact, have not.

Now we on this end must help you by sending some tangible representation of what we are talking about. Perhaps the enclosed sketches will serve the purpose. They are not IT, but they convey the feeling. At the very least, they may give you a sense of participation should your friend Malvina Hoffman break into brisk conversation on radiator caps.

Sincerely yours,

DAVID WALLACE

Special Products Division

DEAR MR. WALLACE:

The sketches. They are indeed exciting; they have quality, and the toucan tones lend tremendous allure—confirmed by the wheels. Half the magic—sustaining effects of this kind. Looked at upside down, furthermore, there is a sense of fish buoyancy. Immediately your word "impeccable" sprang to mind. Might it be a possibility? The Impeccable. In any case, the baguette lapidary glamour you have achieved certainly spurs the imagination. Car-innovation is like launching a ship—"drama."

I am by no means sure that I can help you to the right thing, but performance with elegance casts a spell. Let me do some thinking in the direction of impeccable, symmechromatic, thunderblender. . . . (The exotics, if I can shape them a little.) Dearborn might come into one.

If the sketches should be returned at once, let me know. Otherwise, let me dwell on them for a time. I am, may I say, a trusty confidante.

I thank you for realizing that under contract esprit could not flower. You owe me nothing, specific or moral.

Sincerely,
MARIANNE MOORE

NOVEMBER 19, 1955

Some other suggestions, Mr. Wallace, for the phenomenon:

THE RESILIENT BULLET
or Intelligent Bullet
or Bullet Cloisonné or Bullet Lavolta

(I have always had a fancy for THE INTELLIGENT WHALE—the little first Navy submarine, shaped like a sweet potato; on view in our Brooklyn Yard.)

THE FORD FABERGE

(That there is also a perfume Fabergé seems to me to do no harm, for here allusion is to the original silversmith.)

THE ARC-en-CIEL (the rainbow)
ARCENCIEL?

Please do not feel that memoranda from me need acknowledgment. I am not working day and night for you; I feel that etymological hits are partially accidental.

The bullet idea has possibilities, it seems to me, in connection with Mercury (with Hermes and Hermes Trismegistus) and magic (white magic).

Sincerely,
MARIANNE MOORE

NOVEMBER 28, 1955

DEAR MR. WALLACE:

MONGOOSE CIVIQUE

ANTICIPATOR

REGNA RACER (couronne à couronne) sovereign to sovereign

AEROTERRE

Fée Rapide (Aérofée, Aéro Faire, Fée Aiglette, Magi-faire) Comme Il Faire

Tonnerre Alifére (winged thunder)

Aliforme Alifère (wing-slender, a-wing)

TURBOTORC (used as an adjective by Plymouth)

THUNDERBIRD Allié (Cousin Thunderbird)

THUNDER CRESTER

DEARBORN Diamante

MAGIGRAVURE

PASTELOGRAM

I shall be returning the sketches very soon.

M. M.

DECEMBER 6, 1955

DEAR MR. WALLACE:

Regina-rex

Taper Racer   Taper Acer

Varsity Stroke

Angelastro

Astranaut

Chaparral

Tir à l'arc (bull's eye)

Cresta Lark

Triskelion (three legs running)

Pluma Piluma (hairfine, featherfoot)

Andante con Moto (description of a good motor?)

My findings thin, so I terminate them and am returning the sketches. Two principles I have not been able to capture: 1, the topknot of the peacock and topnotcher of speed. 2, the swivel-axis (emphasized elsewhere), like the Captain's bed on the whaleship, Charles Morgan—balanced so that it levelled whatever the slant of the ship.

If I stumble on a hit, you shall have it. Anything so far has been pastime. Do not ponder appreciation, Mr. Wallace. That was embodied in the sketches.

M. M.

I cannot resist the temptation to disobey my brother and submit

TURCOTINGA (turquoise cotinga—the cotinga being a South-American finch or sparrow) solid indigo.

(I have a three-volume treatise on flowers that might produce something but the impression given should certainly be unlabored.)

DECEMBER 8, 1955

MR. WALLACE:

May I submit UTOPIAN TURTLETOP? Do not trouble to answer unless you like it.

MARIANNE MOORE

DECEMBER 23, 1955

MERRY CHRISTMAS TO OUR FAVORITE TURTLETOPPER.

DAVID WALLACE

DECEMBER 26, 1955

DEAR MR. WALLACE:

An aspiring turtle is certain to glory in spiral eucalyptus, white pine straight from the forest, and innumerable scarlet roses almost too tall for close inspection. Of a temperament susceptible to shock though one may be, to be treated like royalty could not but induce sensations unprecedented august.

Please know that a carfancyer's allegiance to the Ford automotive turtle—extending from the Model T Dynasty to the Wallace Utopian Dynasty—can never waver; impersonal gratitude surely becoming infinite when made personal. Gratitude to unmiserly Mr. Wallace and his idealistic associates.

MARIANNE MOORE

NOVEMBER 8, 1956

DEAR MISS MOORE:

Because you were so kind to us in our early days of looking for a suitable name, I feel a deep obligation to report on events that have ensued.

And I feel I must do so before the public announcement of same come Monday, November 19.

We have chosen a name out of the more than six thousand-odd candidates that we gathered. It fails somewhat of the resonance, gaiety, and zest we were seeking. But it has a personal dignity and meaning to many of us here. Our name, dear Miss Moore, is—Edsel.

I hope you will understand.

Cordially,
DAVID WALLACE
Special Products Division

JAMES AGEE*

James Agee (1909–1955), author of A Death in the Family, *reveals his sensitive nature in his letters. A young man, he died in 1955.*

JAMES AGEE TO FATHER FLYE

[*New York City*]
[*March 2, 1948*]

Dear Father:

I'm very puzzled in realizing how long it is since I've written, to say nothing of being very sorry. I've thought of you very often, and every time, realized I haven't written, and every time have expected and intended to write the next chance I got. But I haven't done it. Not in attempted self-excuse, I am curious why, and realize several reasons. I've been very much pre-occupied for several months with a piece of writing I'm trying to do, that has so soaked up my interest that I've felt relatively little else to think or talk about. Added to this, I've been unable to do much of it except during my vacation last fall, but week after week has gone by in frustration compounded of my job, unexpected pieces of hard work for the job, the NATION, or in personal relationships, and besides, my own inertia, inefficiency and capacity for waste of time. This has gradually brought on an unusually deep and lasting depression, mental and physical, from which for several weeks now I've had only a few hours escape per week. In that kind of apathy I'm incapable of anything except, by desperate effort and willpower, doing my job. But any coherent talking is out of the question. Just now I seem to be on a tight rope between such depression and reasonable well-being, so I'm seizing the chance to write you at least a note to tell you I realize how long it is since I've written, and why, so well as I understand it, and to wish you well and send my love.

I think I'd better not talk much about the piece of writing. A novel, short but longer than I had foreseen or thought best for it, about my first 6 years, ending the day of my father's burial.[1] I read you the little I had done of it. On the whole, I feel hopeful about it, and I certainly need to feel hopeful. Underlying the hopefulness is utter lack of confidence, apathy, panic and

---

* George Braziller, Inc.—from *Letters of James Agee to Father Flye;* reprinted with the permission of the publisher. Copyright © 1962 by James Harold Flye and The James Agee Trust.
[1] Ultimately, this became *A Death in the Family* (McDowell, Obolensky, 1957).

despair. And I'd better not dwell on that just now, either, for I could much too easily slip into it . . .

I find I am incapable of leisure without fear and guilt, and that seems a far from healthy state to be in.

There is a very beautiful French movie here now, which I hope will be around this summer for you to see. It is called *Farrabique*, the name of a farm in Southwestern France. It is without actors or a fictional story; it is simply a chronicle of a full year in the life of a farm family. It seems to me one of the finest things of any such kind—i.e. agricultural poetry—that I know. It hasn't the absolute mastery and beauty of the *Georgics*, but it doesn't by any means fall to pieces under the comparison.

Two very differing heroes of mine have died lately: Gandhi, and Sergei Eisenstein. Gandhi seems to me the best reason why this is not merely the horrible Dark Age it certainly is, but also one of wonderful accomplishment,—and conceivable hope for a future. Eisenstein is the perfect image of the Promethean type in this time. Well I can't write about them.

On about everything else, I guess, I'm overtaken with the realization that by Wednesday morning I'm due with as good a piece as I can write about Eisenstein for *The Nation*. I must quit and try to do it.

God bless you . . .

RUFUS

☙ Short Stories

AN UPHEAVAL*

ANTON CHEKHOV (1860–1904)

MASHENKA PAVLETSKY, A YOUNG GIRL WHO HAD ONLY JUST FINISHED HER studies at a boarding school, returning from a walk to the house of the Kushkins, with whom she was living as a governess, found the household in a terrible turmoil. Mihailo, the porter who opened the door to her, was excited and red as a crab.

Loud voices were heard from upstairs.

"Madame Kushkin is in a fit, most likely, or else she has quarrelled with her husband," thought Mashenka.

In the hall and in the corridor she met maid-servants. One of them was crying. Then Mashenka saw, running out of her room, the master of the house himself, Nikolay Sergeitch, a little man with a flabby face and a bald head, though he was not old. He was red in the face and twitching all over. He passed the governess without noticing her, and throwing up his arms, exclaimed:

"Oh, how horrible it is! How tactless! How stupid! How barbarous! Abominable!"

Mashenka went into her room, and then, for the first time in her life, it was her lot to experience in all its acuteness the feeling that is so familiar to persons in dependent positions, who eat the bread of the rich and powerful, and cannot speak their minds. There was a search going on in her room. The lady of the house, Fedosya Vassilyevna, a stout, broad-shouldered, uncouth woman with thick black eyebrows, a faintly perceptible moustache, and red hands, who was exactly like a plain, illiterate cook in face and manners, was standing, without her cap on, at the table, putting back into Mashenka's work-bag balls of wool, scraps of materials, and bits of paper. . . . Evidently the governess's arrival took her by surprise, since, on looking round and seeing the girl's pale and astonished face, she was a little taken aback, and muttered:

"*Pardon.* I . . . I upset it accidentally. . . . My sleeve caught in it. . . ."

And saying something more, Madame Kushkin rustled her long skirts and went out. Mashenka looked round her room with wondering eyes, and, unable to understand it, not knowing what to think, shrugged her shoulders,

* Reprinted with permission of The Macmillan Company from *The Lady with the Dog and Other Stories* by Anton Chekhov. Translated from the Russian by Constance Garnett. Copyright 1917 by The Macmillan Company, renewed 1945 by Constance Garnett.

and turned cold with dismay. What had Fedosya Vassilyevna been looking for in her work-bag? If she really had, as she said, caught her sleeve in it and upset everything, why had Nikolay Sergeitch dashed out of her room so excited and red in the face? Why was one drawer of the table pulled out a little way? The money-box, in which the governess put away ten kopeck pieces and old stamps, was open. They had opened it, but did not know how to shut it, though they had scratched the lock all over. The whatnot with her books on it, the things on the table, the bed—all bore fresh traces of a search. Her linen-basket, too. The linen had been carefully folded, but it was not in the same order as Mashenka had left it when she went out. So the search had been thorough, most thorough. But what was it for? Why? What had happened? Mashenka remembered the excited porter, the general turmoil which was still going on, the weeping servant-girl; had it not all some connection with the search that had just been made in her room? Was not she mixed up in something dreadful? Mashenka turned pale, and feeling cold all over, sank on to her linen-basket.

A maid-servant came into the room.

"Liza, you don't know why they have been rummaging in my room?" the governess asked her.

"Mistress has lost a brooch worth two thousand," said Liza.

"Yes, but why have they been rummaging in my room?"

"They've been searching every one, miss. They've searched all my things, too. They stripped us all naked and searched us. . . . God knows, miss, I never went near her toilet-table, let alone touching the brooch. I shall say the same at the police-station."

"But . . . why have they been rummaging here?" the governess still wondered.

"A brooch has been stolen, I tell you. The mistress has been rummaging in everything with her own hands. She even searched Mihailo, the porter, herself. It's a perfect disgrace! Nikolay Sergeitch simply looks on and cackles like a hen. But you've no need to tremble like that, miss. They found nothing here. You've nothing to be afraid of if you didn't take the brooch."

"But, Liza, it's vile . . . it's insulting," said Mashenka, breathless with indignation. "It's so mean, so low! What right had she to suspect me and to rummage in my things?"

"You are living with strangers, miss," sighed Liza. "Though you are a young lady, still you are . . . as it were . . . a servant. . . . It's not like living with your papa and mamma."

Mashenka threw herself on the bed and sobbed bitterly. Never in her life had she been subjected to such an outrage, never had she been so deeply insulted. . . . She, well-educated, refined, the daughter of a teacher, was suspected of theft; she had been searched like a street-walker! She could not imagine a greater insult. And to this feeling of resentment was added an oppressive dread of what would come next. All sorts of absurd ideas came into her mind. If they could suspect her of theft, then they might arrest her, strip her naked, and search her, then lead her through the street with an escort of soldiers, cast her into a cold, dark cell with mice and woodlice, exactly like the dungeon in which Princess Tarakanov was imprisoned. Who would stand up for her? Her parents lived far away in the provinces; they had not the money to come to her. In the capital she was as solitary as in a desert, without friends or kindred. They could do what they liked with her.

"I will go to all the courts and all the lawyers," Mashenka thought, trembling. "I will explain to them, I will take an oath. . . . They will believe that I could not be a thief!"

Mashenka remembered that under the sheets in her basket she had some sweetmeats, which, following the habits of her schooldays, she had put in her pocket at dinner and carried off to her room. She felt hot all over, and was ashamed at the thought that her little secret was known to the lady of the house; and all this terror, shame, resentment, brought on an attack of palpitation of the heart, which set up a throbbing in her temples, in her heart, and deep down in her stomach.

"Dinner is ready," the servant summoned Mashenka.

"Shall I go, or not?"

Mashenka brushed her hair, wiped her face with a wet towel, and went into the dining-room. There they had already begun dinner. At one end of the table sat Fedosya Vassilyevna with a stupid, solemn, serious face; at the other end Nikolay Sergeitch. At the sides there were the visitors and the children. The dishes were handed by two footmen in swallowtails and white gloves. Every one knew that there was an upset in the house, that Madame Kushkin was in trouble, and every one was silent. Nothing was heard but the sound of munching and the rattle of spoons on the plates.

The lady of the house, herself, was the first to speak.

"What is the third course?" she asked the footman in a weary, injured voice.

"*Esturgeon à la russe*," answered the footman.

"I ordered that, Fenya," Nikolay Sergeitch hastened to observe. "I wanted some fish. If you don't like it, *ma chère*, don't let them serve it. I just ordered it. . . ."

Fedosya Vassilyevna did not like dishes that she had not ordered herself, and now her eyes filled with tears.

"Come, don't let us agitate ourselves," Mamikov, her household doctor, observed in a honeyed voice, just touching her arm, with a smile as honeyed. "We are nervous enough as it is. Let us forget the brooch! Health is worth more than two thousand roubles!"

"It's not the two thousand I regret," answered the lady, and a big tear rolled down her cheek. "It's the fact itself that revolts me! I cannot put up with thieves in my house. I don't regret it—I regret nothing; but to steal from me is such ingratitude! That's how they repay me for my kindness. . . ."

They all looked into their plates, but Mashenka fancied after the lady's

SHORT STORIES

words that every one was looking at her. A lump rose in her throat; she
began crying and put her handkerchief to her lips.

"*Pardon*," she muttered. "I can't help it. My head aches. I'll go away."

And she got up from the table, scraping her chair awkwardly, and went
out quickly, still more overcome with confusion.

"It's beyond everything!" said Nikolay Sergeitch, frowning. "What need
was there to search her room? How out of place it was!"

"I don't say she took the brooch," said Fedosya Vassilyevna, "but can you
answer for her? To tell the truth, I haven't much confidence in these
learned paupers."

"It really was unsuitable, Fenya. . . . Excuse me, Fenya, but you've no
kind of legal right to make a search."

"I know nothing about your laws. All I know is that I've lost my brooch.
And I will find the brooch!" She brought her fork down on the plate with a
clatter, and her eyes flashed angrily. "And you eat your dinner, and don't
interfere in what doesn't concern you!"

Nikolay Sergeitch dropped his eyes mildly and sighed. Meanwhile Mashenka, reaching her room, flung herself on her bed. She felt now neither
alarm nor shame, but she felt an intense longing to go and slap the cheeks of
this hard, arrogant, dull-witted, prosperous woman.

Lying on her bed she breathed into her pillow and dreamed of how nice
it would be to go and buy the most expensive brooch and fling it into the
face of this bullying woman. If only it were God's will that Fedosya
Vassilyevna should come to ruin and wander about begging, and should
taste all the horrors of poverty and dependence, and that Mashenka, whom
she had insulted, might give her alms! Oh, if only she could come in for a
big fortune, could buy a carriage, and could drive noisily past the windows
so as to be envied by that woman!

But all these were only dreams, in reality there was only one thing left to
do—to get away as quickly as possible, not to stay another hour in this
place. It was true it was terrible to lose her place, to go back to her parents,
who had nothing; but what could she do? Mashenka could not bear the
sight of the lady of the house nor of her little room; she felt stifled and
wretched here. She was so disgusted with Fedosya Vassilyevna, who was so
obsessed by her illnesses and her supposed aristocratic rank, that everything
in the world seemed to have become coarse and unattractive because this
woman was living in it. Mashenka jumped up from the bed and began
packing.

"May I come in?" asked Nikolay Sergeitch at the door; he had come up
noiselessly to the door, and spoke in a soft, subdued voice. "May I?"

"Come in."

He came in and stood still near the door. His eyes looked dim and his red
little nose was shiny. After dinner he used to drink beer, and the fact was
perceptible in his walk, in his feeble, flabby hands.

"What's this?" he asked, pointing to the basket.

"I am packing. Forgive me, Nikolay Sergeitch, but I cannot remain in
your house. I feel deeply insulted by this search!"

"I understand. . . . Only you are wrong to go. . . . Why should you? They've searched your things, but you . . . what does it matter to you? You will be none the worse for it."

Mashenka was silent and went on packing. Nikolay Sergeitch pinched his moustache, as though wondering what he should say next, and went on in an ingratiating voice:

"I understand, of course, but you must make allowances. You know my wife is nervous, headstrong; you mustn't judge her too harshly."

Mashenka did not speak.

"If you are so offended," Nikolay Sergeitch went on, "well, if you like, I'm ready to apologise. I ask your pardon."

Mashenka made no answer, but only bent lower over her box. This exhausted, irresolute man was of absolutely no significance in the household. He stood in the pitiful position of a dependent and hanger-on, even with the servants, and his apology meant nothing either.

"H'm! . . . You say nothing! That's not enough for you. In that case, I will apologise for my wife. In my wife's name. . . . She behaved tactlessly, I admit it as a gentleman. . . ."

Nikolay Sergeitch walked about the room, heaved a sigh, and went on:

"Then you want me to have it rankling here, under my heart. . . . You want my conscience to torment me. . . ."

"I know it's not your fault, Nikolay Sergeitch," said Mashenka, looking him full in the face with her big tear-stained eyes. "Why should you worry yourself?"

"Of course, no. . . . But still, don't you . . . go away. I entreat you."

Mashenka shook her head. Nikolay Sergeitch stopped at the window and drummed on the pane with his finger-tips.

"Such misunderstandings are simply torture to me," he said. "Why, do you want me to go down on my knees to you, or what? Your pride is wounded, and here you've been crying and packing up to go; but I have pride, too, and you do not spare it! Or do you want me to tell you what I would not tell as Confession? Do you? Listen; you want me to tell you what I won't tell the priest on my deathbed?"

Mashenka made no answer.

"I took my wife's brooch," Nikolay Sergeitch said quickly. "Is that enough now? Are you satisfied? Yes, I . . . took it. . . . But, of course, I count on your discretion. . . . For God's sake, not a word, not half a hint to any one!"

Mashenka, amazed and frightened, went on packing; she snatched her things, crumpled them up, and thrust them anyhow into the box and the basket. Now, after this candid avowal on the part of Nikolay Sergeitch, she could not remain another minute, and could not understand how she could have gone on living in the house before.

"And it's nothing to wonder at," Nikolay Sergeitch went on after a pause. "It's an everyday story! I need money, and she . . . won't give it to me. It was my father's money that bought this house and everything, you know! It's all mine, and the brooch belonged to my mother, and . . . it's all mine!"

And she took it, took possession of everything. . . . I can't go to law with her, you'll admit. . . . I beg you most earnestly, overlook it . . . stay on. *Tout comprendre, tout pardonner.* Will you stay?"

"No!" said Mashenka resolutely, beginning to tremble. "Let me alone, I entreat you!"

"Well, God bless you!" sighed Nikolay Sergeitch, sitting down on the stool near the box. "I must own I like people who still can feel resentment, contempt, and so on. I could sit here forever and look at your indignant face. . . . So you won't stay, then? I understand. . . . It's bound to be so. . . . Yes, of course. . . . It's all right for you, but for me—wo-o-o-o! . . . I can't stir a step out of this cellar. I'd go off to one of your estates, but in every one of them there are some of my wife's rascals . . . stewards, experts, damn them all! They mortgage and remortgage. . . . You mustn't catch fish, must keep off the grass, mustn't break the trees."

"Nikolay Sergeitch!" his wife's voice called from the drawing-room. "Agnia, call your master!"

"Then you won't stay?" asked Nikolay Sergeitch, getting up quickly and going towards the door. "You might as well stay, really. In the evenings I could come and have a talk with you. Eh? Stay! If you go, there won't be a human face left in the house. It's awful!"

Nikolay Sergeitch's pale, exhausted face besought her, but Mashenka shook her head, and with a wave of his hand he went out.

Half an hour later she was on her way.

ROMAN FEVER*

๙๋ EDITH WHARTON (1862–1937)

1

FROM THE TABLE AT WHICH THEY HAD BEEN LUNCHING TWO AMERICAN LADIES
of ripe but well-cared-for middle age moved across the lofty terrace of the
Roman restaurant and, leaning on its parapet, looked first at each other, and
then down on the outspread glories of the Palatine and the Forum, with the
same expression of vague but benevolent approval.

As they leaned there a girlish voice echoed up gaily from the stairs
leading to the court below. "Well, come along, then," it cried, not to them
but to an invisible companion, "and let's leave the young things to their
knitting"; and a voice as fresh laughed back: "Oh, look here, Babs, not
actually *knitting*—" "Well, I mean figuratively," rejoined the first. "After
all, we haven't left our poor parents much else to do . . ." and at that point
the turn of the stairs engulfed the dialogue.

The two ladies looked at each other again, this time with a tinge of
smiling embarrassment, and the smaller and paler one shook her head and
coloured slightly.

"Barbara!" she murmured, sending an unheard rebuke after the mocking
voice in the stairway.

The other lady, who was fuller, and higher in colour, with a small
determined nose supported by vigorous black eyebrows, gave a good-
humoured laugh. "That's what our daughters think of us!"

Her companion replied by a deprecating gesture. "Not of us individually.
We must remember that. It's just the collective modern idea of Mothers.
And you see—" Half guiltily she drew from her handsomely mounted black
hand-bag a twist of crimson silk run through by two fine knitting needles.
"One never knows," she murmured. "The new system has certainly given us
a good deal of time to kill; and sometimes I get tired just looking—even at
this." Her gesture was now addressed to the stupendous scene at their
feet.

The dark lady laughed again, and they both relapsed upon the view,
contemplating it in silence, with a sort of diffused serenity which might
have been borrowed from the spring effulgence of the Roman skies. The
luncheon-hour was long past, and the two had their end of the vast terrace
to themselves. At its opposite extremity a few groups, detained by a

* "Roman Fever" (Copyright 1934 Liberty Magazine; renewal copyright ©
1962 William R. Tyler) is reprinted with the permission of Charles Scribner's
Sons from *The Collected Short Stories of Edith Wharton*.

lingering look at the outspread city, were gathering up guide-books and fumbling for tips. The last of them scattered, and the two ladies were alone on the air-washed height.

"Well, I don't see why we shouldn't just stay here," said Mrs. Slade, the lady of the high colour and energetic brows. Two derelict basket-chairs stood near, and she pushed them into the angle of the parapet, and settled herself in one, her gaze upon the Palatine. "After all, it's still the most beautiful view in the world."

"It always will be, to me," assented her friend Mrs. Ansley, with so light a stress on the "me" that Mrs. Slade, though she noticed it, wondered if it were not merely accidental, like the random underlinings of old-fashioned letter-writers.

"Grace Ansley was always old-fashioned," she thought; and added aloud, with a retrospective smile: "It's a view we've both been familiar with for a good many years. When we first met here we were younger than our girls are now. You remember?"

"Oh, yes, I remember," murmured Mrs. Ansley, with the same undefinable stress.—"There's that head-waiter wondering," she interpolated. She was evidently far less sure than her companion of herself and of her rights in the world.

"I'll cure him of wondering," said Mrs. Slade, stretching her hand toward a bag as discreetly opulent-looking as Mrs. Ansley's. Signing to the head-waiter, she explained that she and her friend were old lovers of Rome, and would like to spend the end of the afternoon looking down on the view— that is, if it did not disturb the service? The head-waiter, bowing over her gratuity, assured her that the ladies were most welcome, and would be still more so if they would condescend to remain for dinner. A full moon night, they would remember . . .

Mrs. Slade's black brows drew together, as though references to the moon were out-of-place and even unwelcome. But she smiled away her frown as the head-waiter retreated. "Well, why not? We might do worse. There's no knowing, I suppose, when the girls will be back. Do you even know back from *where?* I don't!"

Mrs. Ansley again coloured slightly. "I think those young Italian aviators we met at the Embassy invited them to fly to Tarquinia for tea. I suppose they'll want to wait and fly back by moonlight."

"Moonlight—moonlight! What a part it still plays. Do you suppose they're as sentimental as we were?"

"I've come to the conclusion that I don't in the least know what they are," said Mrs. Ansley. "And perhaps we didn't know much more about each other."

"No; perhaps we didn't."

Her friend gave her a shy glance. "I never should have supposed you were sentimental, Alida."

"Well, perhaps I wasn't." Mrs. Slade drew her lids together in retrospect; and for a few moments the two ladies, who had been intimate since childhood, reflected how little they knew each other. Each one, of course, had a label ready to attach to the other's name; Mrs. Delphin Slade, for instance, would have told herself, or any one who asked her, that Mrs. Horace Ansley, twenty-five years ago, had been exquisitely lovely—no, you wouldn't believe it, would you? . . . though, of course, still charming, distinguished . . . Well, as a girl she had been exquisite; far more beautiful than her daughter Barbara, though certainly Babs, according to the new standards at any rate, was more effective—had more *edge*, as they say. Funny where she got it, with those two nullities as parents. Yes; Horace Ansley was—well, just the duplicate of his wife. Museum specimens of old New York. Good-looking, irreproachable, exemplary. Mrs. Slade and Mrs. Ansley had lived opposite each other—actually as well as figuratively—for years. When the drawing-room curtains in No. 20 East 73rd Street were renewed, No. 23, across the way, was always aware of it. And of all the movings, buyings, travels, anniversaries, illnesses—the tame chronicle of an estimable pair. Little of it escaped Mrs. Slade. But she had grown bored with it by the time her husband made his big *coup* in Wall Street, and when they bought in upper Park Avenue had already begun to think: "I'd rather live opposite a speak-easy for a change; at least one might see it raided." The idea of seeing Grace raided was so amusing that (before the move) she launched it at a woman's lunch. It made a hit, and went the rounds—she sometimes wondered if it had crossed the street, and reached Mrs. Ansley. She hoped not, but didn't much mind. Those were the days when respectability was at a discount, and it did the irreproachable no harm to laugh at them a little.

A few years later, and not many months apart, both ladies lost their husbands. There was an appropriate exchange of wreaths and condolences, and a brief renewal of intimacy in the half-shadow of their mourning; and now, after another interval, they had run across each other in Rome, at the same hotel, each of them the modest appendage of a salient daughter. The similarity of their lot had again drawn them together, lending itself to mild jokes, and the mutual confession that, if in old days it must have been tiring to "keep up" with daughters, it was now, at times, a little dull not to.

No doubt, Mrs. Slade reflected, she felt her unemployment more than poor Grace ever would. It was a big drop from being the wife of Delphin Slade to being his widow. She had always regarded herself (with a certain conjugal pride) as his equal in social gifts, as contributing her full share to the making of the exceptional couple they were: but the difference after his death was irremediable. As the wife of the famous corporation lawyer, always with an international case or two on hand, every day brought its exciting and unexpected obligation: the impromptu entertaining of eminent colleagues from abroad, the hurried dashes on legal business to London, Paris or Rome, where the entertaining was so handsomely reciprocated; the amusement of hearing in her wake: "What, that handsome woman with the good clothes and the eyes is Mrs. Slade—*the* Slade's wife? Really? Generally the wives of celebrities are such frumps."

Yes; being *the* Slade's widow was a dullish business after that. In living up to such a husband all her faculties had been engaged; now she had only her daughter to live up to, for the son who seemed to have inherited his father's gifts had died suddenly in boyhood. She had fought through that agony because her husband was there, to be helped and to help; now, after the father's death, the thought of the boy had become unbearable. There was nothing left but to mother her daughter; and dear Jenny was such a perfect daughter that she needed no excessive mothering. "Now with Babs Ansley I don't know that I *should* be so quiet," Mrs. Slade sometimes half-enviously reflected; but Jenny, who was younger than her brilliant friend, was that rare accident, an extremely pretty girl who somehow made youth and prettiness seem as safe as their absence. It was all perplexing—and to Mrs. Slade a little boring. She wished that Jenny would fall in love—with the wrong man, even; that she might have to be watched, out-manoeuvred, rescued. And instead, it was Jenny who watched her mother, kept her out of draughts, made sure that she had taken her tonic . . .

Mrs. Ansley was much less articulate than her friend, and her mental portrait of Mrs. Slade was slighter, and drawn with fainter touches. "Alida Slade's awfully brilliant; but not as brilliant as she thinks," would have summed it up; though she would have added, for the enlightenment of strangers, that Mrs. Slade had been an extremely dashing girl; much more so than her daughter, who was pretty, of course, and clever in a way, but had none of her mother's—well, "vividness", some one had once called it. Mrs. Ansley would take up current words like this, and cite them in quotation marks, as unheard-of audacities. No; Jenny was not like her mother. Sometimes Mrs. Ansley thought Alida Slade was disappointed; on the whole she had had a sad life. Full of failures and mistakes; Mrs. Ansley had always been rather sorry for her . . .

So these two ladies visualized each other, each through the wrong end of her little telescope.

II

For a long time they continued to sit side by side without speaking. It seemed as though, to both, there was a relief in laying down their somewhat futile activities in the presence of the vast Memento Mori which faced them. Mrs. Slade sat quite still, her eyes fixed on the golden slope of the Palace of the Cæsars, and after a while Mrs. Ansley ceased to fidget with her bag, and she too sank into meditation. Like many intimate friends, the two ladies had never before had occasion to be silent together, and Mrs. Ansley was slightly embarrassed by what seemed, after so many years, a new stage in their intimacy, and one with which she did not yet know how to deal.

Suddenly the air was full of that deep clangour of bells which periodically covers Rome with a roof of silver. Mrs. Slade glanced at her wrist-watch. "Five o'clock already," she said, as though surprised.

Mrs. Ansley suggested interrogatively: "There's bridge at the Embassy at five." For a long time Mrs. Slade did not answer. She appeared to be lost in contemplation, and Mrs. Ansley thought the remark had escaped her. But after a while she said, as if speaking out of a dream: "Bridge, did you say? Not unless you want to . . . But I don't think I will, you know."

"Oh, no," Mrs. Ansley hastened to assure her. "I don't care to at all. It's so lovely here; and so full of old memories, as you say." She settled herself in her chair, and almost furtively drew forth her knitting. Mrs. Slade took sideway note of this activity, but her own beautifully cared-for hands remained motionless on her knee.

"I was just thinking," she said slowly, "what different things Rome stands for to each generation of travellers. To our grandmothers, Roman fever; to our mothers, sentimental dangers—how we used to be guarded!—to our daughters, no more dangers than the middle of Main Street. They don't know it—but how much they're missing!"

The long golden light was beginning to pale, and Mrs. Ansley lifted her knitting a little closer to her eyes. "Yes; how we were guarded!"

"I always used to think," Mrs. Slade continued, "that our mothers had a much more difficult job than our grandmothers. When Roman fever stalked the streets it must have been comparatively easy to gather in the girls at the danger hour; but when you and I were young, with such beauty calling us, and the spice of disobedience thrown in, and no worse risk than catching cold during the cool hour after sunset, the mothers used to be put to it to keep us in—didn't they?"

She turned again toward Mrs. Ansley, but the latter had reached a delicate point in her knitting. "One, two, three—slip two; yes, they must have been," she assented, without looking up.

Mrs. Slade's eyes rested on her with a deepened attention. "She can knit—in the face of *this!* How like her . . ."

Mrs. Slade leaned back, brooding, her eyes ranging from the ruins which faced her to the long green hollow of the Forum the fading glow of the church fronts beyond it, and the outlying immensity of the Colosseum. Suddenly she thought: "It's all very well to say that our girls have done away with sentiment and moonlight. But if Babs Ansley isn't out to catch that young aviator—the one who's a Marchese—then I don't know any-thing. And Jenny has no chance beside her. I know that too. I wonder if that's why Grace Ansley likes the two girls to go everywhere together? My poor Jenny as a foil—!" Mrs. Slade gave a hardly audible laugh, and at the sound Mrs. Ansley dropped her knitting.

"Yes—?"

"I—oh, nothing. I was only thinking how your Babs carries everything before her. That Campolieri boy is one of the best matches in Rome. Don't look so innocent, my dear—you know he is. And I was wondering, ever so respectfully, you understand . . . wondering how two such exemplary characters as we and Horace had managed to produce anything quite so dynamic. Mrs. Slade laughed again, with a touch of asperity.

Mrs. Ansley's hands lay inert across her needles. She looked straight out at the great accumulated wreckage of passion and splendour at her feet. But her small profile was almost expressionless. At length she said: "I think you overrate Babs, my dear."

"Mrs. Slade's tone grew easier. "No; I don't. I appreciate her. And perhaps envy you. Oh, my girl's perfect; if I were a chronic invalid I'd— well, I think I'd rather be in Jenny's hands. There must be times . . . but there! I always wanted a brilliant daughter . . . and never quite understood why I got an angel instead."

Mrs. Ansley echoed her laugh in a faint murmur. "Babs is an angel too."

"Of course—of course! But she's got rainbow wings. Well, they're wandering by the sea with their young men; and here we sit . . . and it all brings back the past a little too acutely."

Mrs. Ansley had resumed her knitting. One might almost have imagined (if one had known her less well, Mrs. Slade reflected) that, for her also, too many memories rose from the lengthening shadows of those august ruins. But no; she was simply absorbed in her work. What was there for her to worry about? She knew that Babs would almost certainly come back engaged to the extremely eligible Campolieri. "And she'll sell the New York house, and settle down near them in Rome, and never be in their way . . . she's much too tactful. But she'll have an excellent cook, and just the right people in for bridge and cocktails . . . and a perfectly peaceful old age among her grandchildren."

Mrs. Slade broke off this prophetic flight with a recoil of self-disgust. There was no one of whom she had less right to think unkindly than of Grace Ansley. Would she never cure herself of envying her? Perhaps she had begun too long ago.

She stood up and leaned against the parapet, filling her troubled eyes with the tranquillizing magic of the hour. But instead of tranquillizing her the sight seemed to increase her exasperation. Her gaze turned toward the Colosseum. Already its golden flank was drowned in purple shadow, and above it the sky curved crystal clear, without light or colour. It was the moment when afternoon and evening hang balanced in mid-heaven.

Mrs. Slade turned back and laid her hand on her friend's arm. The gesture was so abrupt that Mrs. Ansley looked up, startled.

"The sun's set. You're not afraid, my dear?"

"Afraid—?"

"Of Roman fever or pneumonia? I remember how ill you were that winter. As a girl you had a very delicate throat, hadn't you?"

"Oh, we're all right up here. Down below, in the Forum, it does get deathly cold, all of a sudden . . . but not here."

"Ah, of course you know because you had to be so careful." Mrs. Slade turned back to the parapet. She thought: "I must make one more effort not to hate her." Aloud she said: "Whenever I look at the Forum from up here, I remember that story about a great-aunt of yours, wasn't she? A dreadfully wicked great-aunt?"

"Oh, yes; Great-aunt Harriet. The one who was supposed to have sent her young sister out to the Forum after sunset to gather a night-blooming flower for her album. All our great-aunts and grand-mothers used to have albums of dried flowers."

Mrs. Slade nodded. "But she really sent her because they were in love with the same man—"

"Well, that was the family tradition. They said Aunt Harriet confessed it years afterward. At any rate, the poor little sister caught the fever and died. Mother used to frighten us with the story when we were children."

"And you frightened *me* with it, that winter when you and I were here as girls. The winter I was engaged to Delphin."

Mrs. Ansley gave a faint laugh. "Oh, did I? Really frightened you? I don't believe you're easily frightened."

"Not often; but I was then. I was easily frightened because I was too happy. I wonder if you know what that means?"

"I—yes . . ." Mrs. Ansley faltered.

"Well, I suppose that was why the story of your wicked aunt made such an impression on me. And I thought: 'There's no more Roman fever, but the Forum is deathly cold after sunset—especially after a hot day. And the Colosseum's even colder and damper'."

"The Colosseum—?"

"Yes. It wasn't easy to get in, after the gates were locked for the night. Far from easy. Still, in those days it could be managed; it was managed, often. Lovers met there who couldn't meet elsewhere. You knew that?"

"I—I daresay. I don't remember."

"You don't remember? You don't remember going to visit some ruins or other one evening, just after dark, and catching a bad chill? You were supposed to have gone to see the moon rise. People always said that expedition was what caused your illness."

There was a moment's silence; then Mrs. Ansley rejoined: "Did they? It was all so long ago."

"Yes. And you got well again—so it didn't matter. But I suppose it struck your friends—the reason given for your illness, I mean—because everybody knew you were so prudent on account of your throat, and your mother took such care of you . . . You *had* been out late sight-seeing, hadn't you, that night?"

"Perhaps I had. The most prudent girls aren't always prudent. What made you think of it now?"

Mrs. Slade seemed to have no answer ready. But after a moment she broke out: "Because I simply can't bear it any longer—!"

Mrs. Ansley lifted her head quickly. Her eyes were wide and very pale. "Can't bear what?"

"Why—your not knowing that I've always known why you went."

"Why I went—?"

"Yes. You think I'm bluffing, don't you? Well, you went to meet the man I was engaged to—and I can repeat every word of the letter that took you there."

While Mrs. Slade spoke Mrs. Ansley had risen unsteadily to her feet. Her bag, her knitting and gloves, slid in a panic-stricken heap to the ground. She looked at Mrs. Slade as though she were looking at a ghost.

"No, no—don't," she faltered out.

"Why not? Listen, if you don't believe me. 'My one darling, things can't go on like this. I must see you alone. Come to the Colosseum immediately after dark tomorrow. There will be somebody to let you in. No one whom you need fear will suspect'—but perhaps you've forgotten what the letter said?"

Mrs. Ansley met the challenge with an unexpected composure. Steading herself against the chair she looked at her friend, and replied: "No, I know it by heart too."

"And the signature? 'Only your D.S.' Was that it? I'm right, am I? That was the letter that took you out that evening after dark?"

Mrs. Ansley was still looking at her. It seemed to Mrs. Slade that a slow struggle was going on behind the voluntarily controlled mask of her small quiet face. "I shouldn't have thought she had herself so well in hand," Mrs. Slade reflected, almost resentfully. But at this moment Mrs. Ansley spoke. "I don't know how you knew. I burnt that letter at once."

"Yes; you would, naturally—you're so prudent!" The sneer was open now. "And if you burnt the letter you're wondering how on earth I know what was in it. That's it, isn't it?"

Mrs. Slade waited, but Mrs. Ansley did not speak.

"Well, my dear, I know what was in that letter because I wrote it!"

"You wrote it?"

"Yes."

The two women stood for a minute staring at each other in the last golden light. Then Mrs. Ansley dropped back into her chair. "Oh," she murmured, and covered her face with her hands.

Mrs. Slade waited nervously for another word or movement. None came, and at length she broke out: "I horrify you."

Mrs. Ansley's hands dropped to her knee. The face they uncovered was streaked with tears. "I wasn't thinking of you. I was thinking—it was the only letter I ever had from him!"

"And I wrote it. Yes; I wrote it! But I was the girl he was engaged to. Did you happen to remember that?"

Mrs. Ansley's head drooped again. "I'm not trying to excuse myself . . . I remembered . . ."

"And still you went?"

"Still I went."

Mrs. Slade stood looking down on the small bowed figure at her side. The flame of her wrath had already sunk, and she wondered why she had ever thought there would be any satisfaction in inflicting so purposeless a wound on her friend. But she had to justify herself.

"You do understand? I'd found out—and I hated you, hated you. I knew you were in love with Delphin—and I was afraid; afraid of you, of your quiet ways, your sweetness . . . your . . . well, I wanted you out of the way, that's all. Just for a few weeks; just till I was sure of him. So in a blind fury I wrote that letter . . . I don't know why I'm telling you now."

"I suppose," said Mrs. Ansley slowly, "it's because you've always gone on hating me."

"Perhaps. Or because I wanted to get the whole thing off my mind." She paused. "I'm glad you destroyed the letter. Of course I never thought you'd die."

Mrs. Ansley relapsed into silence, and Mrs. Slade, leaning above her, was conscious of a strange sense of isolation, of being cut off from the warm current of human communion. "You think me a monster!"

"I don't know . . . It was the only letter I had, and you say he didn't write it?"

"Ah, how you care for him still!"

"I cared for that memory," said Mrs. Ansley.

Mrs. Slade continued to look down on her. She seemed physically reduced by the blow—as if, when she got up, the wind might scatter her like a puff of dust. Mrs. Slade's jealousy suddenly leapt up again at the sight. All these years the woman had been living on that letter. How she must have loved him, to treasure the mere memory of its ashes! The letter of the man her friend was engaged to. Wasn't it she who was the monster?

"You tried your best to get him away from me, didn't you? But you failed; and I kept him. That's all."

"Yes. That's all."

"I wish now I hadn't told you. I'd no idea you'd feel about it as you do; I thought you'd be amused. It all happened so long ago, as you say; and you must do me the justice to remember that I had no reason to think you'd ever taken it seriously. How could I, when you were married to Horace Ansley two months afterward? As soon as you could get out of bed your mother rushed you off to Florence and married you. People were rather surprised—they wondered at its being done so quickly; but I thought I knew. I had an idea you did it out of *pique*—to be able to say you'd got ahead of Delphin and me. Girls have such silly reasons for doing the most serious things. And your marrying so soon convinced me that you'd never really cared."

"Yes. I suppose it would," Mrs. Ansley assented.

The clear heaven overhead was emptied of all its gold. Dusk spread over it, abruptly darkening the Seven Hills. Here and there lights began to twinkle through the foliage at their feet. Steps were coming and going on the deserted terrace—waiters looking out of the doorway at the head of the stairs, then reappearing with trays and napkins and flasks of wine. Tables were moved, chairs straightened. A feeble string of electric lights flickered out. Some vases of faded flowers were carried away, and brought back replenished. A stout lady in a dust-coat suddenly appeared, asking in broken Italian if any one had seen the elastic band which held together her tattered

Baedeker. She poked with her stick under the table at which she had lunched, the waiters assisting.

The corner where Mrs. Slade and Mrs. Ansley sat was still shadowy and deserted. For a long time neither of them spoke. At length Mrs. Slade began again: "I suppose I did it as a sort of joke—"

"A joke?"

"Well, girls are ferocious sometimes, you know. Girls in love especially. And I remember laughing to myself all that evening at the idea that you were waiting around there in the dark, dodging out of sight, listening for every sound, trying to get in—. Of course I was upset when I heard you were so ill afterward."

Mrs. Ansley had not moved for a long time. But now she turned slowly toward her companion. "But I didn't wait. He'd arranged everything. He was there. We were let in at once," she said.

Mrs. Slade sprang up from her leaning position. "Delphin there? They let you in?—Ah, now you're lying!" She burst out with violence.

Mrs. Ansley's voice grew clearer, and full of surprise. "But of course he was there. Naturally he came—"

"Came? How did he know he'd find you there? You must be raving!"

Mrs. Ansley hesitated, as though reflecting. "But I answered the letter. I told him I'd be there. So he came."

Mrs. Slade flung her hands up to her face. "Oh, God—you answered! I never thought of your answering . . ."

"It's odd you never thought of it, if you wrote the letter."

"Yes. I was blind with rage."

Mrs. Ansley rose, and drew her fur scarf about her. "It is cold here. We'd better go . . . I'm sorry for you," she said, as she clasped the fur about her throat.

The unexpected words sent a pang through Mrs. Slade. "Yes; we'd better go." She gathered up her bag and cloak. "I don't know why you should be sorry for me," she muttered.

Mrs. Ansley stood looking away from her toward the dusky secret mass of the Colosseum. "Well—because I didn't have to wait that night."

Mrs. Slade gave an unquiet laugh. "Yes; I was beaten there. But I oughtn't to begrudge it to you, I suppose. At the end of all these years. After all, I had everything; I had him for twenty-five years. And you had nothing but that one letter that he didn't write."

Mrs. Ansley was again silent. At length she turned toward the door of the terrace. She took a step, and turned back, facing her companion.

"I had Barbara," she said, and began to move ahead of Mrs. Slade toward the stairway.

RED*

⤷ W. Somerset Maugham (1874–1965)

The skipper thrust his hand into one of his trouser pockets and with difficulty, for they were not at the sides but in front and he was a portly man, pulled out a large silver watch. He looked at it and then looked again at the declining sun. The Kanaka at the wheel gave him a glance, but did not speak. The skipper's eyes rested on the island they were approaching. A white line of foam marked the reef. He knew there was an opening large enough to get his ship through, and when they came a little nearer he counted on seeing it. They had nearly an hour of daylight still before them. In the lagoon the water was deep and they could anchor comfortably. The chief of the village which he could already see among the coconut trees was a friend of the mate's, and it would be pleasant to go ashore for the night. The mate came forward at that minute and the skipper turned to him.

"We'll take a bottle of booze along with us and get some girls in to dance," he said.

"I don't see the opening," said the mate.

He was a Kanaka, a handsome, swarthy fellow, with somewhat the look of a later Roman emperor, inclined to stoutness; but his face was fine and clean-cut.

"I'm dead sure there's one right here," said the captain, looking through his glasses. "I can't understand why I can't pick it up. Send one of the boys up the mast to have a look."

The mate called one of the crew and gave him the order. The captain watched the Kanaka climb and waited for him to speak. But the Kanaka shouted down that he could see nothing but the unbroken line of foam. The captain spoke Samoan like a native, and he cursed him freely.

"Shall he stay up there?" asked the mate.

"What the hell good does that do?" answered the captain. "The blame fool can't see worth a cent. You bet your sweet life I'd find the opening if I was up there."

He looked at the slender mast with anger. It was all very well for a native who had been used to climbing up coconut trees all his life. He was fat and heavy.

"Come down," he shouted. "You're no more use than a dead dog. We'll just have to go along the reef till we find the opening."

It was a seventy-ton schooner with paraffin auxiliary, and it ran, when there was no head wind, between four and five knots an hour. It was a bedraggled object; it had been painted white a very long time ago, but it was now dirty, dingy, and mottled. It smelt strongly of paraffin and of the copra which was its usual cargo. They were within a hundred feet of the reef now and the captain told the steersman to run along it till they came to the opening. But when they had gone a couple of miles he realized that they had missed it. He went about and slowly worked back again. The white foam of the reef continued without interruption and now the sun was setting. With a curse at the stupidity of the crew the skipper resigned himself to waiting till next morning.

"Put her about," he said. "I can't anchor here."

They went out to sea a little and presently it was quite dark. They anchored. When the sail was furled the ship began to roll a good deal. They said in Apia that one day she would roll right over; and the owner, a German-American who managed one of the largest stores, said that no money was big enough to induce him to go out in her. The cook, a Chinese in white trousers, very dirty and ragged, and a thin white tunic, came to say that supper was ready, and when the skipper went into the cabin he found the engineer already seated at table. The engineer was a long, lean man with a scraggy neck. He was dressed in blue overalls and a sleeveless jersey which showed his thin arms tatooed from elbow to wrist.

"Hell, having to spend the night outside," said the skipper.

The engineer did not answer, and they ate their supper in silence. The cabin was lit by a dim oil lamp. When they had eaten the canned apricots with which the meal finished the Chink brought them a cup of tea. The skipper lit a cigar and went on the upper deck. The island now was only a darker mass against the night. The stars were very bright. The only sound was the ceaseless breaking of the surf. The skipper sank into a deck-chair and smoked idly. Presently three or four members of the crew came up and sat down. One of them had a banjo and another a concertina. They began to play, and one of them sang. The native song sounded strange on these instruments. Then to the singing a couple began to dance. It was a barbaric dance, savage and primeval, rapid, with quick movements of the hands and feet and contortions of the body; it was sensual, sexual even, but sexual without passion. It was very animal, direct, weird without mystery, natural in short, and one might almost say childlike. At last they grew tired. They stretched themselves on the deck and slept, and all was silent. The skipper lifted himself heavily out of his chair and clambered down the companion. He went into his cabin and got out of his clothes. He climbed into his bunk and lay there. He panted a little in the heat of the night.

But next morning, when the dawn crept over the tranquil sea, the opening in the reef which had eluded them the night before was seen a little to the east of where they lay. The schooner entered the lagoon. There was not a ripple on the surface of the water. Deep down among the coral rocks you saw little coloured fish swim. When he had anchored his ship the skipper ate his breakfast and went on deck. The sun shone from an unclouded sky, but in the early morning the air was grateful and cool. It was Sunday, and there was a feeling of quietness, a silence as though nature were at rest, which gave him a peculiar sense of comfort. He sat, looking at the wooded coast, and felt lazy and well at ease. Presently a slow smile moved his lips and he threw the stump of his cigar into the water.

"I guess I'll go ashore," he said. "Get the boat out."

He climbed stiffly down the ladder and was rowed to a little cove. The coconut trees came down to the water's edge, not in rows, but spaced out with an ordered formality. They were like a ballet of spinsters, elderly but flippant, standing in affected attitudes with the simpering graces of a bygone age. He sauntered idly through them, along a path that could be just seen winding its tortuous way, and it led him presently to a broad creek. There was a bridge across it, but a bridge constructed of single trunks of coconut trees, a dozen of them, placed end to end and supported where they met by a forked branch driven into the bed of the creek. You walked on a smooth, round surface, narrow and slippery, and there was no support for the hand. To cross such a bridge required sure feet and a stout heart. The skipper hesitated. But he saw on the other side, nestling among the trees, a white man's house; he made up his mind and, rather gingerly, began to walk. He watched his feet carefully, and where one trunk joined on to the next and there was a difference of level, he tottered a little. It was with a gasp of relief that he reached the last tree and finally set his feet on the firm ground of the other side. He had been so intent on the difficult crossing that he never noticed anyone was watching him, and it was with surprise that he heard himself spoken to.

"It takes a bit of nerve to cross these bridges when you're not used to them."

He looked up and saw a man standing in front of him. He had evidently come out of the house which he had seen.

"I saw you hesitate," the man continued, with a smile on his lips, "and I was watching to see you fall in."

"Not on your life," said the captain, who had now recovered his confidence.

"I've fallen in myself before now. I remember, one evening I came back from shooting, and I fell in, gun and all. Now I get a boy to carry my gun for me."

He was a man no longer young, with a small beard, now somewhat grey, and a thin face. He was dressed in a singlet, without arms, and a pair of duck trousers. He wore neither shoes nor socks. He spoke English with a slight accent.

"Are you Neilson?" asked the skipper.

"I am."

"I've heard about you. I thought you lived somewheres round here."

The skipper followed his host into the little bungalow and sat down heavily in the chair which the other motioned him to take. While Neilson went out to fetch whisky and glasses he took a look round the room. It filled him with amazement. He had never seen so many books. The shelves reached from floor to ceiling on all four walls, and they were closely packed. There was a grand piano littered with music, and a large table on which books and magazines lay in disorder. The room made him feel embarrassed. He remembered that Neilson was a queer fellow. No one knew very much about him, although he had been in the islands for so many years, but those who knew him agreed that he was queer. He was a Swede.

"You've got one big heap of books here," he said, when Neilson returned.

"They do no harm," answered Neilson with a smile.

"Have you read them all?" asked the skipper.

"Most of them."

"I'm a bit of a reader myself. I have the *Saturday Evening Post* sent me regler."

Neilson poured his visitor a good stiff glass of whisky and gave him a cigar. The skipper volunteered a little information.

"I got in last night, but I couldn't find the opening, so I had to anchor outside. I never been this run before, but my people had some stuff they wanted to bring over here. Gray, d'you know him?"

"Yes, he's got a store a little way along."

"Well, there was a lot of canned stuff that he wanted over, an' he's got some copra. They thought I might just as well come over as lie idle at Apia. I run between Apia and Pago-Pago mostly, but they've got smallpox there just now, and there's nothing stirring."

He took a drink of his whisky and lit a cigar. He was a taciturn man, but there was something in Neilson that made him nervous, and his nervousness made him talk. The Swede was looking at him with large dark eyes in which there was an expression of faint amusement.

"This is a tidy little place you've got here."

"I've done my best with it."

"You must do pretty well with your trees. They look fine. With copra at the price it is now. I had a bit of a plantation myself once, in Upolu it was, but I had to sell it."

He looked round the room again, where all those books gave him a feeling of something incomprehensible and hostile.

"I guess you must find it a bit lonesome here though," he said.

"I've got used to it. I've been here for twenty-five years."

Now the captain could think of nothing more to say, and he smoked in silence. Neilson had apparently no wish to break it. He looked at his guest with a meditative eye. He was a tall man, more than six feet high, and very stout. His face was red and blotchy, with a network of little purple veins on the cheeks, and his features were sunk into its fatness. His eyes were blood-shot. His neck was buried in rolls of fat. But for a fringe of long curly hair, nearly white, at the back of his head, he was quite bald; and that immense, shiny surface of forehead, which might have given him a false look of intelligence, on the contrary gave him one of peculiar imbecility. He wore a blue flannel shirt, open at the neck and showing his fat chest covered with a mat of reddish hair, and a very old pair of blue serge trousers. He sat in his chair in a heavy ungainly attitude, his great belly thrust forward and his fat legs uncrossed. All elasticity had gone from his limbs. Neilson wondered idly what sort of man he had been in his youth. It was almost impossible to imagine that this creature of vast bulk had ever been a boy who ran about. The skipper finished his whisky, and Neilson pushed the bottle towards him.

"Help yourself."

The skipper leaned forward and with his great hand seized it.

"And how come you in these parts anyways?" he said.

"Oh, I came out to the islands for my health. My lungs were bad and they said I hadn't a year to live. You see they were wrong."

"I meant, how come you to settle down right here?"

"I am a sentimentalist."

"Oh!"

Neilson knew that the skipper had not an idea what he meant, and he looked at him with an ironical twinkle in his dark eyes. Perhaps just because the skipper was so gross and dull a man the whim seized him to talk further.

"You were too busy keeping your balance to notice, when you crossed the bridge, but this spot is generally considered rather pretty."

"It's a cute little house you've got here."

"Ah, that wasn't here when I first came. There was a native hut, with its beehive roof and its pillars, overshadowed by a great tree with red flowers; and the croton bushes, their leaves yellow and red and golden, made a pied fence around it. And then all about were the coconut trees, as fanciful as women, and as vain. They stood at the water's edge and spent all day looking at their reflections. I was a young man then—Good Heavens, it's a quarter of a century ago—and I wanted to enjoy all the loveliness of the world in the short time allotted to me before I passed into the darkness. I thought it was the most beautiful spot I had ever seen. The first time I saw it I had a catch at my heart, and I was afraid I was going to cry. I wasn't more than twenty-five, and though I put the best face I could on it, I didn't want to die. And somehow it seemed to me that the very beauty of this place made it easier for me to accept my fate. I felt when I came here that all my past life had fallen away, Stockholm and its University, and then Bonn: it all seemed the life of somebody else, as though now at last I had achieved the reality which our doctors of philosophy—I am one myself, you know—had discussed so much. 'A year,' I cried to myself. 'I have a year. I will spend it here and then I am content to die.'

"We are foolish and sentimental and melodramatic at twenty-five, but if we weren't perhaps we should be less wise at fifty.

"Now drink, my friend. Don't let the nonsense I talk interfere with you."

He waved his thin hand towards the bottle, and the skipper finished what remained in his glass.

"You ain't drinking nothin'," he said, reaching for the whisky.

"I am of a sober habit," smiled the Swede. "I intoxicate myself in ways which I fancy are more subtle. But perhaps that is only vanity. Anyhow, the effects are more lasting and the results less deleterious."

"They say there's a deal of cocaine taken in the States now," said the captain.

Neilson chuckled.

"But I do not see a white man often," he continued, "and for once I don't think a drop of whisky can do me any harm."

He poured himself out a little, added some soda, and took a sip.

"And presently I found out why the spot had such an unearthly loveliness. Here love had tarried for a moment like a migrant bird that happens on a ship in mid-ocean and for a little while folds its tired wings. The fragrance of a beautiful passion hovered over it like the fragrance of hawthorn in May in the meadows of my home. It seems to me that the places where men have loved or suffered keep about them always some faint aroma of something that has not wholly died. It is as though they had acquired a spiritual significance which mysteriously affects those who pass. I wish I could make myself clear." He smiled a little. "Though I cannot imagine that if I did you would understand."

He paused.

"I think this place was beautiful because here had been loved beautifully." And now he shrugged his shoulders. "But perhaps it is only that my æsthetic sense is gratified by the happy conjunction of young love and a suitable setting."

Even a man less thick-witted than the skipper might have been forgiven if he were bewildered by Neilson's words. For he seemed faintly to laugh at what he said. It was as though he spoke from emotion which his intellect found ridiculous. He had said himself that he was a sentimentalist, and when sentimentality is joined with scepticism there is often the devil to pay.

He was silent for an instant and looked at the captain with eyes in which there was a sudden perplexity.

"You know, I can't help thinking that I've seen you before somewhere or other," he said.

"I couldn't say as I remember you," returned the skipper.

"I have a curious feeling as though your face were familiar to me. It's been puzzling me for some time. But I can't situate my recollection in any place or at any time."

The skipper massively shrugged his heavy shoulders.

"It's thirty years since I first come to the islands. A man can't figure on remembering all the folk he meets in a while like that."

The Swede shook his head.

"You know how one sometimes has the feeling that a place one has never been to before is strangely familiar. That's how I seem to see you." He gave a whimsical smile. "Perhaps I knew you in some past existence. Perhaps, perhaps you were the master of a galley in ancient Rome and I was a slave at the oar. Thirty years have you been here?"

"Every bit of thirty years."

"I wonder if you knew a man called Red?"

"Red?"

"That is the only name I've ever known him by. I never knew him personally. I never even set eyes on him. And yet I seem to see him more clearly than many men, my brothers, for instance, with whom I passed my daily life for many years. He lives in my imagination with the distinctness of a Paolo Malatesta or a Romeo. But I daresay you have never read Dante or Shakespeare?"

"I can't say as I have," said the captain.

Neilson, smoking a cigar, leaned back in his chair and looked vacantly at the ring of smoke which floated in the still air. A smile played on his lips, but his eyes were grave. Then he looked at the captain. There was in his gross obesity something extraordinarily repellent. He had the plethoric self-satisfaction of the very fat. It was an outrage. It set Neilson's nerves on edge. But the contrast between the man before him and the man he had in mind was pleasant.

"It appears that Red was the most comely thing you ever saw. I've talked to quite a number of people who knew him in those days, white men, and they all agree that the first time you saw him his beauty just took your breath away. They called him Red on account of his flaming hair. It had a natural wave and he wore it long. It must have been of that wonderful colour that the pre-Raphaelites raved over. I don't think he was vain of it, he was much too ingenuous for that, but no one could have blamed him if he had been. He was tall, six feet and an inch or two—in the native house that used to stand here was the mark of his height cut with a knife on the central trunk that supported the roof—and he was made like a Greek god, broad in the shoulders and thin in the flanks; he was like Apollo, with just that soft roundness which Praxiteles gave him, and that suave, feminine grace which has in it something troubling and mysterious. His skin was dazzling white, milky, like satin; his skin was like a woman's."

"I had kind of a white skin myself when I was a kiddie," said the skipper, with a twinkle in his bloodshot eyes.

But Neilson paid no attention to him. He was telling his story now and interruption made him impatient.

"And his face was just as beautiful as his body. He had large blue eyes, very dark, so that some say they were black, and unlike most red-haired people he had dark eyebrows and long dark lashes. His features were perfectly regular and his mouth was like a scarlet wound. He was twenty."

On these words the Swede stopped with a certain sense of the dramatic. He took a sip of whisky.

"He was unique. There never was anyone more beautiful. There was no more reason for him than for a wonderful blossom to flower on a wild plant. He was a happy accident of nature.

"One day he landed at that cove into which you must have put this morning. He was an American sailor, and he had deserted from a man-of-war in Apia. He had induced some good-humoured native to give him a passage on a cutter that happened to be sailing from Apia to Safoto, and he had been put ashore here in a dugout. I do not know why he deserted. Perhaps life on a man-of-war with its restrictions irked him, perhaps he was in trouble, and perhaps it was the South Seas and these romantic islands that got into his bones. Every now and then they take a man strangely, and he finds himself like a fly in a spider's web. It may be that there was a softness of fibre in him, and these green hills with their soft airs, this blue sea, took the northern strength from him as Delilah took the Nazarite's. Anyhow, he wanted to hide himself, and he thought he would be safe in this secluded nook till his ship had sailed from Samoa.

"There was a native hut at the cove and as he stood there, wondering where exactly he should turn his steps, a young girl came out and invited him to enter. He knew scarcely two words of the native tongue and she as little English. But he understood well enough what her smiles meant, and her pretty gestures, and he followed her. He sat down on a mat and she gave him slices of pineapple to eat. I can speak of Red only from hearsay, but I saw the girl three years after he first met her, and she was scarcely nineteen then. You cannot imagine how exquisite she was. She had the passionate grace of the hibiscus and the rich colour. She was rather tall, slim, with the delicate features of her race, and large eyes like pools of still water under the palm trees; her hair, black and curling, fell down her back, and she wore a wreath of scented flowers. Her hands were lovely. They were so small, so exquisitely formed, they gave your heart-strings a wrench. And in those days she laughed easily. Her smile was so delightful that it made your knees shake. Her skin was like a field of ripe corn on a summer day. Good Heavens, how can I describe her? She was too beautiful to be real.

"And these two young things, she was sixteen and he was twenty, fell in love with one another at first sight. That is the real love, not the love that comes from sympathy, common interests, or intellectual community, but love pure and simple. That is the love that Adam felt for Eve when he awoke and found her in the garden gazing at him with dewy eyes. That is the love that draws the beasts to one another, and the Gods. That is the love that makes the world a miracle. That is the love which gives life its pregnant meaning. You have never heard of the wise, cynical French duke who said that with two lovers there is always one who loves and one who lets himself be loved; it is a bitter truth to which most of us have to resign ourselves; but now and then there are two who love and two who let themselves be loved. Then one might fancy that the sun stands still as it stood when Joshua prayed to the God of Israel.

"And even now after all these years, when I think of these two, so young, so fair, so simple, and of their love, I feel a pang. It tears my heart just as my heart is torn when on certain nights I watch the full moon shining on the lagoon from an unclouded sky. There is always pain in the contemplation of perfect beauty.

"They were children. She was good and sweet and kind. I know nothing of him, and I like to think that then at all events he was ingenuous and frank. I like to think that his soul was as comely as his body. But I daresay he had no more soul than the creatures of the woods and forests who made pipes from reeds and bathed in the mountain streams when the world was young, and you might catch sight of little fawns galloping through the glade on the back of a bearded centaur. A soul is a troublesome possession and when man developed it he lost the Garden of Eden.

"Well, when Red came to the island it had recently been visited by one of those epidemics which the white man has brought to the South Seas, and one third of the inhabitants had died. It seems that the girl had lost all her near kin and she lived now in the house of distant cousins. The household consisted of two ancient crones, bowed and wrinkled, two younger women, and a man and a boy. For a few days he stayed there. But perhaps he felt himself too near the shore, with the possibility that he might fall in with white men who would reveal his hiding-place; perhaps the lovers could not bear that the company of others should rob them for an instant of the delight of being together. One morning they set out, the pair of them, with the few things that belonged to the girl, and walked along a grassy path under the coconuts, till they came to the creek you see. They had to cross the bridge you crossed, and the girl laughed gleefully because he was afraid. She held his hand till they came to the end of the first tree, and then his courage failed him and he had to go back. He was obliged to take off all his clothes before he could risk it, and she carried them over for him on her head. They settled down in the empty hut that stood here. Whether she had any rights over it (land tenure is a complicated business in the islands), or whether the owner had died during the epidemic, I do not know, but anyhow no one questioned them, and they took possession. Their furniture consisted of a couple of grass mats on which they slept, a fragment of looking-glass, and a bowl or two. In this pleasant land that is enough to start housekeeping on.

"They say that happy people have no history, and certainly a happy love has none. They did nothing all day long and yet the days seemed all too short. The girl had a native name, but Red called her Sally. He picked up the easy language very quickly, and he used to lie on the mat for hours while she chattered gaily to him. He was a silent fellow, and perhaps his mind was lethargic. He smoked incessantly the cigarettes which she made him out of the native tobacco and pandanus leaf, and he watched her while with deft fingers she made grass mats. Often natives would come in and tell long stories of the old days when the island was disturbed by tribal wars. Sometimes he would go fishing on the reef, and bring home a basket full of coloured fish. Sometimes at night he would go out with a lantern to catch lobster. There were plantains round the hut and Sally would roast them for their frugal meal. She knew how to make delicious messes from coconuts, and the breadfruit tree by the side of the creek gave them its fruit. On feast-days they killed a little pig and cooked it on hot stones. They bathed together in the creek; and in the evening they went down to the lagoon and paddled about in a dugout, with its great outrigger. The sea was deep blue, wine-coloured at sundown, like the sea of Homeric Greece; but in the lagoon the colour had an infinite variety, aquamarine and amethyst and emerald; and the setting sun turned it for a short moment to liquid gold. Then there was the colour of the coral, brown, white, pink, red, purple; and the shapes it took were marvellous. It was like a magic garden, and the hurrying fish were like butterflies. It strangely lacked reality. Among the coral were pools with a floor of white sand and here, where the water was dazzling clear, it was very good to bathe. Then, cool and happy, they wandered back in the gloaming over the soft grass road to the creek, walking hand in hand, and now the mynah birds filled the coconut trees with their clamour. And then the night, with that great sky shining with gold, that seemed to stretch more widely than the skies of Europe, and the soft airs that blow gently through the open hut, the long night again was all too short. She was sixteen and he was barely twenty. The dawn crept in among the wooden pillars of the hut and looked at those lovely children sleeping in one another's arms. The sun hid behind the great tattered leaves of the plantains so that it might not disturb them, and then, with playful malice, shot a golden ray, like the outstretched paw of a Persian cat, on their faces. They opened their sleepy eyes and they smiled to welcome another day. The weeks lengthened into months, and a year passed. They seemed to love one another as—I hesitate to say passionately, for passion has in it always a shade of sadness, a touch of bitterness or anguish, but as whole heartedly, as simply and naturally as on that first day on which, meeting, they had recognized that a god was in them.

"If you had asked them I have no doubt that they would have thought it impossible to suppose their love could ever cease. Do we not know that the essential element of love is a belief in its own eternity? And yet perhaps in Red there was already a very little seed, unknown to himself and unsus- pected by the girl, which would in time have grown to weariness. For one day one of the natives from the cove told them that some way down the coast at the anchorage was a British whaling-ship.

" 'Gee,' he said, 'I wonder if I could make a trade of some nuts and plantains for a pound or two of tobacco.'

"The pandanus cigarettes that Sally made him with untiring hands were strong and pleasant enough to smoke, but they left him unsatisfied; and he yearned on a sudden for real tobacco, hard, rank, and pungent. He had not smoked a pipe for many months. His mouth watered at the thought of it. One would have thought some premonition of harm would have made Sally seek to dissuade him, but love possessed her so completely that it never occurred to her any power on earth could take him from her. They went up into the hills together and gathered a great basket of wild oranges, green, but sweet and juicy; and they picked plantains from around the hut, and coconuts from their trees, and breadfruit and mangoes; and they carried them down to the cove. They loaded the unstable canoe with them, and Red and the native boy who had brought them the news of the ship paddled along outside the reef.

"It was the last time she ever saw him.

"Next day the boy came back alone. He was all in tears. This is the story he told. When after their long paddle they reached the ship and Red hailed it, a white man looked over the side and told them to come on board. They took the fruit they had brought with them and Red piled it up on the deck. The white man and he began to talk, and they seemed to come to some agreement. One of them went below and brought up tobacco. Red took some at once and lit a pipe. The boy imitated the zest with which he blew a great cloud of smoke from his mouth. Then they said something to him and he went into the cabin. Through the open door the boy, watching curiously, saw a bottle brought out and glasses. Red drank and smoked. They seemed to ask him something, for he shook his head and laughed. The man, the first man who had spoken to them, laughed too, and he filled Red's glass once more. They went on talking and drinking, and presently, growing tired of watching a sight that meant nothing to him, the boy curled himself up on the deck and slept. He was awakened by a kick; and, jumping to his feet, he saw that the ship was slowly sailing out of the lagoon. He caught sight of Red seated at the table, with his head resting heavily on his arms, fast asleep. He made a movement towards him, intending to wake him, but a rough hand seized his arm, and a man, with a scowl and words which he did not understand, pointed to the side. He shouted to Red, but in a moment he was seized and flung overboard. Helpless, he swam round to his canoe which was drifting a little way off, and pushed it on to the reef. He climbed in and, sobbing all the way, paddled back to shore.

"What had happened was obvious enough. The whaler, by desertion or sickness, was short of hands, and the captain when Red came aboard had asked him to sign on; on his refusal he had made him drunk and kidnapped him.

"Sally was beside herself with grief. For three days she screamed and cried. The natives did what they could to comfort her, but she would not be comforted. She would not eat. And then, exhausted, she sank into a sullen apathy. She spent long days at the cove, watching the lagoon, in the vain hope that Red somehow or other would manage to escape. She sat on the white sand, hour after hour, with the tears running down her cheeks, and at night dragged herself wearily back across the creek to the little hut, where she had been happy. The people with whom she had lived before Red came to the island wished her to return to them, but she would not; she was convinced that Red would come back, and she wanted him to find her where he had left her. Four months later she was delivered of a still-born

child, and the old woman who had come to help her through her confine-
ment remained with her in the hut. All joy was taken from her life. If her
anguish with time became less intolerable it was replaced by a settled
melancholy. You would not have thought that among these people, whose
emotions, though so violent, are very transient, a woman could be found
capable of so enduring a passion. She never lost the profound conviction
that sooner or later Red would come back. She watched for him, and every
time someone crossed this slender little bridge of coconut trees she looked.
It might at last be he."

Neilson stopped talking and gave a faint sigh.

"And what happened to her in the end?" asked the skipper.

Neilson smiled bitterly.

"Oh, three years afterwards she took up with another white man."

The skipper gave a fat, cynical chuckle.

"That's generally what happens to them," he said.

The Swede shot him a look of hatred. He did not know why that gross,
obese man excited in him so violent a repulsion. But his thoughts wandered
and he found his mind filled with memories of the past. He went back five
and twenty years. It was when he first came to the island, weary of Apia,
with its heavy drinking, its gambling and coarse sensuality, a sick man,
trying to resign himself to the loss of the career which had fired his imagination with ambitious thoughts. He set behind him resolutely all his hopes
of making a great name for himself and strove to content himself with the
few poor months of careful life which was all that he could count on. He
was boarding with a half-caste trader who had a store a couple of miles
along the coast at the edge of a native village; and one day, wandering
aimlessly along the grassy paths of the coconut groves, he had come upon
the hut in which Sally lived. The beauty of the spot had filled him with a
rapture so great that it was almost painful, and then he had seen Sally. She
was the loveliest creature he had ever seen, and the sadness in those dark,
magnificent eyes of hers affected him strangely. The Kanakas were a
handsome race, and beauty was not rare among them, but it was the beauty
of shapely animals. It was empty. But those tragic eyes were dark with
mystery, and you felt in them the bitter complexity of the groping, human
soul. The trader told him the story and it moved him.

"Do you think he'll ever come back?" asked Neilson.

"No fear. Why, it'll be a couple of years before the ship is paid off, and
by then he'll have forgotten all about her. I bet he was pretty mad when he
woke up and found he'd been shanghaied, and I shouldn't wonder but he
wanted to fight somebody. But he'd got to grin and bear it, and I guess in a
month he was thinking it the best thing that had ever happened to him that
he got away from the island."

But Neilson could not get the story out of his head. Perhaps because he
was sick and weakly, the radiant health of Red appealed to his imagination.
Himself an ugly man, insignificant of appearance, he prized very highly
comeliness in others. He had never been passionately in love, and certainly
he had never been passionately loved. The mutual attraction of those two

young things gave him a singular delight. It had the ineffable beauty of the Absolute. He went again to the little hut by the creek. He had a gift for languages and an energetic mind, accustomed to work, and he had already given much time to the study of the local tongue. Old habit was strong in him and he was gathering together material for a paper on the Samoan speech. The old crone who shared the hut with Sally invited him to come in and sit down. She gave him *kava* to drink and cigarettes to smoke. She was glad to have someone to chat with and while she talked he looked at Sally. She reminded him of the Psyche in the museum at Naples. Her features had the same clear purity of line, and though she had borne a child she had still a virginal aspect.

It was not till he had seen her two or three times that he induced her to speak. Then it was only to ask him if he had seen in Apia a man called Red. Two years had passed since his disappearance, but it was plain that she still thought of him incessantly.

It did not take Neilson long to discover that he was in love with her. It was only by an effort of will now that he prevented himself from going every day to the creek, and when he was not with Sally his thoughts were. At first, looking upon himself as a dying man, he asked only to look at her, and occasionally hear her speak, and his love gave him a wonderful happiness. He exulted in its purity. He wanted nothing from her but the opportunity to weave around her graceful person a web of beautiful fancies. But the open air, the equable temperature, the rest, the simple fare, began to have an unexpected effect on his health. His temperature did not soar at night to such alarming heights, he coughed less and began to put on weight; six months passed without his having a hæmorrhage; and on a sudden he saw the possibility that he might live. He had studied his disease carefully, and the hope dawned upon him that with great care he might arrest its course. It exhilarated him to look forward once more to the future. He made plans. It was evident that any active life was out of the question, but he could live on the islands, and the small income he had, insufficient elsewhere, would be ample to keep him. He could grow coconuts; that would give him an occupation; and he would send for his books and a piano; but his quick mind saw that in all this he was merely trying to conceal from himself the desire which obsessed him.

He wanted Sally. He loved not only her beauty, but that dim soul which he divined behind her suffering eyes. He would intoxicate her with his passion. In the end he would make her forget. And in an ecstasy of surrender he fancied himself giving her too the happiness which he had thought never to know again, but had now so miraculously achieved.

He asked her to live with him. She refused. He had expected that and did not let it depress him, for he was sure that sooner or later she would yield. His love was irresistible. He told the old woman of his wishes, and found somewhat to his surprise that she and the neighbours, long aware of them, were strongly urging Sally to accept his offer. After all, every native was glad to keep house for a white man, and Neilson according to the standards of the island was a rich one. The trader with whom he boarded went to her and told her not to be a fool; such an opportunity would not come again, and after so long she could not still believe that Red would ever return. The girl's resistance only increased Neilson's desire, and what had been a very pure love now became an agonizing passion. He was determined that nothing should stand in his way. He gave Sally no peace. At last, worn out by his persistence and the persuasions, by turns pleading and angry, of everyone around her, she consented. But the day after when, exultant, he went to see her he found that in the night she had burnt down the hut in which she and Red had lived together. The old crone ran towards him full of angry abuse of Sally, but he waved her aside; it did not matter; they would build a bungalow on the place where the hut had stood. A European house would really be more convenient if he wanted to bring out a piano and a vast number of books.

And so the little wooden house was built in which he had now lived for many years, and Sally became his wife. But after the first few weeks of rapture, during which he was satisfied with what she gave him, he had known little happiness. She had yielded to him, through weariness, but she had only yielded what she set no store on. The soul which he had dimly glimpsed escaped him. He knew that she cared nothing for him. She still loved Red, and all the time she was waiting for his return. At a sign from him, Neilson knew that, notwithstanding his love, his tenderness, his sympathy, his generosity, she would leave him without a moment's hesitation. She would never give a thought to his distress. Anguish seized him and he battered at that impenetrable self of hers which sullenly resisted him. His love became bitter. He tried to melt her heart with kindness, but it remained as hard as before; he feigned indifference, but she did not notice it. Sometimes he lost his temper and abused her, and then she wept silently. Sometimes he thought she was nothing but a fraud, and that soul simply an invention of his own, and that he could not get into the sanctuary of her heart because there was no sanctuary there. His love became a prison from which he longed to escape, but he had not the strength merely to open the door—that was all it needed—and walk out into the open air. It was torture and at last he became numb and hopeless. In the end the fire burnt itself out and, when he saw her eyes rest for an instant on the slender bridge, it was no longer rage that filled his heart but impatience. For many years now they had lived together bound by the ties of habit and convenience, and it was with a smile that he looked back on his old passion. She was an old woman, for the women on the islands age quickly, and if he had no love for her any more he had tolerance. She left him alone. He was contented with his piano and his books.

His thoughts led him to a desire for words.

"When I look back now and reflect on that brief passionate love of Red and Sally, I think that perhaps they should thank the ruthless fate that separated them when their love seemed still to be at its height. They suffered, but they suffered in beauty. They were spared the real tragedy of love."

"I don't know exactly as I get you," said the skipper.

"The tragedy of love is not death or separation. How long do you think it would have been before one or other of them ceased to care? Oh, it is dreadfully bitter to look at a woman whom you have loved with all your heart and soul, so that you felt you could not bear to let her out of your sight, and realize that you would not mind if you never saw her again. The tragedy of love is indifference."

But while he was speaking a very extraordinary thing happened. Though he had been addressing the skipper he had not been talking to him, he had been putting his thoughts into words for himself, and with his eyes fixed on the man in front of him he had not seen him. But now an image presented itself to them, an image not of the man he saw, but of another man. It was as though he were looking into one of those distorting mirrors that make you extraordinarily squat or outrageously elongate, but here exactly the opposite took place, and in the obese, ugly old man he caught the shadowy glimpse of a stripling. He gave him now a quick, searching scrutiny. Why had a haphazard stroll brought him just to this place? A sudden tremor of his heart made him slightly breathless. An absurd suspicion seized him. What had occurred to him was impossible and yet it might be a fact.

"What is your name?" he asked abruptly.

The skipper's face puckered and he gave a cunning chuckle. He looked then malicious and horribly vulgar.

"It's such a damned long time since I heard it that I almost forget it myself. But for thirty years now in the islands they've always called me Red."

His huge form shook as he gave a low, almost silent laugh. It was obscene. Neilson shuddered. Red was hugely amused, and from his bloodshot eyes tears ran down his cheeks.

Neilson gave a gasp, for at that moment a woman came in. She was a native, a woman of somewhat commanding presence, stout without being corpulent, dark, for the natives grow darker with age, with very grey hair. She wore a black Mother Hubbard, and its thinness showed her heavy breasts. The moment had come.

She made an observation to Neilson about some household matter and he answered. He wondered if his voice sounded as unnatural to her as it did to himself. She gave the man who was sitting in the chair by the window an indifferent glance, and went out of the room. The moment had come and gone.

Neilson for a moment could not speak. He was strangely shaken. Then he said:

"I'd be very glad if you'd stay and have a bit of dinner with me. Pot luck."

"I don't think I will," said Red. "I must go after this fellow Gray. I'll give him his stuff and then I'll get away. I want to be back in Apia to-morrow."

"I'll send a boy along with you to show you the way."

"That'll be fine."

Red heaved himself out of his chair, while the Swede called one of the boys who worked on the plantation. He told him where the skipper wanted to go, and the boy stepped along the bridge. Red prepared to follow him.

"Don't fall in," said Neilson.

"Not on your life."

Neilson watched him make his way across and when he had disappeared among the coconuts he looked still. Then he sank heavily in his chair. Was that the man who had prevented him from being happy? Was that the man whom Sally had loved all these years and for whom she had waited so desperately? It was grotesque. A sudden fury seized him so that he had an instinct to spring up and smash everything around him. He had been cheated. They had seen each other at last and had not known it. He began to laugh, mirthlessly, and his laughter grew till it became hysterical. The Gods had played him a cruel trick. And he was old now.

At last Sally came in to tell him dinner was ready. He sat down in front of her and tried to eat. He wondered what she would say if he told her now that the fat old man sitting in the chair was the lover whom she remembered still with the passionate abandonment of her youth. Years ago, when he hated her because she made him so unhappy, he would have been glad to tell her. He wanted to hurt her then as she hurt him, because his hatred was only love. But now he did not care. He shrugged his shoulders listlessly.

"What did that man want?" she asked presently.

He did not answer at once. She was old too, a fat old native woman. He wondered why he had ever loved her so madly. He had laid at her feet all the treasures of his soul, and she had cared nothing for them. Waste, what waste! And now, when he looked at her, he felt only contempt. His patience was at last exhausted. He answered her question.

"He's the captain of a schooner. He's come from Apia."

"Yes."

"He brought me news from home. My eldest brother is very ill and I must go back."

"Will you be gone long?"

He shrugged his shoulders.

THE KILLERS*

✍ ERNEST HEMINGWAY (1899–1961)

THE DOOR OF HENRY'S LUNCH-ROOM OPENED AND TWO MEN CAME IN. THEY sat down at the counter.

"What's yours?" George asked them.

"I don't know," one of the men said. "What do you want to eat, Al?"

"I don't know," said Al. "I don't knew what I want to eat."

Outside it was getting dark. The street-light came on outside the window. The two men at the counter read the menu. From the other end of the counter Nick Adams watched them. He had been talking to George when they came in.

"I'll have a roast pork tenderloin with apple sauce and mashed potatoes," the first man said.

"It isn't ready yet."

"What the hell do you put it on the card for?"

"That's the dinner," George explained. "You can get that at six o'clock."

George looked at the clock on the wall behind the counter.

"It's five o'clock."

"The clock says twenty minutes past five," the second man said.

"It's twenty minutes fast."

"Oh, to hell with the clock," the first man said. "What have you got to eat?"

"I can give you any kind of sandwiches," George said. "You can have ham and eggs, bacon and eggs, liver and bacon, or a steak."

"Give me chicken croquettes with green peas and cream sauce and mashed potatoes."

"That's the dinner."

"Everything we want's the dinner, eh? That's the way you work it."

"I can give you ham and eggs, bacon and eggs, liver——"

"I'll take ham and eggs," the man called Al said. He wore a derby hat and a black overcoat buttoned across the chest. His face was small and white and he had tight lips. He wore a silk muffler and gloves.

"Give me bacon and eggs," said the other man. He was about the same size as Al. Their faces were different, but they were dressed like twins. Both wore overcoats too tight for them. They sat leaning forward, their elbows on the counter.

---

* "The Killers" (Copyright 1927 Charles Scribner's Sons; renewal copyright © 1955) is reprinted with the permission of Charles Scribner's Sons from *Men Without Women* by Ernest Hemingway.

"Got anything to drink?" Al asked.

"Silver beer, bevo, ginger-ale," George said.

"I mean you got anything to *drink?*"

"Just those I said."

"This is a hot town," said the other. "What do they call it?"

"Summit."

"Ever hear of it?" Al asked his friend.

"No," said the friend.

"What do you do here nights?" Al asked.

"They eat the dinner," his friend said. "They all come here and eat the big dinner."

"That's right," George said.

"So you think that's right?" Al asked George.

"Sure."

"You're a pretty bright boy, aren't you?"

"Sure," said George.

"Well, you're not," said the other little man. "Is he, Al?"

"He's dumb," said Al. He turned to Nick. "What's your name?"

"Adams."

"Another bright boy," Al said. "Ain't he a bright boy, Max?"

"The town's full of bright boys," Max said.

George put the two platters, one of ham and eggs, the other of bacon and eggs, on the counter. He set down two side-dishes of fried potatoes and closed the wicket into the kitchen.

"Which is yours?" he asked Al.

"Don't you remember?"

"Ham and eggs."

"Just a bright boy," Max said. He leaned forward and took the ham and eggs. Both men ate with their gloves on. George watched them eat.

"What are *you* looking at?" Max looked at George.

"Nothing."

"The hell you were. You were looking at me."

"Maybe the boy meant it for a joke, Max," Al said.

George laughed.

"*You* don't have to laugh," Max said to him. "*You* don't have to laugh at all, see?"

"All right," said George.

"So he thinks it's all right." Max turned to Al. "He thinks it's all right. That's a good one."

"Oh, he's a thinker," Al said. They went on eating.

"What's the bright boy's name down the counter?" Al asked Max.

"Hey, bright boy," Max said to Nick. "You go around on the other side of the counter with your boy friend."

"What's the idea?" Nick asked.

"There isn't any idea."

"You better go around, bright boy," Al said. Nick went around behind the counter.

"What's the idea?" George asked.

"None of your damn business," Al said. "Who's out in the kitchen?"

"The nigger."

"What do you mean the nigger?"

"The nigger that cooks."

"Tell him to come in."

"What's the idea?"

"Tell him to come in."

"Where do you think you are?"

"We know damn well where we are," the man called Max said. "Do we look silly?"

"You talk silly," Al said to him. "What the hell do you argue with this kid for? Listen," he said to George, "tell the nigger to come out here."

"What are you going to do to him?"

"Nothing. Use your head, bright boy. What would we do to a nigger?"

George opened the slit that opened back into the kitchen. "Sam," he called. "Come in here a minute."

The door to the kitchen opened and the nigger came in. "What was it?" he asked. The two men at the counter took a look at him.

"All right, nigger. You stand right there," Al said.

Sam, the nigger, standing in his apron, looked at the two men sitting at the counter. "Yes, sir," he said. Al got down from his stool.

"I'm going back to the kitchen with the nigger and bright boy," he said. "Go on back to the kitchen, nigger. You go with him, bright boy." The little man walked after Nick and Sam, the cook, back into the kitchen. The door shut after them. The man called Max sat at the counter opposite George. He didn't look at George but looked in the mirror that ran along back of the counter. Henry's had been made over from a saloon into a lunch-counter.

"Well, bright boy," Max said, looking into the mirror, "why don't you say something?"

"What's it all about?"

"Hey, Al," Max called, "bright boy wants to know what it's all about."

"Why don't you tell him?" Al's voice came from the kitchen.

"What do you think it's all about?"

"I don't know."

"What do you think?"

Max looked into the mirror all the time he was talking.

"I wouldn't say."

"Hey, Al, bright boy says he wouldn't say what he thinks it's all about."

"I can hear you, all right," Al said from the kitchen. He had propped open the slit that dishes passed through into the kitchen with a catsup bottle. "Listen, bright boy," he said from the kitchen to George. "Stand a little further along the bar. You move a little to the left, Max." He was like a photographer arranging for a group picture.

"Talk to me, bright boy," Max said. "What do you think's going to happen?"

George did not say anything.

"I'll tell you," Max said. "We're going to kill a Swede. Do you know a big Swede named Ole Andreson?"

"Yes."

"He come here to eat every night, don't he?"

"Sometimes he comes here."

"He comes here at six o'clock, don't he?"

"If he comes."

"We know all that, bright boy," Max said. "Talk about something else. Ever go to the movies?"

"Once in a while."

"You ought to go to the movies more. The movies are fine for a bright boy like you."

"What are you going to kill Ole Andreson for? What did he ever do to you?"

"He never had a chance to do anything to us. He never even seen us."

"And he's only going to see us once," Al said from the kitchen.

"What are you going to kill him for, then?" George asked.

"We're killing him for a friend. Just to oblige a friend, bright boy."

"Shut up," said Al from the kitchen. "You talk too goddam much."

"Well, I got to keep bright boy amused. Don't I, bright boy?"

"You talk too damn much," Al said. "The nigger and my bright boy are amused by themselves. I got them tied up like a couple of girl friends in the convent."

"I suppose you were in a convent?"

"You never know."

"You were in a kosher convent. That's where you were."

George looked up at the clock.

"If anybody comes in you tell them the cook is off, and if they keep after it, you tell them you'll go back and cook yourself. Do you get that, bright boy?"

"All right," George said. "What you going to do with us afterward?"

"That'll depend," Max said. "That's one of those things you never know at the time."

George looked up at the clock. It was a quarter past six. The door from the street opened. A street-car motorman came in.

"Hello, George," he said. "Can I get supper?"

"Sam's gone out," George said. "He'll be back in about half an hour."

"I'd better go up the street," the motorman said. George looked at the clock. It was twenty minutes past six.

"That was nice, bright boy," Max said. "You're a regular little gentleman."

"He knew I'd blow his head off," Al said from the kitchen.

"No," said Max. "It ain't that. Bright boy is nice. He's a nice boy. I like him."

At six-fifty-five George said: "He's not coming."

Two other people had been in the lunch-room. Once George had gone out to the kitchen and made a ham-and-egg sandwich "to go" that a man wanted to take with him. Inside the kitchen he saw Al, his derby hat tipped back, sitting on a stool beside the wicket with the muzzle of a sawed-off shotgun resting on the ledge. Nick and the cook were back to back in the corner, a towel tied in each of their mouths. George had cooked the sandwich, wrapped it up in oiled paper, put it in a bag, brought it in, and the man had paid for it and gone out.

"Bright boy can do everything," Max said. "He can cook and everything. You'd make some girl a nice wife, bright boy."

"Yes?" George said. "Your friend, Ole Andreson, isn't going to come."

"We'll give him ten minutes," Max said.

Max watched the mirror and the clock. The hands of the clock marked seven o'clock, and then five minutes past seven.

"Come on, Al," said Max. "We better go. He's not coming."

"Better give him five minutes," Al said from the kitchen.

In the five minutes a man came in, and George explained that the cook was sick.

"Why the hell don't you get another cook?" the man asked. "Aren't you running a lunch-counter?" He went out.

"Come on, Al," Max said.

"What about the two bright boys and the nigger?"

"They're all right."

"You think so?"

"Sure. We're through with it."

"I don't like it," said Al. "It's sloppy. You talk too much."

"Oh, what the hell," said Max. "We got to keep amused, haven't we?"

"You talk too much, all the same," Al said. He came out from the kitchen. The cut-off barrels of the shotgun made a slight bulge under the waist of his too tight-fitting overcoat. He straightened his coat with his gloved hands.

"So long, bright boy," he said to George. "You got a lot of luck."

"That's the truth," Max said. "You ought to play the races, bright boy."

The two of them went out the door. George watched them, through the window, pass under the arc-light and cross the street. In their tight overcoats and derby hats they looked like a vaudeville team. George went back through the swinging-door into the kitchen and untied Nick and the cook.

"I don't want any more of that," said Sam, the cook. "I don't want any more of that."

Nick stood up. He had never had a towel in his mouth before.

"Say," he said. "What the hell?" He was trying to swagger it off.

"They were going to kill Ole Andreson," George said. "They were going to shoot him when he came in to eat."

"Ole Andreson?"

"Sure."

The cook felt the corners of his mouth with his thumbs.

"They all gone?" he asked.

"Yeah," said George. "They're gone now."

"I don't like it," said the cook. "I don't like any of it at all."

"Listen," George said to Nick. "You better go see Ole Andreson."

"All right."

"You better not have anything to do with it at all," Sam, the cook, said. "You better stay way out of it."

"Don't go if you don't want to," George said.

"Mixing up in this ain't going to get you anywhere," the cook said. "You stay out of it."

"I'll go see him," Nick said to George. "Where does he live?"

The cook turned away.

"Little boys always know what they want to do," he said.

"He lives up at Hirsch's rooming-house," George said to Nick.

"I'll go up there."

Outside the arc-light shone through the bare branches of a tree. Nick walked up the street beside the car-tracks and turned at the next arc-light down a side-street. Three houses up the street was Hirsch's rooming-house. Nick walked up the two steps and pushed the bell. A woman came to the door.

"Is Ole Andreson here?"

"Do you want to see him?"

"Yes, if he's in."

Nick followed the woman up a flight of stairs and back to the end of a corridor. She knocked on the door.

"Who is it?"

"It's somebody to see you, Mr. Andreson," the woman said.

"It's Nick Adams."

"Come in."

Nick opened the door and went into the room. Ole Andreson was lying on the bed with all his clothes on. He had been a heavyweight prizefighter and he was too long for the bed. He lay with his head on two pillows. He did not look at Nick.

"What was it?" he asked.

"I was up at Henry's," Nick said, "and two fellows came in and tied up me and the cook, and they said they were going to kill you."

It sounded silly when he said it. Ole Andreson said nothing.

"They put us out in the kitchen," Nick went on. "They were going to shoot you when you came in to supper."

Ole Andreson looked at the wall and did not say anything.

"George thought I better come and tell you about it."

"There isn't anything I can do about it," Ole Andreson said.

"I'll tell you what they were like."

"I don't want to know what they were like," Ole Andreson said. He looked at the wall. "Thanks for coming to tell me about it."

"That's all right."

Nick looked at the big man lying on the bed.

"Don't you want me to go and see the police?"

"No," Ole Andreson said. "That wouldn't do any good."

"Isn't there something I could do?"

"No. There ain't anything to do."

"Maybe it was just a bluff."

"No. It ain't just a bluff."

Ole Andreson rolled over toward the wall.

"The only thing is," he said, talking toward the wall, "I just can't make up my mind to go out. I been in here all day."

"Couldn't you get out of town?"

"No," Ole Andreson said. "I'm through with all that running around."

He looked at the wall.

"There ain't anything to do now."

"Couldn't you fix it up some way?"

"No. I got in wrong." He talked in the same flat voice. "There ain't anything to do. After a while I'll make up my mind to go out."

"I better go back and see George," Nick said.

"So long," said Ole Andreson. He did not look toward Nick. "Thanks for coming around."

Nick went out. As he shut the door he saw Ole Andreson with all his clothes on, lying on the bed looking at the wall.

"He's been in his room all day," the landlady said down-stairs. "I guess he don't feel well. I said to him: 'Mr. Andreson, you ought to go out and take a walk on a nice fall day like this,' but he didn't feel like it."

"He doesn't want to go out."

"I'm sorry he don't feel well," the woman said. "He's an awfully nice man. He was in the ring, you know."

"I know it."

"You'd never know it except from the way his face is," the woman said. They stood talking just inside the street door. "He's just as gentle."

"Well, good-night, Mrs. Hirsch," Nick said.

"I'm not Mrs. Hirsch," the woman said. "She owns the place. I just look after it for her. I'm Mrs. Bell."

"Well, good-night, Mrs. Bell," Nick said.

"Good-night," the woman said.

Nick walked up the dark street to the corner under the arc-light, and then along the car-tracks to Henry's eating-house. George was inside, back of the counter.

"Did you see Ole?"

"Yes," said Nick. "He's in his room and he won't go out."

The cook opened the door from the kitchen when he heard Nick's voice.

"I don't even listen to it," he said and shut the door.

"Did you tell him about it?" George asked.

"Sure. I told him but he knows what it's all about."

"What's he going to do?"

"Nothing."

"They'll kill him."

"I guess they will."

"He must have got mixed up in something in Chicago."

"I guess so," said Nick.

"It's a hell of a thing."

"It's an awful thing," Nick said.

They did not say anything. George reached down for a towel and wiped the counter.

"I wonder what he did?" Nick said.

"Double-crossed somebody. That's what they kill them for."

"I'm going to get out of this town," Nick said.

"Yes," said George. "That's a good thing to do."

"I can't stand to think about him waiting in the room and knowing he's going to get it. It's too damned awful."

"Well," said George, "you better not think about it."

THE CHRISTMAS TREE AND THE WEDDING*

⟨ꞟ FEODOR M. DOSTOYEVSKY (1821–1881)

THE OTHER DAY I SAW A WEDDING. . . . BUT NO! I WOULD RATHER TELL YOU about a Christmas tree. The wedding was superb. I liked it immensely. But the other incident was still finer. I don't know why it is that the sight of the wedding reminded me of the Christmas tree. This is the way it happened:

Exactly five years ago, on New Year's Eve, I was invited to a children's ball by a man high up in the business world, who had his connections, his circle of acquaintances, and his intrigues. So it seemed as though the children's ball was merely a pretext for the parents to come together and discuss matters of interest to themselves, quite innocently and casually.

I was an outsider, and, as I had no special matters to air, I was able to spend the evening independently of the others. There was another gentleman present who like myself had just stumbled upon this affair of domestic bliss. He was the first to attract my attention. His appearance was not that of a man of birth or high family. He was tall, rather thin, very serious, and well dressed. Apparently he had no heart for the family festivities. The instant he went off into a corner by himself the smile disappeared from his face, and his thick dark brows knitted into a frown. He knew no one except the host and showed every sign of being bored to death, though bravely sustaining the rôle of thorough enjoyment to the end. Later I learned that he was a provincial, had come to the capital on some important, brain-racking business, had brought a letter of recommendation to our host, and our host had taken him under his protection, not at all *con amore*. It was merely out of politeness that he had invited him to the children's ball.

They did not play cards with him, they did not offer him cigars. No one entered into conversation with him. Possibly they recognised the bird by its feathers from a distance. Thus, my gentleman, not knowing what to do with his hands, was compelled to spend the evening stroking his whiskers. His whiskers were really fine, but he stroked them so assiduously that one got the feeling that the whiskers had come into the world first and afterwards the man in order to stroke them.

There was another guest who interested me. But he was of quite a different order. He was a personage. They called him Julian Mastakovich. At first glance one could tell he was an honoured guest and stood in the same relation to the host as the host to the gentleman of the whiskers. The

* Reprinted from *Best Russian Short Stories*, edited by Thomas Seltzer, by courtesy of Random House, Inc.

host and hostess said no end of amiable things to him, were most attentive, wining him, hovering over him, bringing guests up to be introduced, but never leading him to any one else. I noticed tears glisten in our host's eyes when Julian Mastakovich remarked that he had rarely spent such a pleasant evening. Somehow I began to feel uncomfortable in this personage's presence. So, after amusing myself with the children, five of whom, re- markably well-fed young persons, were our host's, I went into a little sitting- room, entirely unoccupied, and seated myself at the end that was a con- servatory and took up almost half the room.

The children were charming. They absolutely refused to resemble their elders, notwithstanding the efforts of mothers and governesses. In a jiffy they had denuded the Christmas tree down to the very last sweet and had already succeeded in breaking half of their playthings before they even found out which belonged to whom.

One of them was a particularly handsome little lad, dark-eyed, curly- haired, who stubbornly persisted in aiming at one with his wooden gun. But the child that attracted the greatest attention was his sister, a girl of about eleven, lovely as a Cupid. She was quiet and thoughtful, with large, full, dreamy eyes. The children had somehow offended her, and she left them and walked into the same room that I had withdrawn into. There she seated herself with her doll in a corner.

"Her father is an immensely wealthy business man," the guests informed each other in tones of awe. "Three hundred thousand rubles set aside for her dowry already."

As I turned to look at the group from which I heard this news item issuing, my glance met Julian Mastakovich's. He stood listening to the insipid chatter in an attitude of concentrated attention, with his hands behind his back and his head inclined to one side.

All the while I was quite lost in admiration of the shrewdness our host displayed in the dispensing of the gifts. The little maid of the many-rubled dowry received the handsomest doll, and the rest of the gifts were graded in value according to the diminishing scale of the parents' stations in life. The last child, a tiny chap of ten, thin, red-haired, freckled, came into possession of a small book of nature stories without illustrations or even head and tail pieces. He was the governess's child. She was a poor widow, and her little boy, clad in a sorry-looking little nankeen jacket, looked thoroughly crushed and intimidated. He took the book of nature stories and circled slowly about the children's toys. He would have given anything to play with them. But he did not dare to. You could tell he already knew his place.

I like to observe children. It is fascinating to watch the individuality in them struggling for self-assertion. I could see that the other children's things had tremendous charm for the red-haired boy, especially a toy theatre, in which he was so anxious to take a part that he resolved to fawn upon the other children. He smiled and began to play with them. His one and only apple he handed over to a puffy urchin whose pockets were already

crammed with sweets, and he even carried another youngster pickaback—
all simply that he might be allowed to stay with the theatre.

But in a few moments an impudent young person fell on him and gave
him a pummelling. He did not dare even to cry. The governess came and
told him to leave off interfering with the other children's games, and he
crept away to the same room the little girl and I were in. She let him sit
down beside her, and the two set themselves busily to dressing the expensive
doll.

Almost half an hour passed, and I was nearly dozing off, as I sat there in
the conservatory half listening to the chatter of the red-haired boy and the
dowered beauty, when Julian Mastakovich entered suddenly. He had
slipped out of the drawing-room under cover of a noisy scene among the
children. From my secluded corner it had not escaped my notice that a few
moments before he had been eagerly conversing with the rich girl's father,
to whom he had only just been introduced.

He stood still for a while reflecting and mumbling to himself, as if
counting something on his fingers.

"Three hundred—three hundred——eleven—twelve—thirteen—sixteen—
in five years! Let's say four per cent—five times twelve—sixty, and on these
sixty——. Let us assume that in five years it will amount to—well, four
hundred. Hm—hm! But the shrewd old fox isn't likely to be satisfied with
four per cent. He gets eight or even ten, perhaps. Let's suppose five
hundred, five hundred thousand, at least, that's sure. Anything above that
for pocket money—hm—"

He blew his nose and was about to leave the room when he spied the girl
and stood still. I, behind the plants, escaped his notice. He seemed to me to
be quivering with excitement. It must have been his calculations that upset
him so. He rubbed his hands and danced from place to place, and kept
getting more and more excited. Finally, however, he conquered his emotions
and came to a standstill. He cast a determined look at the future bride and
wanted to move toward her, but glanced about first. Then, as if with a
guilty conscience, he stepped over to the child on tip-toe, smiling, and bent
down and kissed her head.

His coming was so unexpected that she uttered a shriek of alarm.

"What are you doing here, dear child?" he whispered, looking around
and pinching her cheek.

"We're playing."

"What, with him?" said Julian Mastakovich with a look askance at the
governess's child. "You should go into the drawing-room, my lad," he said
to him.

The boy remained silent and looked up at the man with wide-open eyes.
Julian Mastakovich glanced round again cautiously and bent down over the
girl.

"What have you got, a doll, my dear?"

"Yes, sir." The child quailed a little, and her brow wrinkled.

"A doll? And do you know, my dear, what dolls are made of?"

"No, sir," she said weakly, and lowered her head.

"Out of rags, my dear. You, boy, you go back to the drawing-room, to the children," said Julian Mastakovich, looking at the boy sternly.

The two children frowned. They caught hold of each other and would not part.

"And do you know why they gave you the doll?" asked Julian Mastakovich, dropping his voice lower and lower.

"No."

"Because you were a good, very good little girl the whole week."

Saying which, Julian Mastakovich was seized with a paroxysm of agitation. He looked round and said in a tone faint, almost inaudible with excitement and impatience:

"If I come to visit your parents will you love me, my dear?"

He tried to kiss the sweet little creature, but the red-haired boy saw that she was on the verge of tears, and he caught her hand and sobbed out loud in sympathy. That enraged the man.

"Go away! Go away! Go back to the other room, to your playmates."

"I don't want him to. I don't want him to! You go away!" cried the girl. "Let him alone! Let him alone!" She was almost weeping.

There was a sound of footsteps in the doorway. Julian Mastakovich started and straightened up his respectable body. The red-haired boy was even more alarmed. He let go the girl's hand, sidled along the wall, and escaped through the drawing-room into the dining-room.

Not to attract attention, Julian Mastakovich also made for the dining-room. He was red as a lobster. The sight of himself in a mirror seemed to embarrass him. Presumably he was annoyed at his own ardour and impatience. Without due respect to his importance and dignity, his calculations had lured and pricked him to the greedy eagerness of a boy, who makes straight for his object—though this was not as yet an object; it only would be so in five years' time. I followed the worthy man into the dining-room, where I witnessed a remarkable play.

Julian Mastakovich, all flushed with vexation, venom in his look, began to threaten the red-haired boy. The red-haired boy retreated farther and farther until there was no place left for him to retreat to, and he did not know where to turn in his fright.

"Get out of here! What are you doing here? Get out, I say, you good-for-nothing! Stealing fruit, are you? Oh, so, stealing fruit! Get out, you freckle face, go to your likes!"

The frightened child, as a last desperate resort, crawled quickly under the table. His persecutor, completely infuriated, pulled out his large linen handkerchief and used it as a lash to drive the boy out of his position.

Here I must remark that Julian Mastakovich was a somewhat corpulent man, heavy, well-fed, puffy-cheeked, with a paunch and ankles as round as nuts. He perspired and puffed and panted. So strong was his dislike (or was it jealousy?) of the child that he actually began to carry on like a madman.

I laughed heartily. Julian Mastakovich turned. He was utterly confused and for a moment, apparently, quite oblivious of his immense importance.

At that moment our host appeared in the doorway opposite. The boy crawled out from under the table and wiped his knees and elbows. Julian Mastakovich hastened to carry his handkerchief, which he had been dangling by the corner, to his nose. Our host looked at the three of us rather suspiciously. But, like a man who knows the world and can readily adjust himself, he seized upon the opportunity to lay hold of his very valuable guest and get what he wanted out of him.

"Here's the boy I was talking to you about," he said, indicating the red-haired child. "I took the liberty of presuming on your goodness in his behalf."

"Oh," replied Julian Mastakovich, still not quite master of himself.

"He's my governess's son," our host continued in a beseeching tone. "She's a poor creature, the widow of an honest official. That's why, if it were possible for you—"

"Impossible, impossible!" Julian Mastakovich cried hastily. "You must excuse me, Philip Alexeyevich, I really cannot. I've made inquiries. There are no vacancies, and there is a waiting list of ten who have a greater right —I'm sorry."

"Too bad," said our host. "He's a quiet, unobtrusive child."

"A very naughty little rascal, I should say," said Julian Mastakovich, wryly. "Go away, boy. Why are you here still? Be off with you to the other children."

Unable to control himself, he gave me a sidelong glance. Nor could I control myself. I laughed straight in his face. He turned away and asked our host, in tones quite audible to me, who that odd young fellow was. They whispered to each other and left the room, disregarding me.

I shook with laughter. Then I, too, went to the drawing-room. There the great man, already surrounded by the fathers and mothers and the host and the hostess, had begun to talk eagerly with a lady to whom he had just been introduced. The lady held the rich little girl's hand. Julian Mastakovich went into fulsome praise of her. He waxed ecstatic over the dear child's beauty, her talents, her grace, her excellent breeding, plainly laying himself out to flatter the mother, who listened scarcely able to restrain tears of joy, while the father showed his delight by a gratified smile.

The joy was contagious. Everybody shared in it. Even the children were obliged to stop playing so as not to disturb the conversation. The atmosphere was surcharged with awe. I heard the mother of the important little girl, touched to her profoundest depths, ask Julian Mastakovich in the choicest language of courtesy, whether he would honour them by coming to see them. I heard Julian Mastakovich accept the invitation with unfeigned enthusiasm. Then the guests scattered decorously to different parts of the room, and I heard them, with veneration in their tones, extol the business man, the business man's wife, the business man's daughter, and, especially, Julian Mastakovich.

"Is he married?" I asked out loud of an acquaintance of mine standing beside Julian Mastakovich.

Julian Mastakovich gave me a venomous look.

"No," answered my acquaintance, profoundly shocked by my—intentional—indiscretion.

. . . .

Not long ago I passed the Church of——. I was struck by the concourse of people gathered there to witness a wedding. It was a dreary day. A drizzling rain was beginning to come down. I made my way through the throng into the church. The bridegroom was a round, well-fed, pot-bellied little man, very much dressed up. He ran and fussed about and gave orders and arranged things. Finally word was passed that the bride was coming. I pushed through the crowd, and I beheld a marvellous beauty whose first spring was scarcely commencing. But the beauty was pale and sad. She looked distracted. It seemed to me even that her eyes were red from recent weeping. The classic severity of every line of her face imparted a peculiar significance and solemnity to her beauty. But through that severity and solemnity, through the sadness, shone the innocence of a child. There was something inexpressibly naïve, unsettled and young in her features, which, without words, seemed to plead for mercy.

They said she was just sixteen years old. I looked at the bridegroom carefully. Suddenly I recognised Julian Mastakovich, whom I had not seen again in all those five years. Then I looked at the bride again.—Good God! I made my way, as quickly as I could, out of the church. I heard gossiping in the crowd about the bride's wealth—about her dowry of five hundred thousand rubles—so and so much for pocket money.

"Then his calculations were correct," I thought, as I pressed out into the street.

THE DAY IT RAINED FOREVER*

Ray Bradbury (1920–)

THE HOTEL STOOD LIKE A HOLLOWED DRY BONE UNDER THE VERY CENTER OF
the desert sky where the sun burned the roof all day. All night, the memory
of the sun stirred in every room like the ghost of an old forest fire. Long
after dusk, since light meant heat, the hotel lights stayed off. The inhabitants
of the hotel preferred to feel their way blind through the halls in their
never-ending search for cool air.

This one particular evening Mr. Terle, the proprietor, and his only
boarders, Mr. Smith and Mr. Fremley, who looked and smelled like two
ancient rags of cured tobacco, stayed late on the long veranda. In their
creaking glockenspiel rockers they gasped back and forth in the dark,
trying to rock up a wind.

"Mr. Terle . . . ? Wouldn't it be *really* nice . . . someday . . . if you
could buy . . . air conditioning . . . ?"

Mr. Terle coasted awhile, eyes shut.

"Got no money for such things, Mr. Smith."

The two old boarders flushed; they hadn't paid a bill now in twenty-one
years.

Much later Mr. Fremley sighed a grievous sigh. "Why, why don't we all
just quit, pick up, get outa here, move to a decent city? Stop this swelterin'
and fryin' and sweatin'."

"Who'd buy a dead hotel in a ghost town?" said Mr. Terle quietly. "No.
No, we'll just set here and wait, wait for that great day, January 29."

Slowly, all three men stopped rocking.

January 29.

The one day in all the year when it really let go and rained.

"Won't wait long." Mr. Smith tilted his gold railroad watch like the
warm summer moon in his palm. "Two hours and nine minutes from now
it'll *be* January 29. But I don't see nary a cloud in ten thousand miles."

"It's rained every January 29 since I was born!" Mr. Terle stopped,
surprised at his own loud voice. "If it's a day late this year, I won't pull
God's shirttail."

Mr. Fremley swallowed hard and looked from east to west across the
desert toward the hills. "I wonder . . . will there ever be a gold rush
hereabouts again?"

"No gold," said Mr. Smith. "And what's more, I'll make you a bet—no rain. No rain tomorrow or the day after the day after tomorrow. No rain all the rest of this year."

The three old men sat staring at the big sun-yellowed moon that burned a hole in the high stillness.

After a long while, painfully, they began to rock again.

The first hot morning breezes curled the calendar pages like a dried snake skin against the flaking hotel front.

The three men, thumbing their suspenders up over their hat rack shoulders, came barefoot downstairs to blink out at that idiot sky.

"January 29 . . ."

"Not a drop of mercy there."

"Day's young."

"*I'm* not." Mr. Fremley turned and went away.

It took him five minutes to find his way up through the delirious hallways to his hot, freshly baked bed.

At noon, Mr. Terle peered in.

"Mr. Fremley . . . ?"

"Damn desert cactus, that's us!" gasped Mr. Fremley, lying there, his face looking as if at any moment it might fall away in a blazing dust on the raw plank floor. "But even the best damn cactus got to have just a sip of water before it goes back to another year of the same damn furnace. I tell you I won't move again, I'll lie here an' die if I don't hear more than birds pattin' around up on that roof!"

"Keep your prayers simple and your umbrella handy," said Mr. Terle and tiptoed away.

At dusk, on the hollow roof a faint pattering sounded.

Mr. Fremley's voice sang out mournfully from his bed.

"Mr. Terle, that ain't rain! That's you with the garden hose sprinklin' well water on the roof! Thanks for tryin', but cut it out, now."

The pattering sound stopped. There was a sigh from the yard below.

Coming around the side of the hotel a moment later, Mr. Terle saw the calendar fly out and down in the dust.

"Damn January 29!" cried a voice. "Twelve more months! Have to wait twelve more months, now!"

Mr. Smith was standing there in the doorway. He stepped inside and brought out two dilapidated suitcases and thumped them on the porch.

"Mr. Smith!" cried Mr. Terle. "You can't leave after thirty years!"

"They say it rains twenty days a month in Ireland," said Mr. Smith. "I'll get a job there and run around with my hat off and my mouth open."

"You can't go!" Mr. Terle tried frantically to think of something; he snapped his fingers. "You owe me nine thousand dollars rent!"

Mr. Smith recoiled; his eyes got a look of tender and unexpected hurt in them.

"I'm sorry." Mr. Terle looked away. "I didn't mean that. Look now—you

just head for Seattle. Pours two inches a week there. Pay me when you can,
or never. But do me a favor: wait till midnight. It's cooler then, anyhow.
Get you a good night's walk toward the city."

"Nothin'll happen between now and midnight."

"You got to have faith. When everything else is gone, you got to believe a
thing'll happen. Just stand here with me, you don't have to sit, just stand
here and think of rain. That's the last thing I'll ever ask of you."

On the desert sudden little whirlwinds of dust twisted up, sifted down.
Mr. Smith's eyes scanned the sunset horizon.

"What do I think? Rain, oh you rain, come along here? Stuff like that?"

"Anything. Anything at all!"

Mr. Smith stood for a long time between his two mangy suitcases and did
not move. Five, six minutes ticked by. There was no sound, save the two
men's breathing in the dusk.

Then at last, very firmly, Mr. Smith stooped to grasp the luggage handles.

Just then, Mr. Terle blinked. He leaned forward, cupping his hand to his
ear.

Mr. Smith froze, his hands still on the luggage.

From away among the hills, a murmur, a soft and tremulous rumble.

"Storm coming!" hissed Mr. Terle.

The sound grew louder; a kind of whitish cloud rose up from the hills.

Mr. Smith stood tall on tiptoe.

Upstairs Mr. Fremley sat up like Lazarus.

Mr. Terle's eyes grew wider and yet wider to take hold of what was
coming. He held to the porch rail like the captain of a calm-foundered
vessel feeling the first stir of some tropic breeze that smelled of lime and the
ice-cool white meat of coconut. The smallest wind stroked over his aching
nostrils as over the flues of a white-hot chimney.

"There!" cried Mr. Terle. "There!"

And over the last hill, shaking out feathers of fiery dust, came the cloud,
the thunder, the racketing storm.

Over the hill the first car to pass in twenty days flung itself down the
valley with a shriek, a thud, and a wail.

Mr. Terle did not dare to look at Mr. Smith.

Mr. Smith looked up, thinking of Mr. Fremley in his room.

Mr. Fremley, at the window, looked down and saw the car expire and die
in front of the hotel.

For the sound that the car made was curiously final. It had come a very
long way on blazing sulphur roads, across salt flats abandoned ten million
years ago by the shingling off of waters. Now, with wire-ravelings like
cannibal hair sprung up from seams, with a great eyelid of canvas top
thrown back and melted to spearmint gum over the rear seat, the auto, a
Kissel car, vintage 1924, gave a final shuddering as if to expel its ghost upon
the air.

The old woman in the front seat of the car waited patiently, looking in at
the three men and the hotel as if to say, Forgive me, my friend is ill; I've

known him a long while, and now I must see him through his final hour. So
she just sat in the car waiting for the faint convulsions to cease and for the
great relaxation of all the bones which signifies that the final process is over.
She must have sat a full half minute longer listening to her car, and there
was something so peaceful about her that Mr. Terle and Mr. Smith leaned
slowly toward her. At last she looked at them with a grave smile and raised
her hand.

Mr. Fremley was surprised to see his hand go out the window, above and
wave back to her.

On the porch Mr. Smith murmured, "Strange. It's not a storm. And I'm
not disappointed. How come?"

But Mr. Terle was down the path and to the car.

"We thought you were . . . that is . . ." He trailed off. "Terle's my
name, Joe Terle."

She took his hand and looked at him with absolutely clear and unclouded
light blue eyes like water that has melted from snow a thousand miles off
and come a long way, purified by wind and sun.

"Miss Blanche Hillgood," she said, quietly. "Graduate of the Grinnell
College, unmarried teacher of music, thirty years high-school glee club and
student orchestra conductor, Green City, Iowa, twenty years private
teacher of piano, harp, and voice, one month retired and living on a pension
and now, taking my roots with me, on my way to California."

"Miss Hillgood, you don't look to be going anywhere from here."

"I had a feeling about that." She watched the two men circle the car
cautiously. She sat like a child on the lap of a rheumatic grandfather,
undecided. "Is there nothing we can do?"

"Make a fence of the wheels, dinner gong of the brake drums, the rest'll
make a fine rock garden."

Mr. Fremley shouted from the sky. "Dead? I say, is the car dead? I can
feel it from here! Well—it's way past time for supper!"

Mr. Terle put out his hand. "Miss Hillgood, that there is Joe Terle's
Desert Hotel, open twenty-six hours a day. Gila monsters and road runners
please register before going upstairs. Get you a night's sleep, free, we'll
knock our Ford off its blocks and drive you to the city come morning."

She let herself be helped from the car. The machine groaned as if in
protest at her going. She shut the door carefully with a soft click.

"One friend gone, but the other still with me. Mr. Terle, could you please
bring her in out of the weather?"

"Her, ma'am?"

"Forgive me, I never think of things but what they're people. The car was
a man, I suppose, because it took me places. But a harp, now, don't you
agree, is female?"

She nodded to the rear seat of the car. There, tilted against the sky like an
ancient scrolled leather ship prow cleaving the wind, stood a case which
towered above any driver who might sit up in front and sail the desert
calms or the city traffics.

"Mr. Smith," said Mr. Terle, "lend a hand."

They untied the huge case and hoisted it gingerly out between them.

"What you got there?" cried Mr. Fremley from above.

Mr. Smith stumbled. Miss Hillgood gasped. The case shifted in the two men's arms.

From within the case came a faint musical humming.

Mr. Fremley, above, heard. It was all the answer he needed. Mouth open, he watched the lady and the two men and their boxed friend sway and vanish in the cavernous porch below.

"What out!" said Mr. Smith. "Some damn fool left his luggage here——" He stopped. "Some damn fool? *Me!*"

The two men looked at each other. They were not perspiring any more. A wind had come up from somewhere, a gentle wind that fanned their shirt collars and flapped the strewn calendar gently in the dust.

"*My* luggage . . ." said Mr. Smith.

Then they all went inside.

"More wine, Miss Hillgood? Ain't had wine on the table in years."

"Just a touch, if you please."

They sat by the light of a single candle which made the room an oven and struck fire from the good silverware and the uncracked plates as they talked and drank warm wine and ate.

"Miss Hillgood, get on with your life."

"All my life," she said, "I've been so busy running from Beethoven to Bach to Brahms, I never noticed I was twenty-nine. Next time I looked up I was forty. Yesterday, seventy-one. Oh, there were men; but they'd given up singing at ten and given up flying when they were twelve. I always figured we were born to fly, one way or other, so I couldn't stand most men shuffling along with all the iron of the earth in their blood. I never met a man who weighed less than nine hundred pounds. In their black business suits, you could hear them roll by like funeral wagons."

"So you flew away?"

"Just in my mind, Mr. Terle. It's taken sixty years to make the final break. All that time I grabbed onto piccolos and flutes and violins because they make streams in the air, you know, like streams and rivers on the ground. I rode every tributary and tried every fresh-water wind from Handel on down to a whole slew of Strausses. It's been the far way around that's brought me here."

"How'd you finally make up your mind to leave?" asked Mr. Smith.

"I looked around last week and said, 'Why, look, you've been flying *alone!*' No one in all Green City really cares *if* you fly or how high you go. It's always, 'Fine, Blanche,' or 'thanks for the recital at the PTA tea, Miss H.' But no one really listening. And when I talked a long time ago about Chicago or New York, folks swatted me and laughed. 'Why be a little frog in a big pond when you can be the biggest frog in all Green City!' So I stayed on, while the folks who gave me advice moved away or died or both.

The rest had wax in their ears. Just last week I shook myself and said, 'Hold on! Since when do *frogs* have wings?' "

"So now you're headin' west?" said Mr. Terle.

"Maybe to play in pictures or in that orchestra under the stars. But somewhere I just must play at last for someone who'll hear and really listen. . . ."

They sat there in the warm dark. She was finished, she had said it all now, foolish or not—and she moved back quietly in her chair.

Upstairs someone coughed.

Miss Hillgood heard, and rose.

It took Mr. Fremley a moment to ungum his eyelids and make out the shape of the woman bending down to place the tray by his rumpled bed.

"What you all talking about down there just now?"

"I'll come back later and tell you word for word," said Miss Hillgood. "Eat now. The salad's fine." She moved to leave the room.

He said, quickly, "You goin' to stay?"

She stopped half out the door and tried to trace the expression on his sweating face in the dark. He, in turn, could not see her mouth or eyes. She stood a moment longer, silently, then went on down the stairs.

"She must not've heard me," said Mr. Fremley.

But he knew she had heard.

Miss Hillgood crossed the downstairs lobby to fumble with the locks on the upright leather case.

"I must pay you for my supper."

"On the house," said Mr. Terle.

"I must pay," she said, and opened the case.

There was a sudden flash of gold.

The two men quickened in their chairs. They squinted at the little old woman standing beside the tremendous heart-shaped object which towered above her with its shining columbined pedestal atop which a calm Grecian face with antelope eyes looked serenely at them even as Miss Hillgood looked now.

The two men shot each other the quickest and most startled of glances, as if each had guessed what might happen next. They hurried across the lobby, breathing hard, to sit on the very edge of the hot velvet lounge, wiping their faces with damp handkerchiefs.

Miss Hillgood drew a chair under her, rested the golden harp gently back on her shoulder, and put her hands to the strings.

Mr. Terle took a breath of fiery air and waited.

A desert wind came suddenly along the porch outside, tilting the chairs so they rocked this way and that like boats on a pond at night.

Mr. Fremley's voice protested from above. "What's goin' on down there?"

And then Miss Hillgood moved her hands.

Starting at the arch near her shoulder, she played her fingers out along the simple tapestry of wires toward the blind and beautiful stare of the

Greek goddess on her column, and then back. Then for a moment she paused and let the sounds drift up through the baked lobby air and into all the empty rooms.

If Mr. Fremley shouted, above, no one heard. For Mr. Terle and Mr. Smith were so busy jumping up to stand riven in the shadows, they heard nothing save the storming of their own hearts and the shocked rush of all the air in their lungs. Eyes wide, mouths dropped, in a kind of pure insanity, they stared at the two women there, the blind Muse proud on her golden pillar, and the seated one, gentle eyes closed, her small hands stretched forth on the air.

Like a girl, they both thought wildly, like a little girl putting her hands out a window to feel what? Why, of course, of course!

To feel the rain.

The echo of the first shower vanished down remote causeways and roof drains, away.

Mr. Fremley, above, rose from his bed as if pulled round by his ears.

Miss Hillgood played.

She played and it wasn't a tune they knew at all, but it was a tune they had heard a thousand times in their long lives, words or not, melody or not. She played and each time her fingers moved, the rain fell pattering through the dark hotel. The rain fell cool at the open windows and the rain rinsed down the baked floor boards of the porch. The rain fell on the roof top and fell on hissing sand, it fell on rusted car and empty stable and dead cactus in the yard. It washed the windows and laid the dust and filled the rain barrels and curtained the doors with beaded threads that might part and whisper as you walked through. But more than anything the soft touch and coolness of it fell on Mr. Smith and Mr. Terle. Its gentle weight and pressure moved them down and down until it had seated them again. By its continuous budding and prickling on their faces it made them shut up their eyes and mouths and raise their hands to shield it away. Seated there, they felt their heads tilt slowly back to let the rain fall where it would.

The flash flood lasted a minute, then faded away as the fingers trailed down the loom, let drop a few last bursts and squalls and then stopped.

The last chord hung in the air like a picture taken when lightning strikes and freezes a billion drops of water on their downward flight. Then the lightning went out. The last drops fell through darkness in silence.

Miss Hillgood took her hands from the strings, her eyes still shut.

Mr. Terle and Mr. Smith opened their eyes to see those two miraculous women way over there across the lobby somehow come through the storm untouched and dry.

They trembled. They leaned forward as if they wished to speak. They looked helpless, not knowing what to do.

And then a single sound from high above in the hotel corridors drew their attention and told them what to do.

The sound came floating down feebly, fluttering like a tired bird beating its ancient wings.

The two men looked up and listened.

It was the sound of Mr. Fremley.

Mr. Fremley, in his room, applauding.

It took five seconds for Mr. Terle to figure out what it was. Then he nudged Mr. Smith and began, himself, to beat his palms together. The two men struck their hands in mighty explosions. The echoes ricocheted around about in the hotel caverns above and below, striking walls, mirrors, windows, trying to fight free of the rooms.

Miss Hillgood opened her eyes now, as if this new storm had come on her in the open, unprepared.

The men gave their own recital. They smashed their hands together so fervently it seemed they had fistfuls of firecrackers to set off, one on another. Mr. Fremley shouted. Nobody heard. Hands winged out, banged shut again and again until fingers puffed up and the old men's breath came short and they put their hands at last on their knees, a heart pounding inside each one.

Then, very slowly, Mr. Smith got up and still looking at the harp, went outside and carried in the suitcases. He stood at the foot of the lobby stairs looking for a long while at Miss Hillgood. He glanced down at her single piece of luggage resting there by the first tread. He looked from her suitcase to her and raised his eyebrows questioningly.

Miss Hillgood looked at her harp, at her suitcase, at Mr. Terle, and at last back to Mr. Smith.

She nodded once.

Mr. Smith bent down and with his own luggage under one arm and her suitcase in the other, he started the long slow climb up the stairs in the gentle dark. As he moved, Miss Hillgood put the harp back on her shoulder and either played in time to his moving or he moved in time to her playing, neither of them knew which.

Half up the flight, Mr. Smith met Mr. Fremley who, in a faded robe, was testing his slow way down.

Both stood there, looking deep into the lobby at the one man on the far side in the shadows, and the two women further over, no more than a motion and a gleam. Both thought the same thoughts.

The sound of the harp playing, the sound of the cool water falling every night and every night of their lives, after this. No spraying the roof with the garden hose now any more. Only sit on the porch or lie in your night bed and hear the falling . . . the falling . . . the falling . . .

Mr. Smith moved on up the stair; Mr. Fremley moved down.

The harp, the harp. Listen, listen!

The fifty years of drought were over.

The time of the long rains had come.

RHODES SCHOLAR*

❧ ALLEN READ (1906–)

OVER ONE OF THE COLLEGE HALLS AT OXFORD UNIVERSITY HUNG AN EXPECTANT
silence. The fifty freshmen gathered on the hard benches for the induction
ceremony realized that the Principal was about to arise. They sat stiff and
self-conscious, timidly glancing about at the gilt-framed portraits on the
walls or looking straight ahead toward the dais at the front. On this
platform, a few steps above the main floor, sat a row of gowned men behind
the heavy oak table. These—actually in the flesh—were the dons that the
freshmen had heard about; and in the center, below the intricate coat-of-
arms, was the most venerable of the group, the Principal, whose scholarly
bearing befitted this somber medieval hall.

One of the new students—he seemed slightly detached—had a more
mature cast of eye than the eighteen year olds about him. The rims of his
glasses were heavier and darker and his clothes had a broad, un-English cut.
He glanced about furtively and the trace of a smile gathered at the corners
of his mouth. He was contrasting this solemn scene with that at an American college. There you waited your turn in the hubbub of your adviser's
office and later filed hurriedly past a registrar's clerk-girl who whisked
papers about in a wicker wire booth.

This student recalled his first American college, where he had got his
B.A.—a denominational institution in a little Iowa town. It was a small
school, but he had some true friends on the faculty. Then at the age of
twenty-one he had gone up to the State University for a year and got a
master's degree in history. He had enjoyed the work and his adviser had
liked his thesis. He had proved that the early Iowa steelers were largely
Southerners, and that ten years before the Civil War Iowa would have sided
with the Southern cause. His biggest ordeal of the year had been trying out
for the Rhodes scholarship to come to Oxford University and he had
trembled before the examining committee. But after a long discussion they
had called in the candidates and announced their decision: "Mr. Ross." Now
Mr. Ross, a freshman again, was starting out at Oxford, waiting for the
induction ceremony.

He sniffed at the faint sour smell of beer that hung over the room. He
would learn later of sconces and convivial "bump suppers."

His eyes and those of all others in the room converged upon the Principal
as the aged man put his hands on the carved arms of the chair and lifted

* Reprinted by permission of *The American Oxonian*.

133

himself up. The long, swinging sleeves of his black academic gown gave his figure a sort of regality. He smiled in a grandfatherly way and squinted as if the dim light hurt his eyes.

His informal words of greeting had a smoothness that made them seem perfunctory. For many years, probably, they had welcomed each new freshman group. "You will first read this Latin oath, placing your hand on the Bible," he intoned, "and then sign your name in the Buttery Book." He nodded toward the Vice-Principal, who sat at the end of the table with a double sized ledger in front of him. "You will then be full members of this ancient and honorable college. Now I shall call the roll of candidates for admission to membership."

From the paper in his hand he began reading the names alphabetically: "Mr. Adcock."

The word "Present" came shakily from a freshman off at the side, and every one turned to look at him.

"Mr. Alford."

The answer was a guttural syllable probably meant to be "Here."

"Mr. Arnold."

This was a man with self-assurance. He might become president of the debating society before he left college. With a soft-turned modulation he enunciated, "Heah." His answer seemed to give courage to those who followed.

"Mr. Bartlett." "Heah."

"Mr. Broadhead." "Heah."

The Iowa Rhodes scholar noticed that they used the kind of "r" that he called "Eastun." He affected it jocularly when he put a note-book ring to his eye for a monocle and pretended to have "cultuah." But it seemed to come natural to them. Probably it did come natural. His own "r," he reflected, was actually pronounced in a word.

There was a long list of c's, about a dozen, and the answer came with regularity. "Heah." "Heah." "Heah." "Heah."

With a squirm of the tongue he formed the word as he pronounced it: "He-er." How outlandish it would sound in this group, he realized.

"Mr. Dallam." "Heah."

"Mr. Dunsworth." "Heah."

The Rhodes scholar edged forward on the hard bench and a sort of panic came over him. Why, he couldn't flout this whole group of people, this whole University. He'd have to give in to their pronunciation, of course. He could force himself to say "Heah" if he wanted to.

But he was an American.

"Mr. Edmonds." "Heah."

And a Middle-Westerner at that.

"Mr. Farrell." "Heah."

As the steady march continued, the muscles in his shoulders tensed. The r's would come along now in a matter of minutes, and he would have to decide one way or the other. He loved the Middle West. People seldom talked about it, but he knew that he did. He remembered his flare of wrath upon reading an article in a big magazine by a man from the Rockies who said that prairie was monotonous and no one could love it. Why, the prairie was something you could bathe yourself in.

He remembered a certain afternoon during his high school years when the feeling had taken hold of him possessively. He had driven out with his mother from their town home to the farm she had inherited. As she talked about the place with the renter, the son had climbed to the rear door of the haymow that overlooked the fields beyond. The summer's heat held the corn rows in a gelatinous silence and pressed so heavily on the crumbly loam that a soil-whiff rolled up and sent a twinge deep in his throat. These fruity undulations of prairie made a homeland. In cultivating these fields here—

"Mr. Hassall." "Heah."

—his grandfather had spent his life. The boy had thought of his grandfather's stories of early days, stories of hardships and failures and victories, stories that gave this soil a history and a background. This was the boy's region by inheritance.

"Mr. Huddleston." "Heah."

But there are circumstances—, he began to himself with a feverish compression of his lips.

"Mr. Janson-Smith." "Heah."

The Rhodes scholar recalled the thesis he had written for his master's degree at his State University. He had fairly immersed himself in the early history of his state. What fun it had been, sitting in the State Historical Library, slowly working through the several panels of county histories. These bulky, old-fashioned volumes, padded with Civil War rosters and records of early business machinations, had chapters that effervesced with pioneers' lives—their dreams, their brawlings, their courage in breaking sod that was matted with roots of prairie grass.

"Mr. Knox." "Heah."

The scholar gripped the bench. Were they already at the n's? No, a Knox was a k. At that only a few more moments remained until the fatal words "Mr. Ross."

"Mr. Lansdowne." "Heah."

Perhaps he could say "Present" and avoid the difficulty. No, no one had said it since the very first man, and that would be sidestepping the issue anyway. He would have to bend his action one way or the other all during his Oxford time.

"Mr. Lawrence." "Heah."

He darted his eyes feverishly among the English boys. They were still and intent with "first-day" stiffness. They all had on the little commoner's gown, like his own. Each person in front of him was an item of black uniformity. Could he stand out against them all with his own kind of a "here"?

"Mr. Martin." "Heah."

Isn't it the better part of discretion to "fit in"? Didn't his grandparent pioneers adapt themselves to the prairie? Every one had told him not to remain an outsider in Oxford.

"Mr. Murray." "Heah."

He didn't want to be an outsider.

"Mr. Niblett." "Heah."

He was becoming part of an "ancient and honorable" college, with centuries behind it. Shouldn't he submit to its ways? He was sent here to fit in, to get what Oxford was supposed to give. Everybody said "Heah." That was the way. It doesn't pay to make a fool of yourself.

"Mr. Otley." "Heah."

He could change his pronunciation. People had done it before. But it was nasty business, he realized. His teacher in freshman composition had been brought up in Iowa and had got her master's degree at the State University, and then after one summer session at Columbia in New York City she had come back with a full-fledged Eastern accent. How people had razzed her behind her back and recounted incidents where she had forgotten for the moment!

"Mr. Padwick." "Heah."

God, the p's!

And there was that fat returned Rhodes scholar at his American college whom everybody had disliked. He had lifted his hat whenever he met another man. He was the kind who said "Heah."

The scholar formed the syllables on his lips, experimentally—"He-ah." How—a—perverted it sounded. He gulped laboriously and swayed forward with his head bent.

"Don't be an outsider," he snarled at himself. "Don't make a show of yourself here at the beginning!"

"Mr. Partridge." "Heah."

"But I'd be a traitor!" he gasped. "I'm an American, and I know I love my Middle West, my prairie."

"Mr. Pennington." "Heah."

"Don't be a fool!"

"Mr. Radford." "Heah."

"Mr. Ross."

The eyes of the few who had learned his name turned upon him, and before making his answer he rumbled his throat in a preliminary way.

YOU KNOW ME, AL*

℞ RING LARDNER (1885–1933)

Detroit, Michigan, April 28

FRIEND AL: WHAT DO YOU THINK OF A ROTTEN MANAGER THAT BAWLS ME OUT and fines me $50.00 for loosing a 1 to 0 game in 10 innings when it was my 1st start this season? And no wonder I was a little wild in the 10th when I had not had no chance to work and get control. I got a good notion to quit this rotten club and jump to the Federals where a man gets some kind of treatment. Callahan says I throwed the game away on purpose but I did not do no such a thing Al because when I throwed that ball at Joe Hill's head I forgot that the bases was full and besides if Gleason had not of starved me to death the ball that hit him in the head would of killed him.

And how could a man go to 1st base and the winning run be forced in if he was dead which he should ought to of been the lucky left handed stiff if I had of had my full strength to put on my fast one instead of being ½ starved to death and weak. But I guess I better tell you how it come off. The papers will get it all wrong like they generally allways does.

Callahan asked me this A.M. if I thought I was hard enough to work and I was tickled to death, because I seen he was going to give me a chance. I told him Sure I was in good shape and if them Tigers scored a run off me he could keep me setting on the bench the rest of the summer. So he says All right I am going to start you and if you go good maybe Gleason will let you eat some supper.

Well Al when I begin warming up I happened to look up in the grand stand and who do you think I seen? Nobody but Violet. She smiled when she seen me but I bet she felt more like crying. Well I smiled back at her because she probily would of broke down and made a seen or something if I had not of. They was not nobody warming up for Detroit when I begin warming up but pretty soon I looked over to their bench and Joe Hill Violet's husband was warming up. I says to myself Well here is where I show that bird up if they got nerve enough to start him against me but probily Jennings don't want to waste no real pitcher on this game which he knows we got cinched and we would of had it cinched Al if they had of got a couple of runs or even 1 run for me.

Well, Jennings come passed our bench just like he allways does and tried

---

to pull some of his funny stuff. He says Hello are you still in the league? I
says Yes but I come pretty near not being. I came pretty near being with
Detroit. I wish you could of heard Gleason and Callahan laugh when I
pulled that one on him. He says something back but it was not no hot
comeback like mine.

Well Al if I had of had any work and my regular control I guess I would
of pitched a o hit game because the only time they could touch me was
when I had to ease up to get them over. Cobb was out of the game and they
told me he was sick but I guess the truth is that he knowed I was going to
pitch. Crawford got a couple of lucky scratch hits off of me because I got in
the hole to him and had to let up. But the way that lucky left handed Hill
got by was something awful and if I was as lucky as him I would quit
pitching and shoot craps or something.

Our club can't hit nothing anyway. But batting against this bird was just
like hitting fungos. His curve ball broke about ½ a inch and you could of
wrote your name and address on his fast one while it was comeing up there.
He had good control but who would not when they put nothing on the
ball?

Well Al we could not get started against the lucky stiff and they could
not do nothing with me even if my suport was rotten and I give a couple or
3 or 4 bases on balls but when they was men waiting to score I zipped them
threw there so as they could not see them let alone hit them. Every time I
come to the bench between innings I looked up to where Violet was setting
and give her a smile and she smiled back and once I seen her clapping her
hands at me after I had made Moriarty pop up in the pinch.

Well we come along to the 10th inning, o and o, and all of a sudden we
got after him. Bodie hits one and Schalk gets 2 strikes and 2 balls and then
singles. Callahan tells Alcock to bunt and he does it but Hill sprawls all over
himself like the big boob he is and the bases is full with nobody down. Well
Gleason and Callahan argued about should they send somebody up for me
or let me go up there and I says Let me go up there because I can murder
this bird and Callahan says Well they is nobody out so go up and take a
wallop.

Honest Al if this guy had of had anything at all I would of hit i out of
the park, but he did not have even a glove. And how can a man hit pitching
which is not no pitching at all but just slopping them up? When I went up
there I hollered to him and says Stick i over here now you yellow stiff. And
he says Yes I can stick them over allright and that is where I got something
on you.

Well Al I hit a foul off of him that would of been a fare ball and broke
up the game if the wind had not of been against it. Then I swung and
missed a curve that I don't see how I missed it. The next i was a yard
outside and this Evans calls it a strike. He has had it in for me ever since last
year when he tried to get funny with me and I says something back to him
that stung him. So he calls this 3d strike on me and I felt like murdering
him. But what is the use?

I throwed down my bat and come back to the bench and I was glad Callahan and Gleason was out on the coaching line or they probily would of said something to me and I would of cut loose and beat them up. Well Al Weaver and Blackburne looked like a couple of rums up there and we don't score where we ought to of had 3 or 4 runs with any kind of hitting.

I would of been all O. K. in spite of that peace of rotten luck if this Hill had of walked to the bench and not said nothing like a real pitcher. But what does he do but wait out there till I start for the box and I says Get on to the bench you lucky stiff or do you want me to hand you something? He says I don't want nothing more of yourn. I allready got your girl and your goat.

Well Al what do you think of a man that would say a thing like that? And nobody but a left hander could of. If I had of had a gun I would of killed him deader than a doornail or something. He starts for the bench and I hollered at him Wait till you get up to that plate an then I am going to bean you.

Honest Al I was so mad I could not see the plate or nothing. I don't even know who it was come up to bat 1st but whoever it was I hit him in the arm and he walks to first base. The next guy bunts and Chase tries to pull off 1 of them plays of hisn instead of playing safe and he don't get nobody. Well I kept getting madder and madder and I walks Stanage who if I had of been myself would not foul me.

Callahan has Scotty warming up and Gleason runs out from the bench and tells me I am threw but Callahan says Wait a minute he is going to let Hill hit and this big stiff ought to be able to get him out of the way and that will give Scotty a chance to get warm. Gleason says You better not take a chance because the big busher is hogwild, and they kept argueing till I got sick of listening to them and I went back to the box and got ready to pitch. But when I seen this Hill up there I forgot all about the ball game and I cut loose at his bean.

Well Al my control was all O. K. this time and I catched him square on the fourhead and he dropped like as if he had been shot. But pretty soon he gets up and gives me the laugh and runs to first base. I did not know the game was over till Weaver come up and pulled me off the field. But if I had not of been ½ starved to death and weak so as I could not put all my stuff on the ball you can bet that Hill never would of run to first base and Violet would of been a widow and probily a lot better off than she is now. At that I never should ought to of tried to kill a left-hander by hitting him in the head.

Well Al they jumped all over me in the clubhouse and I had to hold myself back or I would of gave somebody the beating of their life. Callahan tells me I am fined $50.00 and suspended without no pay. I asked him What for and he says They would not be no use in telling you because you have not got no brains. I says Yes I have to got some brains and he says Yes but they is in your stumach. And then he says I wish we had of sent you to Milwaukee and I come back at him. I says I wish you had of.

Well Al I guess they is no chance of getting square treatment on this club and you won't be supprised if you hear of me jumping to the Federals where a man is treated like a man and not like no white slave.

Yours truly,
JACK.

THE PRODIGAL'S RETURN*

⟨⟩ Margaret Linton (1907–)

"Psst! Rab! Rab!"

Johnnie's voice was neither very steady nor very strong as he tried to attract the attention of the young man reading by lamplight at the upstairs window. Johnnie was unprepared for the strong surge of feeling which swept over him at the sight of the familiar figure. The dusk of a late March evening had settled over Glasgow and Johnnie hesitated to knock on the door of Rab's lodgings in case his unkempt appearance would frighten the landlady into slamming the door in his face before he had time to state his business. He looked around for some pebbles to throw up at the window but this was the city and pebbles were scarce. He moistened his lips and tried again—but his lips trembled and he finished up between a squeak and a whisper.

"Damn it! I might as well be a lassie," he fumed, brushing his eyes with his sleeve. "I've spent five hours walkin' aboot this bloody toon just trying to locate this lad and now that I've foun' him I'm too dagnabbit delicate tae name him." He filled his lungs and yelled "RAB!"

Rab looked up from his book and cocked his head as if listening, then went on reading.

"Gawd an' if that's no just like the professor," Johnnie seethed. "His ears tellt him somebody cried his name but the mighty intellect reasoned that there was naebody in Glesca wha'd be crying 'Rab' an' that settled it. In five years he hasna changed a ----"

"Hey! You there! What are you hangin' aboot for? Did you want something?"

A burly middle-aged man stood in the open doorway.

"Yes sir, I'm looking for Rab Lindsay. He lodges here. I see him at the window."

The man appraised Johnnie but made no move to invite him in.

"What does the likes o' you want wi' Mr. Robert Lindsay? Is he expectin' you?"

"No sir,—but I have to see him." Seeing the man's still suspicious look John added, "I knew him when we were boys. He'll recognise me."

"Come in." The man grudgingly moved aside. "But I'm coming with you to his room and if you are less than welcome you'll come out o' there quicker than you went in."

---

* Printed by permission of Margaret Linton Bahn.

Johnnie followed him up a carpeted stairway. The man knocked and Rab opened his door. "This fellow claims to ken you, Mr. Robert." The landlord jerked his head in Johnnie's direction.

"Rab—It's me!" Johnnie stepped forward into the light from the doorway. In the dim light of the landing, Rab hesitated a split second and then almost lost the power of speech from the shock of seeing who his visitor was.

"Jock! Oh Jock! Is't possible? Come on in, man. It's all right Mr. Carruthers. It's my brother."

"Your *brither?*" The landlord shook his head and left them to their handshaking and back slapping, muttering as he went that "nae doot there's mony a black sheep even in professors' families."

"You're a sight for sore eyes and nae mistake! Sit doon, lad," said Rab pulling up a chair for his visitor. "By sangs, Mother's goin' to be the prood woman the morrow when her favourite son walks in. She's all but given up hope o' ever seein' you again tho she wouldna' admit it."

"Happy, maybe—but hardly prood. How is she? How's everybody?"

"Fine—an goin' to be better now that you have shown up."

"Are you sure o' that?" There was a curl to Johnnie's lip.

"I'm sure," Rab answered quietly. "But Guid sakes, man, where ha'e ye been? It's nigh on to three years since we had word o' you."

Rab looked at his brother keenly, noting the dirty, tattered clothes and the tired droop of the shoulders. Was this the gay light-hearted Johnnie to whom they had entrusted the family savings when he set out almost five years ago to make his fortune in America? The brown curly hair was still the same but the once ruddy cheeks were hollow and the light had gone out of his eye. The old Johnnie would never have presented himself anywhere, at seven o'clock in the evening, with a three day's growth of beard on his face.

"Ye may well look, Professor," Johnnie said and could not keep the bitterness out of his voice. "Doubtless you seldom see sich a poor excuse for a human being. Indeed the word 'human' is just a sort o' courtesy title when applied to me nowadays. I'm at the stage where humanity would like to class me wi' the pigs, but the pigs is under nae obligation tae accept me. In fact I talked the whole thing over with a fat sow one nicht I was feedin' her, and she summed up my character wi' a grunt and a snort that left me in nae doubt I wad be nae great success as a pig either."

"Wait a minute, Jock. I'll ask Mrs. Carruthers to get us a bite to eat and then we can talk a' nicht if we like."

"Fine. I'll no deny the thought o' something inside me is pleasant. Maybe, while she is readying it, I could borrow your razor and a bit soap and we can see what's under the stink and the stubble."

"Help yoursel'. They're in the corner there. You'll find clean clothes in the closet there—and if they are ower big for you, we can just keep on feeding you 'till you fill them."

"Ach Rab——." Johnnie struggled for words but his bravado was wearing thin and he was near tears. Seeing this, Rab hurried off to order supper, for though the two were worlds apart in their interests and abilities, they were brothers to the innermost core of their hearts; and their reunion, though outwardly calm, was an emotional whirlwind for them both.

When they had eaten and the supper things had been cleared away, Rab built up the fire and the two settled down to eliminate the five years' separation which had just ended.

"I never did congratulate you an bein' made a professor, Rab. I should have."

"That's a' right" Rab shrugged. "They pay you just the same whether your brother congratulates you or no'. But my story will keep. Let's hear yours."

"You can guess mine."

"Some of it, maybe. You are broke. You've been ill—or starved. But why? Where? What were you doing to get as bedraggled as you looked when you came in tonight?"

"Rab, I got dirty outside, inside, all the way through, stoking coal on a boat from New York tae Glesca. We docked at the Broomielaw pier this forenoon and I started lookin' for you. I never did ken Glesca very weel an' it took me hours tae find the place where you used to lodge when you were a student. Mrs. Monroe, there, was able to tell me where you lived noo and directed me how to get here."

"Aye, well. That's the end o' the story. What aboot the beginning? Last time you wrote you were doing fine in Chicago."

"My Gawd! Is that the last time I wrote? It's a while since I was doin' fine onywhere and if I claimed to be doin' well in Chicago I was lyin'. By the time I got to Chicago, naebody would have given you tuppence for me and all I possessed."

"Start at the beginning and let's hear the true version all the way through."

"Startin' on the night we first landed in New York. . . . Tam Cullen and me (I'd made up wi' Tam on the boat) was just standin' on the pier lookin' aboot us and saying what a pleasure it was to have your feet on terra firma again when a pair o' porters cam up and asked us where we were headed. We said we thought we would just tak a couple o' days in New York and then head oot west somewhere. They were friendly kinna lads and told us we'd best take the ferry to the main part o' the town and put up at the Highlandman's hotel."

"They recognised your origins, I'm thinkin'."

"Oh, aye. They were smart fellows. We thought that sounded like a guid place to stay, so the porters took oor bags to put them on the ferry for us and showed us where to buy oor tickets at the far end o' the pier. To mak' a lang story short, there was nae sich ferry an' that was the last we ever saw o' the porters or oor baggage. Folk laughed at us when we told them how easily we had been taken in. We gaed up to a guard and told him we had been robbed but he laughed in oor faces for being sae green. Then, bein' as we were thunderin' mad anyway, Tam let fly an' hit the guard a clout for laughin' at us instead o' huntin' the culprits as he was paid to do. This breach o' etiquette angered the guard, of coorse, so before you could say 'whoopmaleerie' the hale o' New York joined in and a grand fight ensued.

"A fine start to conquerin' the new world."

"It was a' that, but we gave as good as we got, an' we celebrated by gettin' rip roarin' drunk."

"Drunk? *You?*"

"Aye. *Me!* It's no a hard thing to do, you ken. Tam an' me wandered into this pub, just meanin' to get a bite to eat. We happened to sit doon at a table where a young swell was conscientiously workin' at gettin' drunk. He was a nice, friendly sort o' chap and the first body we found that was sympathetic aboot what had happened to us at the pier. He ordered drinks, and then Tam, to be polite, ordered drinks and then I did the same and after that naebody kenned what was orderin' what. I'd nae idea how much o' the stuff a fellow could drink withoot losin' his wits but I must have passed the place withoot noticin' it, for the first thing I knew, Tam, the swell an' me was gettin' thrown oot the pub. And then he took us home wi' him. He lived wi' his mother. It was a big hoose fair crawlin' wi' servants. In the state we were in at the time we maybe saw twice as mony as there were, but, even so, it was a lot. The next mornin' one o' them came in an' told us Mr. Roy Carver (that was the fellow's name) was waitin' for us on the verandah. He wanted to know what plans we had for the day."

"Plans were somethin' Tam an' me hadna' had time to think about so we said all we knew, for sure, was that we would have to buy some new clothes to replace what had been stolen at the pier. 'Fine,' says Roy, 'have some breakfast and then we'll get you fixed up. I know just the place.' "

"Weel Rab, I might have known better than to let the likes o' Carver show us where to buy clothes. We landed in a fancy establishment so almichty genteel ye werena' even supposed tae ask the price o' onything and if ye did ask, they let on not tae hear ye. Tam an' me bought as little as possible but, even so, we was staggered when we got the reckonin' as we came oot. We didna' want to say onything for fear o' embarrassing Carver so we paid up."

"How much?"

"May I be struck dumb if I ever tell a livin' soul what we paid for they duds, but I'll tell ye this . . . when we got back to the hoose and changed into oor new finery, I'll no deny I felt like a new man. They were gentleman's clothes all right an' we felt like Royalty. As we looked at ourselves in the lang mirrors Cullen whispers tae me, 'Jock, does it occur tae ye that naebody here kens onything aboot us? For a' they ken we could be gentry. Lots o' spare aristocrats, wi' nae hope o' inheritin', come tae the colonies.' "

" 'How's your Lordship feelin'?' says I. 'No sae bad, your Grace,' says he. An' we entered the aristocracy. How the word spread I'll never ken but, from then on, there was a definite change in the way we were treated."

"What kind o' a difference?"

"Rab, withoot you join the aristocracy you'll never ken. Nothin' you could put your finger on; but it was there. The biggest change was in Carver's mother. Up 'til then she had been mighty hoity-toity an' of the obvious opinion that we were just aboot what she would expect her wanderin' boy to pick up at a dockside pub."

"Now she introduced us to her friends an' always explained in a whisper you could have heard in Glesca that we had titles, but were too genteel to use them in a land that had given up sich fripperies. Mony a laugh we had. Tam turned into quite a conversationalist. You shoulda heard him."

" 'I'm just plain Tam Cullen,' he would say wi' a simper which made it clear he was goin' the last mile to get doon to the level o' other folk. Then he would casually mention what the Marquis of Langthaple said at the Ayr races and say 'and—do any of you know the Lady Sophia of Derwent?' Naebody did, of course, there bein' nae sich lady, but he managed to make them feel it was a real pity they'd missed Sophia."

"Weel—this was all verra weel for a while but we were invited so mony places we had to get more fancy clothes an', of coorse, we took our turn to stand treat, an' we had to gie presents everywhere we were invited, especially to the servants, an' what wi' one thing and anither, it didna' tak' lang to spend what it had taken mony a year to save up an' at last we were oot o' funds. Cullen settled this to everybody's satisfaction by marryin' Carver's sister and gettin' a job wi' her father. To this day, that lassie firmly believes she would be the Duchess o' Marlborough but for skulduggery at the court o' Victoria. Me, I hadna gone a' the lang way to America just to get wrecked on the rocks o' matrimony so I took my last ten quid and headed west which was what I'd had in mind all along. It was harder to get work than I had thought, or maybe I had just gotten big ideas aboot the sort o' work my lordship should do. I got ower that tho', before the finish, as you saw. But to get back to my story—I had learned to like a dram and I'd had a go at high society but I had, at last, to pawn my good clothes and eat the proceeds and bring doon my standards o' what kind o' work was suitable for a temporary lord. But I would spend all I'd earned in a day just to buy mysel' a couple o' hours o' feelin' like the Prince o' Wales."

"An apt likeness! But I'm thinkin' two hours out of twenty-four was a poor percentage in return for your health and self respect."

"Nae preachin', Rab! No' 'til you've been broke among strangers: no 'til you have wandered sae far frae the coast you are out o' smell o' the sea. Man, I never thocht how I'd miss the sea! And the hills, Rab. It's as true as I'm tellin' ye, one farm where I worked I could face ony point o' the compass and from me to the far horizon no' even a hillock broke the flat level plain. It gave me the creeps. I felt as if somebody had stolen all the furnishings of the world and that I had been left behind at a global flittin'."

"That's when I decided to come hame. I thocht I was goin' daft. Bit by bit I worked my way back to the coast an' there I just haunted the docks 'til I got a job on a ship headed for Glesca. So here I am. I came to you before goin' doon hame to ask you what I should do. Should I slink hame, hat in hand, an' ask Father for a job on the farm again after all the arguing I did to leave in the first place? He'll have plenty to say about the mess I've made o' things—an' even Mother is goin' to be on the rampage about the damage I've done to my immortal soul, but if you think I can mak' amends I'm willin' to take my medicine frae the baith o' them. I've put them through a lot."

Rab laughed. "If it'll ease your conscience any I can tell you one lad who's goin' to be thankful you're back, and that's Willie. Besides that he's always hero-worshipped you and missed you badly, there's the practical consideration that he's real sick o' farmin' and, bein' the youngest, there's nobody comin' up to tak' his place. You'll be more than welcome to his job I can tell you."

"And what will he do?"

"He wants to start a factory. He's machinery daft."

"The wee deevil! You don't suppose he was prayin' sae hard that I'd come back that he wrecked a' my fine plans for buildin' up America single-handed?"

"I wadna put it past him, but let's get to bed. The morrow is Saturday and we have twenty-five miles to walk hame, so we'd best get an early start if we want to get to the farm before the Sabbath settles doon on it."

"I doot even the Sabbath will have to wait 'til Father has his say!" said Johnnie.

"You stupid gomeril," said Rab with his hand on Johnnie's shoulder, "when you walk in at the farm door, all anybody'll have to say will go into two words: 'Johnnie's Hame!'"

And Rab was right.

Poetry

GEORGE HERBERT (1593–1633)

UNKINDNESSE

Lord, make me coy and tender to offend:
In friendship, first I think, if that agree,
    Which I intend,
  Unto my friends intent and end.
I would not use a friend, as I use Thee.

If any touch my friend, or his good name;
It is my honour and my love to free
    His blasted fame
  From the least spot or thought of blame.
I could not use a friend, as I use Thee.

My friend may spit upon my curious floore:
Would he have gold? I lend it instantly;
    But let the poore,
  And thou within them starve at doore.
I cannot use a friend, as I use Thee.

When that my friend pretendeth to a place,
I quit my interest, and leave it free:
    But when thy grace
  Sues for my heart, I thee displace,
Nor would I use a friend, as I use Thee.

Yet can a friend what thou hast done fulfill?
O write in brasse, *My God upon a tree*
    His bloud did spill
  Onely to purchase my good-will:
Yet use I not my foes, as I use thee.

THE STORM

If as the windes and waters here below
                    Do flie and flow,
My sighs and tears as busie were above;
                    Sure they would move
And much affect thee, as tempestuous times
Amaze poore mortals, and object their crimes.

Starres have their storms, ev'n in a high degree,
                    As well as we.
A throbbing conscience spurred by remorse
                    Hath a strange force:
It quits the earth, and mounting more and more,
Dares to assault thee, and besiege thy doore.

There it stands knocking, to thy musicks wrong,
                    And drowns the song.
Glorie and honour are set by till it
                    An answer get.
Poets have wrong'd poore storms: such dayes are best;
They purge the aire without, within the breast.

THE METHOD

                    Poore heart, lament.
For since thy God refuseth still,
There is some rub, some discontent,
                    Which cools his will.

                    Thy Father *could*
Quickly effect, what thou dost move;
For he is *Power:* and sure he *would;*
                    For he is *Love.*

Go search this thing,
Tumble thy breast, and turn thy book.
If thou hadst lost a glove or ring,
Wouldst thou not look?

What do I see
Written above there? *Yesterday*
I did behave me carelesly,
When I did pray.

And should Gods eare
To such indifferents chained be,
Who do not their own motions heare?
Is God lesse free?

But stay! what's there?
Late when I would have something done,
I had a motion to forbear,
Yet I went on.

And should Gods eare,
Which needs not man, be ty'd to those
Who heare not him, but quickly heare
His utter foes?

Then once more pray:
Down with thy knees, up with thy voice.
Seek pardon first, and God will say,
Glad heart rejoyce.

ABRAHAM COWLEY (1618–1667)

GOLD

A mighty pain *to Love* it is,
And 'tis a pain that pain to *miss.*
But of all pains the greatest pain
It is to love, but love in vain.
Virtue now nor noble *Blood,*
Nor *Wit* by *Love* is understood,
Gold alone does passion move,
Gold Monopolizes love!
A *curse* on her, and on the Man
Who this traffick first began!
A *curse* on him who found the Ore!
A *curse* on him who digg'd the store!
A *curse* on him who did refine it!
A *curse* on him who first did coyn it!
A *Curse* all curses else above
On him, who us'd it first in *Love!*
Gold begets in Brethren hate,
Gold in *Families* debate;
Gold does Friendships separate,
Gold does Civil Wars create.
These the smallest harms of it!
Gold, alas, does *Love beget.*

THE USURPATION

I

Thou'hadst to my *Soul* no *title* or *pretence;*
I was mine own, and *free,*
Till I had *giv'n* my self to Thee;
But thou hast kept me *Slave* and *Prisoner* since.
Well, since so insolent thou'rt grown,

Fond *Tyrant,* I'll *depose* thee from thy Throne;
Such outrages must not admitted be
   In an *Elective Monarchy.*

2

Part of my *Heart* by *Gift* did to Thee fall;
   My Country, Kindred, and my best
   Acquaintance were to share the rest;
But thou, their *Cov'etous Neighbour,* drav'est out all:
   Nay more; thou mak'st me worship *Thee,*
And would'st the rule of my *Religion* be;
Was ever *Tyrant* claim'd such power as you,
   To be both *Emp'rour,* and *Pope* too?

3

The *publick Mise'ries,* and my *private fate*
   Deserve some tears: but greedy Thou
   (*Insatiate Maid!*) wilt not allow
That I one drop from thee should *alienate.*
   Nor wilt thou grant my sins a part,
Though the sole cause of most of them thou art,
Counting my *Tears* thy *Tribute* and thy *Due,*
   Since first mine *Eyes* I gave to *You.*

4

Thou all my *Joys* and all my *Hopes* dost claim,
   Thou ragest like a *Fire* in me,
   Converting all things into *Thee;*
Nought can resist, or *not encrease* the *Flame.*
   Nay every *Grief* and every *Fear,*
Thou dost devour, unless thy stamp it bear.
Thy presence, like the crowned *Basilisks* breath,
   All other *Serpents* puts to death.

5

As men in *Hell* are from *Diseases* free,
   So from all other ills am I;
   Free from their known *Formality:*
But all pains *Eminently* lye in *Thee:*
   Alas, alas, I hope in vain
My conquer'd Soul from out thine hands to gain.
Since all the *Natives* there thou'st overthrown,
   And planted *Gar'isons* of thine own.

HENRY VAUGHAN (1621–1695)

AFFLICTION

PEACE! peace! it is not so. Thou dost miscall
   Thy physic: pills that change
Thy sick accessions into settled health;
This is the great elixir, that turns gall
To wine and sweetness, poverty to wealth;
   And brings man home when he doth range.
   Did not He, Who ordain'd the day,
          Ordain night too?
   And in the greater world display
   What in the lesser He would do?
All flesh is clay, thou know'st; and but that God
      Doth use His rod,
And by a fruitful change of frosts and showers
     Cherish, and bind thy pow'rs,
Thou wouldst to weeds and thistles quite disperse,
   And be more wild than is thy verse.
Sickness is wholesome, and crosses are but curbs
   To check the mule, unruly man;
They are heaven's husbandry, the famous fan,
   Purging the floor which chaff disturbs.
Were all the year one constant sunshine, we
       Should have no flowers;
All would be drought and leanness; not a tree
       Would make us bowers.
Beauty consists in colours; and that's best
   Which is not fix'd, but flies and flows;
The settled red is dull, and whites that rest
   Something of sickness would disclose.
     Vicissitude plays all the game;
       Nothing that stirs,
       Or hath a name,
   But waits upon this wheel;
Kingdoms too have their physic, and for steel
   Exchange their peace and furs.
Thus doth God key disorder'd man,
     Which none else can,
Tuning his breast to rise or fall;
And by a sacred, needful art
Like strings stretch ev'ry part,
Making the whole most musical.

ROBERT BURNS (1759–1796)

TO A MOUSE, ON TURNING HER UP IN HER NEST WITH THE PLOUGH, NOVEMBER, *1785*

WEE, sleekit, cow'rin, tim'rous beastie,
O, what a panic's in thy breastie!
Thou need na start awa sae hasty,
   Wi' bickering brattle!
I wad be laith to rin an' chase thee,
   Wi' murd'ring pattle!

I'm truly sorry man's dominion
Has broken Nature's social union,
An' justifies that ill opinion,
   Which makes thee startle,
At me, thy poor, earth-born companion,
   An' fellow-mortal!

I doubt na, whiles, but thou may thieve;
What then? poor beastie, thou maun live!
A daimen-icker in a thrave
   'S a sma' request:
I'll get a blessin wi' the lave,
   And never miss't!

Thy wee bit housie, too, in ruin!
Its silly wa's the win's are strewin!
An' naething, now, to big a new ane,
   O' foggage green!
An' bleak December's winds ensuin,
   Baith snell an' keen!

Thou saw the fields laid bare and waste,
An' weary winter comin fast,
An' cozie here, beneath the blast,
   Thou thought to dwell,
Till crash! the cruel coulter past,
   Out thro' thy cell.

That wee bit heap o' leaves an' stibble,
Has cost thee mony a weary nibble!

Now thou's turn'd out, for a' thy trouble,
    But house or hald,
To thole the winter's sleety dribble,
    An' cranreuch cauld!

But, Mousie, thou art no thy lane,
In proving foresight may be vain:
The best laid schemes o' mice an' men
    Gang aft a-gley,
An' lea'e us naught but grief an' pain,
    For promis'd joy.

Still thou art blest, compar'd wi' me!
The present only toucheth thee:
But, Och! I backward cast my e'e
    On prospects drear!
An' forward, tho' I canna see,
    I guess an' fear!

WINTER

A DIRGE

The wintry west extends his blast,
    And hail and rain does blaw;
Or, the stormy north sends driving forth,
    The blinding sleet and snaw:
While, tumbling brown, the burn comes down,
    And roars frae bank to brae:
And bird and beast in covert rest,
    And pass the heartless day.

"The sweeping blast, the sky o'ercast,"
    The joyless winter-day,
Let others fear, to me more dear
    Than all the pride of May:
The tempest's howl, it soothes my soul,
    My griefs it seems to join;
The leafless trees my fancy please,
    Their fate resembles mine!

Thou Pow'r Supreme, whose mighty scheme
    These woes of mine fulfil,

Here, firm, I rest, they must be best,
  Because they are Thy will!
Then all I want, (Oh! do thou grant
  This one request of mine!)
Since to enjoy thou dost deny
  Assist me to resign.

O, WERT THOU IN THE CAULD BLAST

TUNE—"THE LASS OF LIVINGSTONE"

O, WERT thou in the cauld blast,
  On yonder lea, on yonder lea,
My plaidie to the angry airt,
  I'd shelter thee, I'd shelter thee.
Or did misfortune's bitter storms
  Around thee blaw, around thee blaw,
Thy bield should be my bosom,
  To share it a', to share it a'.

Or were I in the wildest waste,
  Of earth and air, of earth and air,
The desert were a paradise,
  If thou wert there, if thou wert there.
Or were I monarch o' the globe,
  Wi' thee to reign, wi' thee to reign,
The only jewel in my crown
  Wad be my queen, wad be my queen.

WILLIAM WORDSWORTH (1770–1850)

ODE

INTIMATIONS OF IMMORALITY FROM RECOLLECTIONS OF
EARLY CHILDHOOD

The Child is Father of the Man;
And I could wish my days to be
Bound each to each by natural piety.

I

THERE was a time when meadow, grove, and stream,
The earth, and every common sight,
      To me did seem
      Apparelled in celestial light,
The glory and the freshness of a dream.
It is not now as it hath been of yore;—
      Turn wheresoe'er I may,
      By night or day,
The things which I have seen I now can see no more.

II

      The Rainbow comes and goes,
      And lovely is the Rose,
      The Moon doth with delight
Look round her when the heavens are bare;
      Waters on a starry night
      Are beautiful and fair;
      The sunshine is a glorious birth;
      But yet I know, where'er I go,
That there hath past away a glory from the earth.

III

Now, while the birds thus sing a joyous song,
      And while the young lambs bound
      As to the tabor's sound,
To me alone there came a thought of grief:
A timely utterance gave that thought relief,
      And I again am strong:
The cataracts blow their trumpets from the steep;

No more shall grief of mine the season wrong;
I hear the Echoes through the mountains throng,
The Winds come to me from the fields of sleep,
    And all the earth is gay;
        Land and sea
    Give themselves up to jollity,
        And with the heart of May
    Doth every Beast keep holiday;—
        Thou Child of Joy,
Shout round me, let me hear thy shouts, thou happy
    Shepherd-boy!

IV

Ye blessed Creatures, I have heard the call
  Ye to each other make; I see
The heavens laugh with you in your jubilee;
    My heart is at your festival,
      My head hath its coronal,
The fulness of your bliss, I feel—I feel it all.
      Oh evil day! if I were sullen
      While Earth herself is adorning,
        This sweet May-morning,
      And the Children are culling
        On every side,
    In a thousand valleys far and wide,
    Fresh flowers; while the sun shines warm,
And the Babe leaps up on his Mother's arm:—
    I hear, I hear, with joy I hear!
    —But there's a Tree, of many one,
A single Field which I have looked upon,
Both of them speak of something that is gone:
      The Pansy at my feet
      Doth the same tale repeat:
Whither is fled the visionary gleam?
Where is it now, the glory and the dream?

V

Our birth is but a sleep and a forgetting:
The Soul that rises with us, our life's Star,
      Hath had elsewhere its setting,
      And cometh from afar:
    Not in entire forgetfulness,
    And not in utter nakedness,
But trailing clouds of glory do we come
    From God, who is our home:

Heaven lies about us in our infancy!
Shades of the prison-house begin to close
      Upon the growing Boy,
But He beholds the light, and whence it flows,
      He sees it in his joy;
The Youth, who daily farther from the east
      Must travel, still is Nature's Priest,
      And by the vision splendid
      Is on his way attended;
At length the Man perceives it die away,
And fade into the light of common day.

VI

Earth fills her lap with pleasures of her own;
Yearnings she hath in her own natural kind,
And, even with something of a Mother's mind,
      And no unworthy aim,
      The homely Nurse doth all she can
To make her Foster-child, her Inmate Man,
      Forget the glories he hath known,
And that imperial palace whence he came.

VII

Behold the Child among his new-born blisses,
A six years' Darling of a pigmy size!
See, where 'mid work of his own hand he lies,
Fretted by sallies of his mother's kisses,
With light upon him from his father's eyes!
See, at his feet, some little plan or chart,
Some fragment from his dream of human life,
Shaped by himself with newly-learned art;
      A wedding or a festival,
      A mourning or a funeral;
        And this hath now his heart,
      And unto this he frames his song:
        Then will he fit his tongue
To dialogues of business, love, or strife;
      But it will not be long
      Ere this be thrown aside,
      And with new joy and pride
The little Actor cons another part;
Filling from time to time his 'humorous stage'
With all the Persons, down to palsied Age,
That Life brings with her in her equipage;
      As if his whole vocation
      Were endless imitation.

SONNETS

XIV

LONDON, 1802

MILTON! thou should'st be living at this hour:
England hath need of thee: she is a fen
Of stagnant waters: altar, sword, and pen,
Fireside, the heroic wealth of hall and bower,
Have forfeited their ancient English dower
Of inward happiness. We are selfish men;
Oh! raise us up, return to us again;
And give us manners, virtue, freedom, power.
Thy soul was like a Star, and dwelt apart:
Thou hadst a voice whose sound was like the sea:
Pure as the naked heavens, majestic, free,
So didst thou travel on life's common way,
In cheerful godliness; and yet thy heart
The lowliest duties on herself did lay.

XXIX

COMPOSED UPON WESTMINSTER BRIDGE, SEPT. 3, 1803

EARTH has not any thing to show more fair:
Dull would he be of soul who could pass by
A sight so touching in its majesty:
This City now doth, like a garment, wear
The beauty of the morning; silent, bare,
Ships, towers, domes, theatres, and temples lie
Open unto the fields, and to the sky;
All bright and glittering in the smokeless air.
Never did sun more beautifully steep
In his first splendour, valley, rock, or hill;
Ne'er saw I, never felt, a calm so deep!
The river glideth at his own sweet will:
Dear God! the very houses seem asleep;
And all that mighty heart is lying still!

THOMAS CAMPBELL (1777–1844)

LORD ULLIN'S DAUGHTER

A chieftain to the Highlands bound,
   Cries, 'Boatman, do not tarry!
And I'll give thee a silver pound,
   To row us o'er the ferry."

"Now, who be ye would cross Loch-Gyle
   This dark and stormy water?"
"Oh! I'm the chief of Ulva's isle,
   And this, Lord Ullin's daughter.

"And fast before her father's men
   Three days we've fled together,
For should he find us in the glen,
   My blood would stain the heather.

"His horsemen hard behind us ride;
   Should they our steps discover,
Then who will cheer my bonny bride,
   When they have slain her lover?"

Out spoke the hardy Highland wight
   "I'll go, my chief—I'm ready:
It is not for your silver bright,
   But for your winsome lady:

And, by my word! the bonny bird
   In danger shall not tarry;
So, though the waves are raging white,
   I'll row you o'er the ferry."

By this, the storm grew loud apace,
   The water-wraith was shrieking;
And, in the scowl of heaven, each face
   Grew dark as they were speaking.

But still, as wilder grew the wind,
   And as the night grew drearer,

Adown the glen rode armèd men,
   Their trampling sounded nearer.

"Oh! haste thee, haste!" the lady cries,
   "Though tempests round us gather,
I'll meet the raging of the skies,
   But not an angry father."

The boat has left the stormy land,
   A stormy sea before her;
When, oh! too strong for human hand
   The tempest gathered o'er her.

And still they rowed, amid the roar
   Of waters fast prevailing;
Lord Ullin reached that fatal shore,
   His wrath was changed to wailing.

For sore dismayed through storm and shade
   His child he did discover;
One lovely hand she stretched for aid,
   And one was round her lover.

"Come back! come back!" he cried, in grief,
   "Across this stormy water;
And I'll forgive your Highland chief,
   My daughter! O, my daughter!"

'Twas vain: the loud waves lashed the shore,
   Return or aid preventing:
The waters wild, went o'er his child,
   And he was left lamenting.

LORD BYRON (1788–1824)

FROM CHILDE HAROLD'S PILGRIMAGE
CANTO III

88

Ye stars! which are the poetry of heaven
If in your bright leaves we would read the fate
Of men and empires,—'t is to be forgiven,
That in our aspirations to be great,
Our destinies o'erleap their mortal state,
And claim a kindred with you; for ye are
A beauty and a mystery, and create
In us such love and reverence from afar,
That fortune, fame, power, life, have named themselves a star.

89

All heaven and earth are still—though not in sleep,
But breathless, as we grow when feeling most;
And silent, as we stand in thoughts too deep:—
All heaven and earth are still: From the high host
Of stars, to the lull'd lake and mountain-coast,
All is concenter'd in a life intense,
Where not a beam, nor air, nor leaf is lost,
But hath a part of being, and a sense
Of that which is of all Creator and defence.

90

Then stirs the feeling infinite, so felt
In solitude, where we are least alone;
A truth, which through our being then doth melt
And purifies from self: it is a tone,
The soul and source of music, which makes known
Eternal harmony, and sheds a charm,
Like to the fabled Cytherea's zone,
Binding all things with beauty;—'t would disarm
The spectre Death, had he substantial power to harm.

CANTO IV (THE OCEAN)

There is a pleasure in the pathless woods,
    There is a rapture on the lonely shore,
There is society, when none intrudes,
    By the deep Sea, and music in its roar:
I love not Man the less, but nature more,
    From these our interviews; in which I steal
From all I may be, or have been before,
    To mingle with the Universe, and feel
What I can ne'er express, yet can not all conceal.

Roll on, thou deep and dark-blue ocean—roll!
    Ten thousand fleets sweep over thee in vain;
Man marks the earth with ruin—his control
    Stops with the shore;—upon the watery plain
The wrecks are all thy deed, nor doth remain
    A shadow of man's ravage, save his own;
When, for a moment, like a drop of rain,
    He sinks into thy depths with bubbling groan
Without a grave, unknell'd, uncoffin'd, and unknown!

His steps are not upon thy paths,—thy fields
    Are not a spoil for him,—thou dost arise
And shake him from thee; the vile strength he wields
    For earth's destruction thou dost all despise,
Spurning him from thy bosom to the skies,
    And send'st him, shivering in thy playful spray
And howling, to his Gods, where haply lies
    His petty hope in some near port or bay,
And dashes him again to earth:—there let him lay.

The armaments which thunderstrike the walls
    Of rock-built cities, bidding nations quake,
And monarchs tremble in their capitals—
    The oak leviathans, whose huge ribs make
Their clay creator the vain title take
    Of lord of thee, and arbiter of war—
These are thy toys, and, as the snowy flake,

They melt into thy yeast of waves, which mar
Alike the Armada's pride, or spoils of Trafalgar.

Thy shores are empires, changed in all save thee—
    Assyria, Greece, Rome, Carthage, what are they?
Thy waters wasted them while they were free,
    And many a tyrant since; their shores obey
The stranger, slave, or savage; their decay
    Has dried up realms to deserts:—not so thou,
Unchangeable save to thy wild waves' play—
    Time writes no wrinkle on thine azure brow—
Such as Creation's dawn beheld, thou rollest now!

Thou glorious mirror, where the Almighty's form
    Glasses itself in tempests!—in all time—
Calm or convulsed, in breeze or gale or storm,
    Icing the pole, or in the torrid clime
Dark-heaving—boundless, endless, and sublime!
    The image of Eternity!—the throne
Of the invisible!—Even from out thy slime
    The monsters of the deep are made! Each zone
Obeys thee! Thou goest forth, dread! fathomless!
    alone!

PERCY BYSSHE SHELLEY (1792–1822)

THE CLOUD

I BRING fresh showers for the thirsting flowers,
    From the seas and the streams;
I bear light shade for the leaves when laid
    In their noonday dreams.
From my wings are shaken the dews that waken
    The sweet birds every one,
When rocked to rest on their mother's breast,
    As she dances about the sun.
I wield the flail of the lashing hail,
    And whiten the green plains under;
And then again I dissolve it in rain,
    And laugh as I pass in thunder.

2

I sift the snow on the mountains below,
    And their great pines groan aghast;
And all the night 't is my pillow white,
    While I sleep in the arms of the blast.
Sublime on the towers of my skyey bowers
    Lightning, my pilot, sits;
In a cavern under it fettered the thunder;
    It struggles and howls by fits;
Over earth and ocean, with gentle motion,
    This pilot is guiding me,
Lured by the love of the genii that move
    In the depths of the purple sea;
Over the rills, and the crags, and the hills,
    Over the lakes and the plains,
Wherever he dreams, under mountain or stream,
    The spirit he loves remains;
And I all the while bask in heaven's blue smile,
    While he is dissolving in rains.

3

The sanguine sunrise, with his meteor eyes,
    And his burning plumes outspread,
Leaps on the back of my sailing rack

When the morning star shines dead;
As on the jag of a mountain crag,
   Which an earthquake rocks and swings,
An eagle alit one moment may sit
   In the light of its golden wings.
And when sunset may breathe, from the lit sea beneath,
   Its ardors of rest and of love,
And the crimson pall of eve may fall
   From the depth of heaven above,
With wings folded I rest on my airy nest,
   As still as a brooding dove.

4

That orbèd maiden, with white fire laden,
   Whom mortals call the moon,
Glides glimmering o'er my fleece-like floor,
   By the midnight breezes strewn;
And wherever the beat of her unseen feet,
   Which only the angels hear,
May have broken the woof of my tent's thin roof,
   The stars peep behind her and peer;
And I laugh to see them whirl and flee,
   Like a swarm of golden bees,
When I widen the rent in my wind-built tent,
   Till the calm river, lakes, and seas,
Like strips of the sky fallen through me on high,
   Are each paved with the moon and these.

5

I bind the sun's throne with a burning zone,
   And the moon's with a girdle of pearl:
The volcanoes are dim, and the stars reel and swim,
   When the whirlwinds my banner unfurl.
From cape to cape, with a bridge-like shape,
   Over a torrent sea,
Sunbeam proof, I hang like a roof,
   The mountains its columns be.
The triumphal arch through which I march,
   With hurricane, fire, and snow,
When the powers of the air are chained to my chair,
   Is the million-colored bow;
The sphere-fire above its soft colors wove,
   While the moist earth was laughing below.

6

I am the daughter of the earth and water,
    And the nursling of the sky;
I pass through the pores of the ocean and shores;
    I change, but I cannot die.
For after the rain, when, with never a stain,
    The pavilion of heaven is bare,
And the winds and sunbeams, with their convex gleams,
    Build up the blue dome of air,
I silently laugh at my own cenotaph,
    And out of the caverns of rain,
Like a child from the womb, like a ghost from the tomb,
    I arise and unbuild it again.

FROM *ADONAIS*

LII

The One remains, the many change and pass;
Heaven's light forever shines, Earth's shadows fly;
Life, like a dome of many-coloured glass,
Stains the white radiance of Eternity,
Until Death tramples it to fragments.—Die,
If thou wouldst be with that which thou dost seek!
Follow where all is fled!—Rome's azure sky,
Flowers, ruins, statues, music, words, are weak
The glory they transfuse with fitting truth to speak.

LIII

Why linger, why turn back, why shrink, my Heart?
Thy hopes are gone before: from all things here
They have departed; thou shouldst now depart!
A light is past from the revolving year,
And man, and woman; and what still is dear
Attracts to crush, repels to make thee wither.
The soft sky smiles,—the low wind whispers near;
'Tis Adonais calls! oh, hasten thither,
No more let Life divide what Death can join together.

LIV

That Light whose smile kindles the Universe,
That Beauty in which all things work and move,
That Benediction which the eclipsing Curse
Of birth can quench not, that sustaining Love
Which through the web of being blindly wove
By man and beast and earth and air and sea,
Burns bright or dim, as each are mirrors of
The fire for which all thirst; now beams on me,
Consuming the last clouds of cold mortality.

LV

The breath whose might I have invoked in song
Descends on me; my spirit's bark is driven,
Far from the shore, far from the trembling throng
Whose sails were never to the tempest given;
The massy earth and spherèd skies are riven!
I am borne darkly, fearfully, afar;
Whilst burning through the inmost veil of Heaven,
The soul of Adonais, like a star,
Beacons from the abode where the Eternal are.

JOHN KEATS (1795–1821)

TO AUTUMN

1

SEASON of mists and mellow fruitfulness,
  Close bosom-friend of the maturing sun;
Conspiring with him how to load and bless
  With fruit the vines that round the thatch-eves run;
To bend with apples the moss'd cottage-trees,
  And fill all fruit with ripeness to the core;
    To swell the gourd, and plump the hazel shells
With a sweet kernel; to set budding more,
  And still more, later flowers for the bees,
  Until they think warm days will never cease,
    For Summer has o'er-brimm'd their clammy cells.

2

Who hath not seen thee oft amid thy store?
  Sometimes whoever seeks abroad may find
Thee sitting careless on a granary floor,
  Thy hair soft-lifted by the winnowing wind;
Or on a half-reap'd furrow sound asleep,
  Drows'd with the fume of poppies, while thy hook
    Spares the next swath and all its twined flowers:
And sometimes like a gleaner thou dost keep
  Steady thy laden head across a brook;
  Or by a cyder-press, with patient look,
    Thou watchest the last oozings hours by hours.

3

Where are the songs of Spring? Ay, where are they?
  Think not of them, thou hast thy music too,—
While barred clouds bloom the soft-dying day,
  And touch the stubble-plains with rosy hue;
Then in a wailful choir the small gnats mourn
  Among the river sallows, borne aloft
    Or sinking as the light wind lives or dies;
And full-grown lambs loud bleat from hilly bourn;

Hedge-crickets sing; and now with treble soft
The red-breast whistles from a garden-croft;
And gathering swallows twitter in the skies.

ON THE GRASSHOPPER AND CRICKET

THE poetry of earth is never dead:
  When all the birds are faint with the hot sun,
  And hide in cooling trees, a voice will run
From hedge to hedge about the new-mown mead;
That is the Grasshopper's—he takes the lead
  In summer luxury,—he has never done
  With his delights; for when tired out with fun
He rests at ease beneath some pleasant weed.
The poetry of earth is ceasing never:
  On a lone winter evening, when the frost
    Has wrought a silence, from the stove there shrills
The Cricket's song, in warmth increasing ever,
  And seems to one in drowsiness half lost,
    The Grasshopper's among some grassy hills.

EDGAR ALLAN POE (1809–1849)

TO HELEN

HELEN, thy beauty is to me
  Like those Nicéan barks of yore,
That gently, o'er a perfumed sea,
  The weary, wayworn wanderer bore
  To his own native shore.

On desperate seas long wont to roam,
  Thy hyacinth hair, thy classic face,
Thy Naiad airs have brought me home
  To the glory that was Greece
And the grandeur that was Rome.

Lo! in yon brilliant window-niche
  How statue-like I see thee stand,
  The agate lamp within thy hand!
Ah, Psyche, from the regions which
  Are Holy Land!

HENRY DAVID THOREAU (1817–1862)

CONSCIENCE

Conscience is instinct bred in the house,
Feeling and Thinking propagate the sin
By an unnatural breeding in and in.
I say, Turn it out doors,
Into the moors.
I love a life whose plot is simple,
And does not thicken with every pimple,
A soul so sound no sickly conscience binds it,
That makes the universe no worse than't finds it.
I love an earnest soul,
Whose mighty joy and sorrow
Are not drowned in a bowl,
And brought to life to-morrow;
That lives one tragedy,
And not seventy;
A conscience worth keeping,
Laughing not weeping;
A conscience wise and steady,
And for ever ready;
Not changing with events,
Dealing in compliments;
A conscience exercised about
Large things, where one *may* doubt.
I love a soul not all of wood,
Predestinated to be good,
But true to the backbone
Unto itself alone,
And false to none;
Born to its own affairs,
Its own joys and own cares;
By whom the work which God begun
Is finished, and not undone;
Taken up where he left off,
Whether to worship or to scoff;
If not good, why then evil,
If not good god, good devil.
Goodness!—you hypocrite, come out of that,

174

Live your life, do your work, then take your hat.
I have no patience towards
Such conscientious cowards.
Give me simple laboring folk,
Who love their work,
Whose virtue is a song
To cheer God along.

WALT WHITMAN (1819–1892)

THERE WAS A CHILD WENT FORTH*

THERE was a child went forth every day,
And the first object he look'd upon, that object he became,
And that object became part of him for the day or a certain part of the day,
Or for many years or stretching cycles of years.

The early lilacs became part of this child,
And grass and white and red morning-glories, and white and red clover, and
the song of the phœbe-bird,
And the Third-month lambs and the sow's pink-faint litter, and the mare's
foal and the cow's calf,
And the noisy brood of the barnyard or by the mire of the pond-side,
And the fish suspending themselves so curiously below there, and the beauti-
ful curious liquid,
And the water-plants with their graceful flat heads, all became part of him.

The field-sprouts of Fourth-month and Fifth-month became part of him,
Winter-grain sprouts and those of the light-yellow corn, and the esculent
roots of the garden,
And the apple-trees cover'd with blossoms and the fruit afterward, and
wood-berries, and the commonest weeds by the road,
And the old drunkard staggering home from the outhouse of the tavern
whence he had lately risen,
And the schoolmistress that pass'd on her way to the school,
And the friendly boys that pass'd, and the quarrelsome boys,
And the tidy and fresh-cheek'd girls, and the barefoot negro boy and girl,
And all the changes of city and country wherever he went.

His own parents, he that had father'd him and she that had conceiv'd him in
her womb and birth'd him,
They gave this child more of themselves than that,
They gave him afterward every day, they became part of him.

The mother at home quietly placing the dishes on the supper-table,
The mother with mild words, clean her cap and gown, a wholesome odor
falling off her person and clothes as she walks by,

The father, strong, self-sufficient, manly, mean, anger'd, unjust,
The blow, the quick loud word, the tight bargain, the crafty lure,
The family usages, the language, the company, the furniture, the yearning
    and swelling heart,
Affection that will not be gainsay'd, the sense of what is real, the thought if
    after all it should prove unreal,
The doubts of day-time and the doubts of night-time, the curious whether
    and how,
Whether that which appears so is so, or is it all flashes and specks?
Men and women crowding fast in the streets, if they are not flashes and
    specks what are they?
The streets themselves and the façades of houses, and goods in the windows,
Vehicles, teams, the heavy-plank'd wharves, the huge crossing at the ferries,
The village on the highland seen from afar at sunset, the river between,
Shadows, aureola and mist, the light falling on roofs and gables of white or
    brown two miles off,
The schooner near by sleepily dropping down the tide, the little boat slack-
    tow'd astern,
The hurrying tumbling waves, quick-broken crests, slapping,
The strata of color'd clouds, the long bar of maroon-tint away solitary by
    itself, the spread of purity it lies motionless in,
The horizon's edge, the flying sea-crow, the fragrance of salt marsh and
    shore mud,
These became part of that child who went forth every day, and who now
    goes, and will always go forth every day.

DIRGE FOR TWO VETERANS*

THE last sunbeam
Lightly falls from the finish'd Sabbath,
On the pavement here, and there beyond it is looking,
    Down a new-made double grave.

Lo, the moon ascending,
Up from the east the silvery round moon,
Beautiful over the house-tops, ghastly, phantom moon,
    Immense and silent moon.

I see a sad procession,
And I hear the sound of coming full-key'd bugles,
All the channels of the city streets they're flooding,
    As with voices and with tears.

I hear the great drums pounding,
And the small drums steady whirring,
And every blow of the great convulsive drums,
    Strikes me through and through.

For the son is brought with the father,
(In the foremost ranks of the fierce assault they fell,
Two veterans son and father dropt together,
    And the double grave awaits them.)

Now nearer blow the bugles,
And the drums strike more convulsive,
And the daylight o'er the pavement quite has faded,
    And the strong dead-march enwraps me.

In the eastern sky up-buoying,
The sorrowful vast phantom moves illumin'd,
('T is some mother's large transparent face,
    In heaven brighter growing.)

O strong dead-march you please me!
O moon immense with your silvery face you soothe me!
O my soldiers twain! O my veterans passing to burial!
    What I have I also give you.

The moon gives you light,
And the bugles and the drums give you music,
And my heart, O my soldiers, my veterans,
    My heart gives you love.

EMILY DICKINSON (1830–1886)

I CANNOT LIVE WITH YOU

I cannot live with you,
It would be life,
And life is over there
Behind the shelf

The sexton keeps the key to,
Putting up
Our life, his porcelain,
Like a cup

Discarded of the housewife,
Quaint or broken;
A newer Sèvres pleases,
Old ones crack.

I could not die with you,
For one must wait
To shut the other's gaze down,—
You could not.

And I, could I stand by
And see you freeze,
Without my right of frost,
Death's privilege?

Nor could I rise with you,
Because your face
Would put out Jesus',
That new grace

Glow plain and foreign
On my homesick eye,
Except that you, than he
Shone closer by.

They'd judge us—how?
For you served Heaven, you know,
Or sought to;
I could not,

Because you saturated sight,
And I had no more eyes
For sordid excellence
As Paradise.

And were you lost, I would be,
Though my name
Rang loudest
On the heavenly fame.

And were you saved,
And I condemned to be
Where you were not,
That self were hell to me.

So we must keep apart,
You there, I here,
With just the door ajar
That oceans are,
And prayer,
And that pale sustenance,
Despair!

GERARD MANLEY HOPKINS (1844–1889)

THE CAGED SKYLARK*

As a dare-gale skylark scanted in a dull cage
  Man's mounting spirit in his bone-house, mean house, dwells—
  That bird beyond the remembering his free fells;
This in drudgery, day-labouring-out life's age.

Though aloft on turf or perch or poor low stage,
  Both sing sometímes the sweetest, sweetest spells,
  Yet both droop deadly sómetimes in their cells
Or wring their barriers in bursts of fear or rage.

Not that the sweet-fowl, song-fowl, needs no rest—
Why, hear him, hear him babble and drop down to his nest,
  But his own nest, wild nest, no prison.

Man's spirit will be flesh-bound when found at best,
But uncumbered: meadow-down is not distressed
  For a rainbow footing it nor he for his bónes rísen.

THE SEA AND THE SKYLARK

On ear and ear two noises too old to end
  Trench—right, the tide that ramps against the shore;
  With a flood or a fall, low lull-off or all roar,
Frequenting there while moon shall wear and wend.

Left hand, off land, I hear the lark ascend,
  His rash-fresh re-winded new-skeinèd score
  In crisps of curl off wild winch whirl, and pour
And pelt music, till none 's to spill nor spend.

---

* This, and the following selection, from *Poems of* Gerard Manley Hopkins, Third Edition, edited by W. H. Gardner. Copyright 1948 by Oxford University Press, Inc. Reprinted by permission.

How these two shame this shallow and frail town!
　How ring right out our sordid turbid time,
Being pure! We, life's pride and cared-for crown,

　Have lost that cheer and charm of earth's past prime:
Our make and making break, are breaking, down
　To man's last dust, drain fast towards man's first slime.

ROBERT FROST (1874–1963)

'OUT, OUT—'*

The buzz saw snarled and rattled in the yard
And made dust and dropped stove-length sticks of wood,
Sweet-scented stuff when the breeze drew across it.
And from there those that lifted eyes could count
Five mountain ranges one behind the other
Under the sunset far into Vermont.
And the saw snarled and rattled, snarled and rattled,
As it ran light, or had to bear a load.
And nothing happened: day was all but done.
Call it a day, I wish they might have said
To please the boy by giving him the half hour
That a boy counts so much when saved from work.
His sister stood beside them in her apron
To tell them 'Supper.' At the word, the saw,
As if to prove saws knew what supper meant,
Leaped out at the boy's hand, or seemed to leap—
He must have given the hand. However it was,
Neither refused the meeting. But the hand!
The boy's first outcry was a rueful laugh,
As he swung toward them holding up the hand
Half in appeal, but half as if to keep
The life from spilling. Then the boy saw all—
Since he was old enough to know, big boy
Doing a man's work, though a child at heart—
He saw all spoiled. 'Don't let him cut my hand off—
The doctor, when he comes. Don't let him, sister!'
So. But the hand was gone already.
The doctor put him in the dark of ether.
He lay and puffed his lips out with his breath.
And then—the watcher at his pulse took fright.
No one believed. They listened at his heart.
Little—less—nothing!—and that ended it.
No more to build on there. And they, since they
Were not the one dead, turned to their affairs.

ACQUAINTED WITH THE NIGHT*

I have been one acquainted with the night.
I have walked out in rain—and back in rain.
I have outwalked the furthest city light.

I have looked down the saddest city lane.
I have passed by the watchman on his beat
And dropped my eyes, unwilling to explain.

I have stood still and stopped the sound of feet
When far away an interrupted cry
Came over houses from another street,

But not to call me back or say good-by;
And further still at an unearthly height,
One luminary clock against the sky

Proclaimed the time was neither wrong nor right.
I have been one acquainted with the night.

WALLACE STEVENS (1879–1955)

THE GLASS OF WATER*

That the glass would melt in heat,
That the water would freeze in cold,
Shows that this object is merely a state,
One of many, between two poles. So,
In the metaphysical, there are these poles.

Here in the centre stands the glass. Light
Is the lion that comes down to drink. There
And in that state, the glass is a pool.
Ruddy are his eyes and ruddy are his claws
When light comes down to wet his frothy jaws

And in the water winding weeds move round.
And there and in another state—the refractions,
The *metaphysica*, the plastic parts of poems
Crash in the mind—But, fat Jocundus, worrying
About what stands here in the centre, not the glass,

But in the centre of our lives, this time, this day,
It is a state, this spring among the politicians
Playing cards. In a village of the indigenes,
One would have still to discover. Among the dogs and dung,
One would continue to contend with one's ideas.

SOMNAMBULISMA*

On an old shore, the vulgar ocean rolls
Noiselessly, noiselessly, resembling a thin bird,
That thinks of settling, yet never settles, on a nest.

The wings keep spreading and yet are never wings.
The claws keep scratching on the shale, the shallow shale,
The sounding shallow, until by water washed away.

The generations of the bird are all
By water washed away. They follow after.
They follow, follow, follow, in water washed away.

Without this bird that never settles, without
Its generations that follow in their universe,
The ocean, falling and falling on the hollow shore,

Would be a geography of the dead: not of that land
To which they may have gone, but of the place in which
They lived, in which they lacked a pervasive being,

In which no scholar, separately dwelling,
Poured forth the fine fins, the gawky beaks, the personalia,
Which, as a man feeling everything, were his.

OF MODERN POETRY*

The poem of the mind in the act of finding
What will suffice. It has not always had
To find: the scene was set; it repeated what
Was in the script.
                    Then the theatre was changed
To something else. Its past was a souvenir.
It has to be living, to learn the speech of the place.
It has to face the men of the time and to meet
The women of the time. It has to think about war
And it has to find what will suffice. It has
To construct a new stage. It has to be on that stage
And, like an insatiable actor, slowly and
With meditation, speak words that in the ear,
In the delicatest ear of the mind, repeat,
Exactly, that which it wants to hear, at the sound
Of which, an invisible audience listens,
Not to the play, but to itself, expressed
In an emotion as of two people, as of two
Emotions becoming one. The actor is
A metaphysician in the dark, twanging
An instrument, twanging a wiry string that gives
Sounds passing through sudden rightnesses, wholly
Containing the mind, below which it cannot descend,
Beyond which it has no will to rise.
                                    It must
Be the finding of a satisfaction, and may
Be of a man skating, a woman dancing, a woman
Combing. The poem of the act of the mind.

ROBINSON JEFFERS (1887–1962)

NEW MEXICAN MOUNTAIN*

I watch the Indians dancing to help the young corn at Taos pueblo. The old
men squat in a ring
And make the song, the young women with fat bare arms, and a few shame-
faced young men, shuffle the dance.

The lean-muscled young men are naked to the narrow loins, their breasts
and backs daubed with white clay,
Two eagle-feathers plume the black heads. They dance with reluctance,
they are growing civilized; the old men persuade them.

Only the drum is confident, it thinks the world has not changed; the beating
heart, the simplest of rhythms,
It thinks the world has not changed at all; it is only a dreamer, a brainless
heart, the drum has no eyes.

These tourists have eyes, the hundred watching the dance, white Americans,
hungrily too, with reverence, not laughter;
Pilgrims from civilization, anxiously seeking beauty, religion, poetry; pilgrims from the vacuum.

People from cities, anxious to be human again. Poor show how they suck
you empty! The Indians are emptied,
And certainly there was never religion enough, nor beauty nor poetry
here . . . to fill Americans.

Only the drum is confident, it thinks the world has not changed. Apparently
only myself and the strong
Tribal drum, and the rockhead of Taos mountain, remember that civilization is a transient sickness.

SHINE, REPUBLIC*

The quality of these trees, green height; of the sky, shining, of water, a
clear flow; of the rock, hardness
And reticence: each is noble in its quality. The love of freedom has been
the quality of Western man.

There is a stubborn torch that flames from Marathon to Concord, its
dangerous beauty binding three ages
Into one time; the waves of barbarism and civilization have eclipsed but
have never quenched it.

For the Greeks the love of beauty, for Rome of ruling; for the present age
the passionate love of discovery;
But in one noble passion we are one; and Washington, Luther, Tacitus,
Aeschylus, one kind of man.

And you, America, that passion made you. You were not born to prosperity,
you were born to love freedom.
You did not say "en masse," you said "independence." But we cannot have
all the luxuries and freedom also.

Freedom is poor and laborious; that torch is not safe but hungry, and often
requires blood for its fuel.
You will tame it against it burn too clearly, you will hood it like a kept
hawk, you will perch it on the wrist of Caesar.

But keep the tradition, conserve the forms, the observances, keep the spot
sore. Be great, carve deep your heel-marks.
The states of the next age will no doubt remember you, and edge their
love of freedom with contempt of luxury.

T. S. ELIOT (1888–1965)

ASH-WEDNESDAY*

1930

I

Because I do not hope to turn again
Because I do not hope
Because I do not hope to turn
Desiring this man's gift and that man's scope
I no longer strive to strive towards such things
(Why should the agèd eagle stretch its wings?)
Why should I mourn
The vanished power of the usual reign?

Because I do not hope to know again
The infirm glory of the positive hour
Because I do not think
Because I know I shall not know
The one veritable transitory power
Because I cannot drink
There, where trees flower, and springs flow, for there is nothing again

Because I know that time is always time
And place is always and only place
And what is actual is actual only for one time
And only for one place
I rejoice that things are as they are and
I renounce the blessèd face
And renounce the voice
Because I cannot hope to turn again
Consequently I rejoice, having to construct something
Upon which to rejoice

And pray to God to have mercy upon us
And I pray that I may forget

These matters that with myself I too much discuss
Too much explain
Because I do not hope to turn again
Let these words answer
For what is done, not to be done again
May the judgement not be too heavy upon us

Because these wings are no longer wings to fly
But merely vans to beat the air
The air which is now thoroughly small and dry
Smaller and dryer than the will
Teach us to care and not to care
Teach us to sit still.

Pray for us sinners now and at the hour of our death
Pray for us now and at the hour of our death.

GUS: THE THEATRE CAT*

Gus is the Cat at the Theatre Door.
His name, as I ought to have told you before,
Is really Asparagus. That's such a fuss
To pronounce, that we usually call him just Gus.
His coat's very shabby, he's thin as a rake,
And he suffers from palsy that makes his paw shake.
Yet he was, in his youth, quite the smartest of Cats—
But no longer a terror to mice and to rats.
For he isn't the Cat that he was in his prime;
Though his name was quite famous, he says, in its time.
And whenever he joins his friends at their club
(Which takes place at the back of the neighbouring pub)
He loves to regale them, if someone else pays,
With anecdotes drawn from his palmiest days.
For he once was a Star of the highest degree—
He has acted with Irving, he's acted with Tree.
And he likes to relate his success on the Halls,

Where the Gallery once gave him seven cat-calls.
But his grandest creation, as he loves to tell,
Was Firefrorefiddle, the Fiend of the Fell.

"I have played," so he says, "every possible part,
And I used to know seventy speeches by heart.
I'd extemporize back-chat, I knew how to gag,
And I knew how to let the cat out of the bag.
I knew how to act with my back and my tail;
With an hour of rehearsal, I never could fail.
I'd a voice that would soften the hardest of hearts,
Whether I took the lead, or in character parts.
I have sat by the bedside of poor Little Nell;
When the Curfew was rung, then I swung on the bell.
In the Pantomime season I never fell flat,
And I once understudied Dick Whittington's Cat.
But my grandest creation, as history will tell,
Was Firefrorefiddle, the Fiend of the Fell."

Then, if someone will give him a toothful of gin,
He will tell how he once played a part in *East Lynne*.
At a Shakespeare performance he once walked on pat,
When some actor suggested the need for a cat.
He once played a Tiger—could do it again—
Which an Indian Colonel pursued down a drain.
And he thinks that he still can, much better than most,
Produce blood-curdling noises to bring on the Ghost.
And he once crossed the stage on a telegraph wire,
To rescue a child when a house was on fire.
And he says: "Now, these kittens, they do not get trained
As we did in the days when Victoria reigned.
They never get drilled in a regular troupe,
And they think they are smart, just to jump through a hoop."
And he'll say, as he scratches himself with his claws,
"Well, the Theatre's certainly not what it was.
These modern productions are all very well,
But there's nothing to equal, from what I hear tell,
That moment of mystery
When I made history
As Firefrorefiddle, the Fiend of the Fell."

JOHN CROWE RANSOM (1888–   )

LADY LOST*

This morning, flew up the lane
A timid lady bird to our birdbath
And eyed her image dolefully as death;
This afternoon, knocked on our windowpane
To be let in from the rain.

And when I caught her eye
She looked aside, but at the clapping thunder
And sight of the whole world blazing up like tinder
Looked in on us again most miserably,
Indeed as if she would cry.

So I will go out into the park and say,
"Who has lost a delicate brown-eyed lady
In the West End section? Or has anybody
Injured some fine woman in some dark way
Last night, or yesterday?

"Let the owner come and claim possession,
No questions will be asked. But stroke her gently
With loving words, and she will evidently
Return to her full soft-haired white-breasted fashion
And her right home and her right passion."

JANET WAKING*

Beautifully Janet slept
Till it was deeply morning. She woke then
And thought about her dainty-feathered hen,
To see how it had kept.

One kiss she gave her mother.
Only a small one gave she to her daddy
Who would have kissed each curl of his shining baby;
No kiss at all for her brother.

"Old Chucky, old Chucky!" she cried,
Running across the world upon the grass
To Chucky's house, and listening. But alas,
Her Chucky had died.

It was a transmogrifying bee
Came droning down on Chucky's old bald head
And sat and put the poison. It scarcely bled,
But how exceedingly

And purply did the knot
Swell with the venom and communicate
Its rigor! Now the poor comb stood up straight
But Chucky did not.

So there was Janet
Kneeling on the wet grass, crying her brown hen
(Translated far beyond the daughters of men)
To rise and walk upon it.

And weeping fast as she had breath
Janet implored us, "Wake her from her sleep!"
And would not be instructed in how deep
Was the forgetful kingdom of death.

CONRAD AIKEN (1889–)

SONNET III*

Think, when a starry night of bitter frost
Is ended, and the small pale winter sun
Shines on the garden trellis, ice-embossed,
And the stiff frozen flower-stalks, every one,
And turns their fine embroideries of ice
Into a loosening silver, skein by skein,
Warming cold sticks and stones, till, in a trice,
The garden sighs, and smiles, and breathes again:
And further think how the poor frozen snail
Creeps out with trembling horn to feel that heat,
And thaws the snowy mildew from his mail,
Stretching with all his length from his retreat:
Will he not praise, with his whole heart, the sun?
Then think at last I too am such an one.

E. E. CUMMINGS (1894–1962)

147*

"next to of course god america i
love you land of the pilgrims' and so forth oh
say can you see by the dawn's early my
country 'tis of centuries come and go
and are no more what of it we should worry
in every language even deafanddumb
thy sons acclaim your glorious name by gorry
by jingo by gee by gosh by gum
why talk of beauty what could be more beautiful than these heroic happy dead
who rushed like lions to the roaring slaughter
they did not stop to think they died instead
then shall the voice of liberty be mute?"

He spoke. And drank rapidly a glass of water

104†

little tree
little silent Christmas tree
you are so little
you are more like a flower

who found you in the green forest
and were you very sorry to come away?
see   i will comfort you
because you smell so sweetly

i will kiss your cool bark
and hug you safe and tight
just as your mother would,
only don't be afraid

look   the spangles
that sleep all the year in a dark box
dreaming of being taken out and allowed to shine,
the balls the chains red and gold the fluffy threads,

put up your little arms
and i'll give them all to you to hold
every finger shall have its ring
and there won't be a single place dark or unhappy

then when you're quite dressed
you'll stand in the window for everyone to see
and how they'll stare!
oh but you'll be very proud

and my little sister and i will take hands
and looking up at our beautiful tree
we'll dance and sing
"Noel Noel"

KENNETH FEARING (1902–1961)

PORTRAIT OF A COG*

You have forgotten the monthly conference. Your four o'clock appointment
    waits in the ante-room. The uptown bureau is on the wire again.
Most of your correspondence is still unanswered, these bills have not been
    paid, and one of your trusted agents has suddenly resigned.
And where are this morning's reports? They must be filed at once, at once.

It is an hour you do not fully understand, a mood you have had so many
    times but cannot quite describe,
It is a fantastic situation repeated so often it is commonplace and dull,
It is an unlikely plot, a scheme, a conspiracy you helped to begin but do not,
    any longer, control at all.

Perhaps you are really in league with some maniac partner whom you have
    never met, whose voice you have never heard, whose name you do not
    even know.
It is a destiny that is yours, yours, all yours and only yours, a fate you have
    long ago disowned and disavowed.

When they dig you up, in a thousand years, they will find you in just this
    pose,
One hand upon the buzzer, the other reaching for the phone, eyes fixed
    upon the calendar, feet firmly on the office rug.

Shall you ask the operator for an outside wire? And then dictate this memo:
No (overwhelming) passions. No (remarkable) vices. No (memorable)
    virtues. No (terrific) motives.

Yes, when they dig you up, like this, a thousand years from now,
They will say: Just as he was in life. A man typical of the times, engaged in
    typical affairs.
Notice the features, especially, they will say. How self-assured they are, and
    how serene.

* With permission of the copyright owners, reprinted from *New and Selected Poems* by Kenneth Fearing, published by Indiana University Press.

HOMAGE*

They said to him, "It is a very good thing that you have done,
yes, both good and great, proving this other passage to the
Indies. Marvelous," they said. "Very. But where, Señor,
is the gold?"
They said: "We like it, we admire it very much, don't mis-
understand us, in fact we think it's almost great. But isn't
there, well, a little too much of this Prince of Denmark?
After all, there is no one quite like you in your lighter
vein."
"Astonishing," they said. "Who would have thought you had
it in you, Orville?" They said, "Wilbur, this machine of
yours is amazing, if it works, and perhaps some day we
can use it to distribute eggs, or to advertise."

And they were good people, too. Decent people.
They did not beat their wives. They went to church. And they
kept the law.

---

* With permission of the copyright owners, reprinted from *New and Selected
Poems* by Kenneth Fearing, published by Indiana University Press.

ANY MAN'S ADVICE TO HIS SON*

If you have lost the radio beam, then guide yourself by the sun or the stars.
(By the North Star at night, and in daytime by the compass and the sun.)
Should the sky be overcast and there are neither stars nor a sun, then steer
by dead reckoning.
If the wind and direction and speed are not known, then trust to your wits
and your luck.

---

* With permission of the copyright owners, reprinted from *New and Selected
Poems* by Kenneth Fearing, published by Indiana University Press.

Do you follow me? Do you understand? Or is this too difficult to learn?
But you must and you will, it is important that you do,
Because there may be troubles even greater than these that I have said.

Because, remember this: Trust no man fully.
Remember: If you must shoot at another man squeeze, do not jerk the
     trigger. Otherwise you may miss and die, yourself, at the hand of some
     other man's son.

And remember: In all this world there is nothing so easily squandered, or
     once gone, so completely lost as life.

I tell you this because I remember you when you were small,
And because I remember all your monstrous infant boasts and lies,
And the way you smiled, and how you ran and climbed, as no one else quite
     did, and how you fell and were bruised,
And because there is no other person, anywhere on earth, who remembers
     these things as clearly as I do now.

RANDALL JARRELL (1914–1965)

JONAH*

As I lie here in the sun
And gaze out, a day's journey, over Nineveh,
The sailors in the dark hold cry to me:
"What meanest thou, O sleeper? Arise and call upon
Thy God; pray with us, that we perish not."

All thy billows and thy waves passed over me.
The waters compassed me, the weeds were wrapped about my head;
The earth with her bars was about me forever.
A naked worm, a man no longer,
I writhed beneath the dead:

But thou art merciful.
When my soul was dead within me I remembered thee,
From the depths I cried to thee. For thou art merciful:
Thou hast brought my life up from corruption,
O Lord my God. . . . When the king said, "Who can tell

But God may yet repent, and turn away
From his fierce anger, that we perish not?"
My heart fell; for I knew thy grace of old—
In my own country, Lord, did I not say
Thou thou art merciful?

Now take, Lord, I beseech thee,
My life from me; it is better that I die . . .
But I hear, "Doest thou well, then, to be angry?"
And I say nothing, and look bitterly
Across the city; a young gourd grows over me

And shades me—and I slumber, clean of grief.
I was glad of the gourd. But God prepared
A worm that gnawed the gourd; but God prepared
The east wind, the sun beat upon my head
Till I cried, "Let me die!" And God said, "Doest thou well

* "Jonah," by Randall Jarrell, from *Selected Poems*. Harcourt, Brace & Co., Copyright 1955. Reprinted by permission of Mrs. Randall Jarrell.

To be angry for the gourd?"
And I said in my anger, "I do well
To be angry, even unto death." But the Lord God
Said to me, "Thou hast had pity on the gourd"—
And I wept, to hear its dead leaves rattle—

"Which came up in a night, and perished in a night.
And should I not spare Nineveh, that city
Wherein are more than six-score thousand persons
Who cannot tell their left hand from their right;
And also much cattle?"

THEODORE ROETHKE (1908–1963)

THE SONG*

1

I met a ragged man;
He looked beyond me when
I tried to meet his eyes.
What have I done to you?
I cried, and backed away.
Dust in a corner stirred,
And the walls stretched wide.

2

I went running down a road,
In a country of bleak stone,
And shocks of ragged corn;
When I stayed for breath, I lay
With the saxifrage and fern
At the edge of a raw field.

I stared at a fissure of ground
Ringed round with crumbled clay:
The old house of a crab;
Stared, and began to sing.

3

I sang to whatever had been
Down in that watery hole:
I wooed with a low tune;
You could say I was mad.

And a wind woke in my hair,
And the sweat poured from my face,
When I heard, or thought I heard,
Another join my song
With the small voice of a child,
Close, and yet far away.

Mouth upon mouth, we sang,
My lips pressed upon stone.

DYLAN THOMAS (1914–1953)

FERN HILL*

Now as I was young and easy under the apple boughs
About the lilting house and happy as the grass was green,
    The night above the dingle starry,
       Time let me hail and climb
    Golden in the heydays of his eyes,
And honoured among wagons I was prince of the apple towns
And once below a time I lordly had the trees and leaves
       Trail with daisies and barley
    Down the rivers of the windfall light.

And as I was green and carefree, famous among the barns
About the happy yard and singing as the farm was home,
    In the sun that is young once only,
       Time let me play and be
    Golden in the mercy of his means,
And green and golden I was huntsman and herdsman, the calves
Sang to my horn, the foxes on the hills barked clear and cold,
       And the sabbath rang slowly
    In the pebbles of the holy streams.

All the sun long it was running, it was lovely, the hay
Fields high as the house, the tunes from the chimneys, it was air
       And playing, lovely and watery
       And fire green as grass.
    And nightly under the simple stars
As I rode to sleep the owls were bearing the farm away,
All the moon long I heard, blessed among stables, the nightjars
       Flying with the ricks, and the horses
       Flashing into the dark.

And then to awake, and the farm, like a wanderer white
With the dew, come back, the cock on his shoulder: it was all
       Shining, it was Adam and maiden,
       The sky gathered again
       And the sun grew round that very day.

So it must have been after the birth of the simple light
In the first, spinning place, the spellbound horses walking warm
    Out of the whinnying green stable
       On to the fields of praise.

And honoured among foxes and pheasants by the gay house
Under the new made clouds and happy as the heart was long,
    In the sun born over and over,
       I ran my heedless ways,
     My wishes raced through the house high hay
And nothing I cared, at my sky blue trades, that time allows
In all his tuneful turning so few and such morning songs
    Before the children green and golden
       Follow him out of grace,

Nothing I cared, in the lamb white days, that time would take me
Up to the swallow thronged loft by the shadow of my hand,
    In the moon that is always rising,
       Nor that riding to sleep
    I should hear him fly with the high fields
And wake to the farm forever fled from the childless land.
Oh as I was young and easy in the mercy of his means,
       Time held me green and dying
       Though I sang in my chains like the sea.

IN MY CRAFT OR SULLEN ART*

In my craft or sullen art
Exercised in the still night
When only the moon rages
And the lovers lie abed
With all their griefs in their arms,
I labour by singing light
Not for ambition or bread
Or the strut and trade of charms
On the ivory stages
But for the common wages
Of their most secret heart.

Not for the proud man apart
From the raging moon I write
On these spindrift pages
Not for the towering dead
With their nightingales and psalms
But for the lovers, their arms
Round the griefs of the ages,
Who pay no praise or wages
Nor heed my craft or art.

DO NOT GO GENTLE INTO THAT GOOD NIGHT*

Do not go gentle into that good night,
Old age should burn and rave at close of day;
Rage, rage against the dying of the light.

Though wise men at their end know dark is right,
Because their words had forked no lightning they
Do not go gentle into that good night.

Good men, the last wave by, crying how bright
Their frail deeds might have danced in a green bay,
Rage, rage against the dying of the light.

Wild men who caught and sang the sun in flight,
And learn, too late, they grieved it on its way,
Do not go gentle into that good night.

Grave men, near death, who see with blinding sight
Blind eyes could blaze like meteors and be gay,
Rage, rage against the dying of the light.

And you, my father, there on the sad height,
Curse, bless, me now with your fierce tears, I pray.
Do not go gentle into that good night.
Rage, rage against the dying of the light.

NAOMI LONG MADGETT (1923–)

THE LOST MUSE*

I used to be a poet once, but now
My lyre is silent
And its strings are unfamiliar to my touch.

Once when I seethed with youth's indignant rage
And burned with fiercer loves than later years recall,
I strummed my chords incessantly and purely
With fresh, new phrases never heard before.

Now when I touch the strings uncertainly,
Seeking to assure my heart it has not faltered,
The tune I labor with has some familiar, tiresome ring;
The melody is stale and cold and inharmonious,
And I forsake with rue my once-articulate refrain.

Maturity has brought its compensations, I suppose:
Love's steadier flame,
A quiet calm with which to greet the days.
I have come to terms with life
And know that right and wrong are separated
Only by a fog.
I do not trust so implicitly
Nor regret so deeply
Nor laugh so quickly
Nor weep so profusely
Nor love so tenderly
Nor hate so bitterly
Nor fight so courageously
Nor surrender with so much hurt pride.

Nor do I care so much what happens
To a fallen sparrow
Or myself
Or the world.

But I do not sing.
I have no song.

* "The Lost Muse," "September Lament," "The Divorcee" and "Sarah Street,"
by Naomi Long Madgett, from *One and the Many*, Exposition Press, Copyright by
Naomi Long Madgett. Reprinted with the permission of Naomi Long Madgett.

SEPTEMBER LAMENT

The leaves turn brown and fall, turn brown and fall
And that is all.

One long-dead autumn it was otherwise:
Bright flamed the treetops, cloudless gleamed the skies
And love and laughter mingled in your eyes.

In other times and in another place
I looked with wonder on your tender face
And found a warmth no winter could erase.

But I have lost it since. The leafless bough
Becomes a symbol of a cancelled vow.
Once fall was beautiful and gay; but now

The ugly dying leaves turn brown and fall
And that is all.

THE DIVORCEE

This house was gay once, once upon a time;
Its lamps burned bright and laughter shook its walls.
Its doors were wide, and many feet would climb
Its stairs to enter into welcome halls.

But there were, too, anxieties and fears
And sleepless nights that held no hope for day;
The laughter was too burdened with the tears,
And I was wise to go another way.

Now I am lonely and the house is still
And no one comes into its darkened room
Or sees the dust upon the window sill,
And no one cares, and no one shares my gloom.

And here in bitter thought I sit and weep,
Remembering when a baby used to cry;
And here I pass my nights and cannot sleep
And curse the dawn and wish that I could die.

SARAH STREET

(St. Louis)

Once again I float down
The enchanted streets of my town

In a gray
Foggy dream; and the gay
Honky-tonk and tin-horn rattle
Of the bars and dance halls, and the battle
Of the street
Greet
Me with nostalgia. But I know
That I will never go
Back,
For the reality is a black
Abyss.
Only this
Remains—
Only the dream retains
Its shape, its mood and hue
And is true.

But in remembering
I see the dead years blossom into spring.
Once more the scene is new,
And I view
The super three-dimension screen
Of sudden, flashing red and green
With quick excitement and intensity.
Here alone for me
The night
Is strangely full of neon splendor and delight.

Even alleys here look beautiful and fair,
Though the air
Is foul with cat-scents reeking.

I am seeking
Symphony of cloud and smoke and fog.
Can a dog,
Yelping from some neighbor's backyard, shake
My love of cities? Should I wake?
Do I mean
To return to neatly-fenced and clean
White houses in a row?
No!
I was caged
And enraged
In my small New Jersey town.
Now I frown
On its shy propriety.
I am free!

Someone asks me what it means, being here,
Feeling near
To a place that masquerades as a city:
Not a pretty
Sight, this pseudo-metropole
Sprawling like a country town in a soft-coal
Haze; sultry, painted-faced,
Embraced
Like a harlot by the Mississippi; loud
With its laughter, proud
Of old memories and touchy of old pains.
It complains
And is insulted to be called The South—
With a drooping mouth,
Calls itself midwestern. What or where
It claims to be, should I care?

Being there was looking life in the face,
Taking up the race
That may never cease
For peace
Of thought; but knowing, while I ran,
How it all began,
And understanding that the quest
Was best
By far of all pursuits.
Were its fruits
Other than this one,
I was done.

But how many fitful years
Have gone by since then! How many tears!
How many loves degraded or decayed,
Promises made
And broken, reveries dissolved in smoke,
Gilded visions tarnished! I awoke
From the youthful dream I lived, long ago.
Even so,
Once again,
Now and then,
I float down enchanted ways
In a haze—
Though reality will never yearn
For return.

Drama

THE WAY OF THE WORLD*

৶ WILLIAM CONGREVE (1670–1729)

William Congreve's Restoration comedy The Way of the World *has long been considered one of the wittiest English plays ever written. The plot involves the courtship of Millamant by Mirabell, and it is full of intrigue, cynicism and considerable laxity of decorum.*

There are several scenes in this play which require vocal flexibility and good pacing on the part of the oral interpreter. One of the most challenging is the bargaining scene, in which Millamant and Mirabell put forward explicit provisos which each must adhere to if their union is to be consummated.

Joseph Wood Krutch believes that the scene printed below ". . . stands at the very summit of English comedy."[1]

MIRABELL.

Like Daphne she, as lovely and as coy.
Do you lock yourself up from me, to make my search more   135
curious? Or is this pretty artifice contrived, to signify that
here the chase must end and my pursuit be crowned, for
you can fly no further?

MILLAMANT.

Vanity! No. I'll fly and be followed to the last moment.
Though I am upon the very verge of matrimony, I expect   140
you should solicit me as much as if I were wavering at the
grate of a monastery, with one foot over the threshold. I'll
be solicited to the very last, nay and afterwards.

MIRABELL.

What, after the last?

MILLAMANT.

Oh, I should think I was poor and had nothing to bestow,   145
if I were reduced to an inglorious ease and freed from the
agreeable fatigues of solicitation.

---

* From *The Way of the World,* by William Congreve, edited by Kathleen M. Lynch. Published by the University of Nebraska Press, Lincoln. Copyright © 1965 by The University of Nebraska Press. Reprinted by permission.
[1] *Nation,* Dec. 3, 1924, Vol. 119, No. 3100, p. 607.
136. *curious*] complicated.

MIRABELL.

But do not you know that when favors are conferred upon instant and tedious solicitation, that they diminish in their value, and that both the giver loses the grace, and the receiver lessens his pleasure? 150

MILLAMANT.

It may be in things of common application; but never sure in love. Oh, I hate a lover that can dare to think he draws a moment's air independent on the bounty of his mistress. There is not so impudent a thing in nature as the saucy look 155 of an assured man, confident of success. The pedantic arrogance of a very husband has not so pragmatical an air. Ah! I'll never marry, unless I am first made sure of my will and pleasure.

MIRABELL.

Would you have 'em both before marriage? Or will you be 160 contented with the first now, and stay for the other till after grace?

MILLAMANT.

Ah! don't be impertinent. —My dear liberty, shall I leave thee? My faithful solitude, my darling contemplation, must I bid you then adieu? Ay-h adieu—my morning thoughts, 165 agreeable wakings, indolent slumbers, all ye *douceurs*, ye *sommeils du matin*, adieu? —I can't do't, 'tis more than impossible. Positively, Mirabell, I'll lie abed in a morning as long as I please.

MIRABELL.

Then I'll get up in a morning as early as I please. 170

MILLAMANT.

Ah! Idle creature, get up when you will. —And d'ye hear, I won't be called names after I'm married; positively I won't be called names.

MIRABELL.

Names!

MILLAMANT.

Aye, as wife, spouse, my dear, joy, jewel, love, sweetheart, 175 and the rest of that nauseous cant, in which men and their

---

152. *things of common application*] affairs of everyday life.
157. *pragmatical*] matter-of-fact.
161–162. *after grace*] referring to the prayer concluding the marriage ceremony.
166. *douceurs*] sweetnesses.
167. *sommeils du matin*] morning slumbers.

wives are so fulsomely familiar—I shall never bear that.
—Good Mirabell, don't let us be familiar or fond, nor kiss
before folks, like my Lady Fadler and Sir Francis; nor go
to Hyde Park together the first Sunday in a new chariot, to   180
provoke eyes and whispers; and then never to be seen there
together again; as if we were proud of one another the
first week, and ashamed of one another ever after. Let us
never visit together, nor go to a play together. But let us be
very strange and well-bred; let us be as strange as if we had   185
been married a great while, and as well-bred as if we were
not married at all.

MIRABELL.
Have you any more conditions to offer? Hitherto your
demands are pretty reasonable.

MILLAMANT.
Trifles! —As liberty to pay and receive visits to and from   190
whom I please; to write and receive letters, without interro-
gatories or wry faces on your part; to wear what I please;
and choose conversation with regard only to my own taste;
to have no obligation upon me to converse with wits that
I don't like, because they are your acquaintance; or to be   195
intimate with fools, because they may be your relations.
Come to dinner when I please; dine in my dressing room
when I'm out of humor, without giving a reason. To have my
closet inviolate; to be sole empress of my tea table, which
you must never presume to approach without first asking   200
leave. And lastly, wherever I am, you shall always knock at
the door before you come in. These articles subscribed, if
I continue to endure you a little longer, I may by degrees
dwindle into a wife.

MIRABELL.
Your bill of fare is something advanced in this latter   205
account. Well, have I liberty to offer conditions—that
when you are dwindled into a wife, I may not be beyond
measure enlarged into a husband?

MILLAMANT.
You have free leave. Propose your utmost; speak and spare
not.   210

---

179. *Fadler*] To faddle is to fondle.
181. never to be] *Q1;* never be *W1.*
183. ever after] *Q2, W1;* for ever after *Q1.*
185. *strange*] reserved.

MIRABELL.

I thank you. *Imprimis* then, I covenant that your acquaintance be general; that you admit no sworn confidante, or intimate of your own sex; no she-friend to screen her affairs under your countenance, and tempt you to make trial of a mutual secrecy. No decoy-duck to wheedle you a fop, 215 scrambling to the play in a mask; then bring you home in a pretended fright, when you think you shall be found out, and rail at me for missing the play, and disappointing the frolic which you had, to pick me up and prove my constancy.

MILLAMANT.

Detestable *imprimis!* I go to the play in a mask!   220

MIRABELL.

Item, I article that you continue to like your own face as long as I shall; and while it passes current with me, that you endeavor not to new-coin it. To which end, together with all vizards for the day, I prohibit all masks for the night, made of oiled skins and I know now what—hog's 225 bones, hare's gall, pig-water, and the marrow of a roasted cat. In short, I forbid all commerce with the gentlewoman in What-d'ye-call-it Court. *Item*, I shut my doors against all bawds with baskets, and pennyworths of muslin, china, fans, atlases, etc. —*Item*, when you shall be breeding— 230

MILLAMANT.

Ah! name it not.

MIRABELL.

Which may be presumed, with a blessing on our endeavors—

MILLAMANT.

Odious endeavors!

MIRABELL.

I denounce against all strait-lacing, squeezing for a shape, 235 till you mold my boy's head like a sugar loaf, and instead

---

211. *Imprimis*] In the first place.
215-216. *decoy-duck . . . mask*] a female confidante to coax a fop to hurry you, masked, to the theater.
221. *article*] stipulate.
224. *vizards*] masks.
226. *pig-water*] an ingredient in cosmetics.
227. gentlewoman] *Q1, W1;* gentlewomen *Q2.*
227-228. *gentlewoman in What-d'ye-call-it Court*] referring to a seller of cosmetics.
230. *atlases*] a kind of oriental satin.

of a man-child, make me the father to a crooked billet.
Lastly, to the dominion of the tea table I submit, but with
proviso, that you exceed not in your province, but restrain
yourself to native and simple tea-table drinks, as tea,   240
chocolate, and coffee. As likewise to genuine and authorized
tea-table talk—such as mending of fashions, spoiling repu-
tations, railing at absent friends, and so forth; but that on
no account you encroach upon the men's prerogative, and
presume to drink healths, or toast fellows; for prevention of 245
which, I banish all foreign forces, all auxiliaries to the tea
table, as orange brandy, all aniseed, cinnamon, citron, and
Barbadoes waters, together with ratafia and the most
noble spirit of clary. But for cowslip-wine, poppy-water, and
all dormitives, those I allow. These provisos admitted, in   250
other things I may prove a tractable and complying
husband.

MILLAMANT.

Oh, horrid provisos! filthy strong waters! I toast fellows,
odious men! I hate your odious provios.

MIRABELL.

Then we're agreed. Shall I kiss your hand upon the   255
contract? And here comes one to be a witness to the sealing
of the deed.

Enter Mrs. Fainall.

MILLAMANT.

Fainall, what shall I do? Shall I have him? I think I
must have him.

MRS. FAINALL.

Aye, aye, take him, take him, what should you do?   260

MILLAMANT.

Well then—I'll take my death I'm in a horrid fright—
Fainall, I shall never say it—well—I think—I'll endure you.

MRS. FAINALL.

Fie, fie! have him, have him, and tell him so in plain terms;
for I am sure you have a mind to him.

---

237. me the father] *Q1;* me father *W1.*
237. *billet*] small stick.
248. *Barbadoes waters*] brandy flavored with orange and lemon peel.
249. *clary*] clary water, brandy flavored with clary flowers and various spices.
250. *dormitives*] drinks to promote sleep.

MILLAMANT.

Are you? I think I have—and the horrid man looks as if he   265
thought so too. —Well, you ridiculous thing you, I'll have
you—I won't be kissed, nor I won't be thanked—here, kiss
my hand though. —So, hold your tongue now, and don't
say a word.

NATHAN THE WISE*

❧ GOTTHOLD EPHRAIM LESSING (1729–1781)

Gotthold Ephraim Lessing's Nathan the Wise has often been referred to as an immortal poem. Published in 1779 when there was considerable prejudice and discrimination against man and his religion, the poet makes a vital and masterful plea for religious and racial tolerance. Written in blank verse, the story unfolds by means of powerful speeches and graphic parables vividly expressed through the play's three principal characters: Saladin, the Mohammedan; Nathan, the Jew; and The Templar, a Christian.

Lessing's Parable of the Three Rings as related by Nathan points up a truth that bears retelling. In the reading of it the oral interpreter will find that a careful phrasing of ideas, a conversational quality of delivery and natural vocal variety will help to bestow its significant and subtle meaning upon the listener.

In preparation for the reading of the short scenes reprinted below, the poet informs us that Saladin has summoned Nathan before him in order to become better acquainted. The Sultan has heard that Nathan has been called Nathan the Wise by the people, and he remarks,

> *Long have I wished to look upon the man*
> *They call the Wise.*

The Sultan then proceeds to test Nathan:

SALADIN.

—and since it seems
You are so wise, now tell me, I entreat,
What human faith, what theologic law,
Hath struck you as the truest and the best?

NATHAN.

Sire, I'm a Jew.

SALADIN.

And I a Mussulman;
And here we have the Christians to boot.
Of these three faiths one only can be true;
A man like you would never take his stand

---

* From *Nathan the Wise*, by Gotthold Ephraim Lessing, translated from the German by Patrick Maxwell. Published by Bloch Publishing Company, Copyright 1917 and reprinted with permission of the publishers.

Where chance or birth has cast him; or, if so,
'Tis from conviction, reasonable grounds,
And choice of that which is the best,—well, then,
Tell me your view, and let me hear your grounds,
For I myself have ever lacked the time
To rack my brains about it. Let me know
The reasons upon which you found your faith—
In confidence, of course—that I may make
That faith my own. How, Nathan, do you start,
And prove me with your eye?—it well may be
No Sultan e'er before had such a whim;
And yet it seems not utterly beneath
Even a Sultan's notice. Speak then, speak;
Or haply you would wish a little space
To think it over—well, I give it you.—
                    (*Aside.*)
I'd like to know if Sittah's listening now;
I'll go and see; I fain would hear from her
How I have played my part.—Now, Nathan, think,
Think quickly on it—I'll be back anon.
        (*He goes into the adjoining chamber, whither*
        SITTAH *had previously gone.*)

        SCENE VI.—NATHAN *alone.*

'Tis strange, 'tis marvellous! what can it mean?
What can he want? I thought he wanted gold,
And now it seems that what he wants is *Truth!*
And wants it, too, as prompt and plump as if
Truth were a minted coin—nay, if he sought
Some obsolete coinage valued but by weight;
That might have passed. But such a brand-new coin,
Vouched by the stamp and current upon change!
No—truth indeed is not a thing like that.
Can it be hoarded in the head of man
Like gold in bags? Nay, which is here the Jew,
He or myself? And yet, might he not well
In truth have sought the truth? But then, the thought,
The mere suspicion, that he put the case
But as a snare for me! That were *too* small!—
Too small? Nay, what's too petty for the great?
He blurted out the theme so bluntly too;
Your friendly visitor is wont to knock
And give you warning ere he beats you up.
I must be on my guard. How best be that?

I cannot play the downright bigot Jew,
Nor may I wholly cast my Jewish slough,
For if I'm not the Jew, he then might ask
Why not a Mussulman?—I have it now!
Ay, this may serve me—idle tales amuse
Not children only—well, now let him come.

SCENE VII.—SALADIN *and* NATHAN.

SALADIN (*to himself*).
And so the coast was clear.
                    (*To* NATHAN.)
                              I trust I've come
Not too soon back; I hope you've ended now
Your meditation—tell me the result;
There's none to hear us.

NATHAN.

            Would that all the world
Might hear our colloquy!

SALADIN.

            Is Nathan then
So certain of his point? Ha! that I call
A wise man truly—ne'er to blink the truth,
To hazard everything in quest of it;
Body and soul itself, and goods and life.

NATHAN.

Ay, when 'tis needful, or can profit us.

SALADIN.

Henceforth I'll hope to have a right to bear
One of the many names by which I'm dubbed,
"Reformer of the World and of the Law."

NATHAN.

In sooth it is a fair and goodly name;
But, Sultan, ere I tell you all my thought,
Let me relate to you a little tale.

SALADIN.

Why not? I've ever had a love for tales
When well narrated.

NATHAN.

Ah, the telling well,
That scarcely is my forte.

SALADIN.

Again your pride,
Aping humility—tell on, tell on.

NATHAN.

Well then:—In hoar antiquity there dwelt
In eastern lands a man who had received
From a loved hand a ring of priceless worth.
An opal was the stone it bore, which shot
A hundred fair and varied hues around,
And had the mystic power to render dear
Alike to God and man whoever wore
The ring with perfect faith. What wonder, then,
That eastern man would never lay it off,
And further made a fixed and firm resolve
That it should bide for ever with his race.
For this he left it to his dearest son,
Adding a stringent clause that he in turn
Should leave it to the son he loved the most,
And that in every age the dearest son,
Without respect to seniority,
By virtue of the ring alone should be
The lord of all the race. Sultan, I ask
If you have marked me well.

SALADIN.

Ay, ay,—proceed.

NATHAN.

And thus the ring came down from sire to son,
Until it reached a father of three sons
Each equally obedient to his will,
And whom accordingly he was constrained
To love alike. And yet from time to time,
Whene'er the one or other chanced to be
Alone with him, and his o'erflowing heart
Was not divided by the other two,
The one who stood beside him still would seem
Most worthy of the ring; and thus it chanced
That he by kindly weakness had been led

To promise it in turn to each of them.
This state of matters lasted while it could,
But by-and-by he had to think of death,
And then this worthy sire was sore perplexed.
He could not brook the thought of breaking faith
With two dear sons to whom he'd pledged his word;
What now was to be done? He straightway sends
In secret for a skilled artificer,
And charges him to make two other rings
Precisely like the first, at any cost.
This the artificer contrives to do,
And when at last he brings him all three rings
Even the father can't say which is which.
With joyful heart he summons then his sons,
But singly and apart, bestows on each
His special blessing, and his ring—and dies.
You hear me, Sultan?

> SALADIN (*looking aside in perplexity*).
>   Ay, I hear, I hear;
> Come, make an end of it.

NATHAN.

>   I'm at the end;
> For what's to follow may be well conceived.
> Scarce was the father dead, each several son
> Comes with his ring and claims to be the lord
> Of all his kindred. They investigate,
> Recriminate, and wrangle—all in vain—
> Which was the true original genuine ring
> Was undemonstrable——
>   (*After a pause, during which he closely marks the*
>   SULTAN.)
>   Almost as much
> As now by us is undemonstrable
> The one true faith.

SALADIN.

>   Nathan, is this to pass
> For answer to my question?

NATHAN.

>   Sultan, no;
> 'Tis only meant to serve as my excuse
> For better answer. How could I presume
> E'er to pronounce distinction 'tween the rings

The father purposely designed to be
Quite indistinguishable?

SALADIN.

Rings, forsooth!
Trifle not with me thus. I should have thought
The three religions which I named to you
Were easy to distinguish, if alone
By difference of dress and food and drink.

NATHAN.

But not by fundamental difference.
Are they not founded all on history,
Traditional or written? History
Must still be taken upon trust alone;
And who are they who best may claim our trust?
Surely our people, of whose blood we are;
Who from our infancy have proved their love,
And never have deceived us, save, perchance,
When kindly guile was wholesomer for us
Than truth itself. Why should I less rely
Upon my ancestors than you on yours;
Or can I ask of you to give the lie
To your forefathers, merely to agree
With mine?—and all that I have said applies
To Christians as well. Is this not so?

SALADIN (aside).

Now, by the living God, the man is right;
I must be silent.

NATHAN.

Let us now return
Once more unto our rings. As I have said,
The sons now sued each other; each of them
Swore to the judge he had received his ring
Straight from his father's hand—as was the fact—
And that, too, after he had long enjoyed
His father's promise to bequeath the ring
To him alone—which also was the truth;
Each vowed the father never could have proved
So false to him; and rather than believe
A thing like this of such a loving sire,
He was constrained—however loath he was
To think unkindly of his brethren—

To charge them both with some nefarious trick,
And now he would unmask their treachery
And be avenged for such a cruel wrong.

SALADIN.

Well, and the Judge? for I am fain to hear
What you will make *him* say,—tell on, tell on.

NATHAN.

The Judge pronounced—Unless you bring your sire,
And place him here before the judgment-seat,
I must dismiss your suit. Think you I'm here
For solving riddles?—or perhaps you wait
Until the genuine ring declares itself.
Yet stay—you said the genuine ring contains
The magic power to make its wearer loved
More than all else, in sight of God and man;
This must decide the case—the spurious ring
Will not do this—say, which of you is he
The other two most love?—what, no reply?
Your rings would seem to work reflexively,
Not on external objects; since it seems
Each is enamoured of himself alone.
Oh, then, all three of you have been deceived,
And are deceivers too; and all three rings
Are spurious alike—the genuine ring
Was lost, most likely, and to hide its loss,
And to supply its place, your father caused
These three to be made up instead of it.

SALADIN.

Bravo! bravo!

NATHAN.

                    And then the Judge resumed—
Belike ye would not relish my advice
More than the judgment I have now pronounced;
In that case, go—but my advice is this:
Accept the case precisely as it stands;
If each of you in truth received his ring
Straight from his father's hand, let each believe
His own to be the true and genuine ring.
Perhaps your father wished to terminate
The tyranny of that especial ring
'Mid his posterity. Of this be sure,

He loved you all, and loved you all alike,
Since he was loath to injure two of you
That he might favor one alone; well, then,
Let each now rival his unbiased love,
His love so free from every prejudice;
Vie with each other in the generous strife
To prove the virtues of the rings you wear;
And to this end let mild humility,
Hearty forbearance, true benevolence,
And resignation to the will of God,
Come to your aid,—and if, in distant times,
The virtues of the genuine gem be found
Amid your children's children, they shall then,
When many a thousand years have rolled away,
Be called once more before this judgment-seat,
Whereon a wiser man than I shall sit
And give his verdict—now, begone. Thus spake
That sapient Judge.

SALADIN.

My God!

NATHAN.

Oh, Saladin,
Could you but be that wiser promised man!

SALADIN (*stepping forward and grasping* NATHAN's *hand*).

Dust that I am and nothingness!—oh, no,
Oh, no!

NATHAN.

What ails thee, Sultan?

SALADIN.

Nathan, no;
The thousand thousand years of that wise Judge
Are not yet passed; nor is his judgment-seat
For Saladin,—now go—but be my friend.

THE KINGDOM OF GOD*

☙ Gregorio Martinez Sierra (1881–1947)

This play, Reino de Dios, was written in 1915 and translated into English in 1922 under the title of The Kingdom of God. *It was first produced in London in 1927 and in New York in 1928. The play is built around the central character of Sister Gracia, who in the first act is a girl of 19 and an oblate of the Order of St. Vincent de Paul and stationed in a home for poor old men. In the second act, she is 29 years of age and is part of the community of sisters in charge of a maternity home for unwed mothers. Act three, from which our scene for reading is taken, finds Sister Gracia as an old woman of 70 in charge of an orphanage for destitute boys and girls. Although she is suffering from rheumatism and needs to support herself with a stick, she speaks and acts with surety and consecration.*

It is in this act that the point of the play is made—when Sister Gracia, now Reverend Mother, persuades the orphans that the reign of God (or the Kingdom of God) will not come through hate but through love. God would use them and their suffering for His purpose of love. Through suffering can come wisdom, and with His help good can come out of evil.

In the reading of this closing scene we find that Sister Dionisia has been confronted with a strong protest from one of the boys regarding the food that has been prepared for them. Felipe asks:

FELIPE. [*Having dipped his spoon in.*] Look here . . . what sort of stuff is this?

FIRST BOY. It's got no peppers in it!

[*And several of the boys repeat protestingly, "No peppers! It's got no peppers!"*]

SISTER DIONISIA. [*Gently apologetic.*] Now my children . . . what difference does it make?

FELIPE. Well . . . I'm not going to eat it.

[*He gets up in protest and all the others do the same, crying, "Nor am I!" "Nor I!" . . . all but* MORENITO, *who says nothing, but stays in his corner calmly eating away.*]

SISTER DIONISIA. [*Very distressed.*] But, my children, if there's nothing else . . . why, for the love of God . . . eat this!

[FELIPE *stands upon a bench and shouts.*]

FELIPE. We don't want it and we won't eat it! We've had enough of eating bread and water for the love of God!

* From *The Plays of G. Martinez Sierra* (Vol. II), in English versions by Helen and Harley Granville-Barker. Copyright 1923, by E. P. Dutton & Co., Inc. Renewal 1951, by C. D. Medley. Reprinted by permission of the publishers.

[*A chorus of shouting approbation.*]
Sister Dionisia.   But boys . . . boys . . . boys!
Felipe.   Always shaking a crucifix at you . . .
   [*More approbation.*]
Felipe.   . . . whenever they want to cheat you out of something!
   [*There is enthusiastic agreement with this.*]
Sister Dionisia.   Oh boys, do be quiet . . . just because I ask you to.
You're quite right . . . . but do eat your supper. What good will it do you
to go to bed hungry? You shall have something better tomorrow. Now be
good . . . be patient . . . sit down . . . oh, please do as I tell you!
   [*Some of them, thus appealed to, are sitting down when* Felipe *says:*]
Felipe.   The boy that puts his spoon in his plate is a coward.
Sister Dionisia.   Now you be quiet!
Felipe.   I won't be quiet. I say that he's a coward and a sneak.
   [*Those that are down get up again and thus reinforced they all pro-
test, loudly, that "They won't! No, they won't!"*]
Sister Dionisia.   Sit down . . . sit down!
Felipe.   And the boy that sits down to table again is a disgrace to us all!
   [*A great clamour; cries, stamping and hammering on the tables.*]
Sister Dionisia.   [*To* Felipe.]   Will you be good enough to leave the
room this very minute?
Felipe.   Oh, I'm going! But I'm not going alone. Come along, all of you!
Anyone that's not afraid and wants something to eat . . . follow me!
   [*They cheer him and cry that they will, and they are moving off.
   Sister Dionisia darts to the door and tries to block the way.*]
Sister Dionisia.   But where are you going . . . what are you going
to do?
Felipe.   What men do . . . take by force what we can't get by asking
nicely.
   [*Loud cheers and great readiness to be gone.*]
Sister Dionisia.   No . . . no . . . no!
Felipe.   Now you stop interfering or it will be the worse for you. Come
on, boys! They keep us penned up here as if we were brute beasts. We may
shout as loud as we like and we shan't be heard . . . they've forgotten us.
And we're just starved. Well . . . there's bread outside . . . and there's
meat outside . . . and there's wine outside . . . so come outside and get
it. If it has to be stolen we'll steal it . . . and if killing's what's needed . . .
well, we'll do some killing!
   [*Tremendous enthusiasm.*]
Sister Dionisia.   Blessed Jesus . . . Ave Maria . . . help!
Felipe.   [*Beside himself.*]   Into the street with you! We'll let them see
. . . we'll let them hear. It's an everlasting disgrace the way that we're
treated. Well then . . . let's make them treat us better. Throw their bread
and water back in their swine's faces! We weren't born different to anyone
else, were we? Well then . . . we've a right to be as well fed as everyone
else is.

[*They cheer wildly and are marching off.* SISTER DIONISIA *struggles with them in vain, crying, "Get back! Get back!" and then rushes to the bell-rope and pulls it violently. The girls scream.* FELIPE *turns back to them.*]

FELIPE. Well, aren't you coming too? All of us . . . all together . . . where are the rest? Let's have the whole orphanage out in the streets to demand its rights. If we're nobody's children . . . why, we're everybody's children. Come along then . . . March!

[*At this moment* SISTER GRACIA *appears in the doorway.*]

SISTER GRACIA. What's all this?

[*At the sound of her voice and the sight of her, there is something of a lull in the storm, and voices can be heard exclaiming "Reverend Mother! . . . Sister Gracia!"*]

SISTER GRACIA. Oh yes . . . it's Sister Gracia! And what is all this terrible fuss about?

[*The girls have drawn back already and so have some of the boys. The rest stand their ground and the noise has by no means ceased.*]

SISTER DIONISIA. Aie . . . Sister! People must have been giving them wine in the Plaza . . . and there's no holding them.

SISTER GRACIA. So I see. Well . . . we live in a revolutionary age! [*To the girls.*] What . . . you too! [*Then she faces the malcontents.*] Have you had your supper yet?

SISTER DIONISIA. They . . . they didn't like. . . .

SISTER GRACIA. Let me talk to them. Have you had your supper yet?

FELIPE. That's where we're going . . . to get our supper. Well . . . what are you all waiting for? Come on!

SISTER GRACIA. Tsch . . . tsch! [*Looking* FELIPE *squarely in the eyes.*] To get your supper indeed? Where, pray?

FELIPE. Wherever it's to be found.

SISTER GRACIA. And when you've found it . . . do you fancy its owners'll give it you?

FELIPE. If they don't, we'll take it.

[*The few enthusiasts that are left reinforce this with what boldness they can muster.*]

SISTER GRACIA. People keep things that they value locked up, my son.

FELIPE. Then we'll break open the locks.

[*The enthusiasts applaud this also.*]

SISTER GRACIA. [*Quietly now and kindly.*] And do you think if there were any locked door that would open I shouldn't have been there by this to knock at it for you?

FELIPE. Yes . . . but you go asking so prettily. We're going to try if a few stones won't make them attend.

SISTER GRACIA. My son . . . the answer to a stone is often a bullet.

FELIPE. [*Defiantly.*] So much the better! Far better to be left dead in the street once and for all than to stay here and starve to death bit by bit.

SISTER GRACIA. [*Sternly.*] You don't know what you're talking about.

And none of you know what you're doing. Now, there has been enough of this . . . and everybody will be quiet and sit down . . . because I tell them to.

[*They are quiet . . . but they can't make up their minds to obey altogether.*]

Sister Gracia.   Did you hear what I said? Sit down.

[*The boys go slowly towards the benches.*]

Sister Gracia.   Come now . . . be quick about it.

[*They slowly sit down.*]

Sister Gracia.   [*To* Felipe.]   And you.

[*Last of all and much against his will* Felipe *sits down too.*]

Sister Gracia.   Now, Sister Dionisia . . . is there any more broth in the kettle?

Sister Dionisia.   [*Who is still rather frightened.*]   Yes, Señora.

Sister Gracia.   Well then, serve that out . . . then they'll have their supper hot. And let everyone keep quiet. I don't want to have to punish anybody tonight.

[Sister Dionisia *and the girls put more broth in the plates. Then after a moment* Sister Gracia *goes on talking . . . quietly and kindly now, but masterfully still.*]

Sister Gracia.   And d'you think you're the only folk in this world who don't get all they want to eat? No, my children, no. There are people worse off than you . . . some of them so poor that they'd think your plate of supper a luxury. You'll have a roof over your head tonight and a mattress to sleep on and a blanket to cover you. Think of the people who'll sleep in a ditch by the roadside with no roof but the sky, and only the hoarfrost to come down and cover them. Think of the sick people . . . of people without a friend . . . stumbling through the world with not a hand held out to them . . . nobody caring. While you have a home and all the love we can give you. You are sheltered . . . you are taught . . . you are kept in right paths. And then think if you don't owe a few thanks to God after all.

Felipe.   To God . . . to God! There is no God!

[*A stir of horror among the children.* Sister Dionisia *crosses herself and exclaims, "Blessed Jesus!"*]

Sister Gracia.   And whatever do you think you mean by that, you little fool?

Felipe.   Because if there were . . . would he think this was all right?

Sister Gracia.   God does not think this is right. Men break his laws. He made them brothers. Is it his fault if they turn wolves and devour each other? God does not think it right that his children should go hungry . . . and the innocent are not ever disgraced in his eyes. It is by no will of his that some are poor and neglected while some are set up in pride. For God is Love and he loves us all and to each one he gives a share in heaven and in this earth.

Felipe.   Don't listen to her . . . she's just preaching lies to you. Nuns have all sold themselves to the rich. Do they ever go hungry? And as long as they can get us to keep up the sham they're let stuff themselves with food in peace.

SISTER GRACIA.   I am not lying to you. I am telling you the truth and the whole truth. God does not smile upon the injustice of this world. He endures it . . . for how long? . . . ah, that we do not know. But he does not think it right.

FELIPE.   Well then . . . let's go and break the heads of those that do . . . and God will thank us for that.

[*A few of the boys cheer up at this and approve.*]

SISTER GRACIA.   Ah, no, no . . . all that can be done for this wicked world is to help to make it good.

FELIPE.   And who's going to?

SISTER GRACIA.   You . . . you . . . not by hating but through love. Yes, all of you will help do that. For, when you are men . . . and go away from here, it will be because you have suffered from injustice that you'll know how to make . . . and want to make . . . laws that are just. Oh yes, my sons, yes . . . the world is yours . . . for you have won it by hunger and by suffering and pain. So when you hold it in your hands, make it what it ought to be. God is watching you . . . his hopes are all in you. You suffer now that you may succour his world then. God sees you . . . God hears you. Now say with me. Lord, Lord, we thank thee for this food which is given us in thy name. There is not much of it, it is not very good, and we will not forget the taste of this bitter bread. And by thy precious love we swear that thy children on this earth shall eat of it no more . . . say it with me . . . say it . . .

[*The boys repeat after her solemnly and quietly.*]

SISTER GRACIA.   Jesus, Son of God . . . Christ, son of man, by the divine blood that thou didst shed for us we swear to spend our own to the last drop when we are men . . . that children may not be forsaken any more . . . that no more mothers may be wronged and go hungry and be ashamed to carry their children in their arms. My sons . . . my sons, promise me that when you are men you'll try to bring these things to pass . . . that you'll help to build on earth the Kingdom of God.

[*Very quietly, very solemnly, they murmur "Yes."*]

SISTER GRACIA.   Thank you, my children . . . thank you. And now . . . supper's over . . . go to bed and sleep in peace.

[*The boys go slowly out. Only* FELIPE *does not move. He is sitting on his bench, head buried in his arms, and crying.* SISTER GRACIA *goes to him and puts a hand upon his shoulder.*]

SISTER GRACIA.   Don't cry . . . for men don't cry, you know. And they don't complain. They suffer . . . but they work and hope.

CURTAIN

PROLOGUE TO GLORY*

ॐ E. P. CONKLE (1899–)

Prologue to Glory *by E. P. Conkle was first produced by the WPA Federal Theatre in New York, March 17, 1938. This drama of two acts sketches some of the youthful days of Abe Lincoln from the time he worked on his father's farm to his departure for Springfield. In a series of picturesque incidents, which cover a year of Abe's young life, E. P. Conkle has made these formative days entertaining, informative and memorable for the reader and the playgoer. The oral interpreter, likewise, must portray the image of a young Lincoln.*

In the early part of the play we have met Abe as he leaves his father's farm near New Salem to accept an offer from Denton Offut to do some "clerkin" in his country store. We have observed how Abe has proved that he can "out wrastle and throw down any man in Sangamon County" by throwing and pinning Jack Armstrong to the ground. Having completed this feat successfully, Abe is welcomed as a citizen of New Salem, and in addition he meets Ann Rutledge and Mary Cameron. While attending to his "clerkin" duties, he is asked if he would debate against Henry Onstott at the New Salem Forum Society meeting on the subject, "Resolved that bees are more valuable than ants." Although Abe recognizes that they should be debating more sensible subjects, he accepts the challenge. In the following scene a crowd has gathered at the Forum Society meeting place and David Rutledge, Chairman, has just welcomed the people after which they all sing a hymn. Now Mr. Rutledge advances to the table and says:

DAVID *(coming to table)*: The next order of business is the debate. As you probably know, the Society tries always to discuss questions being discussed all over the country. The subject for tonight's debate is: Resolved that bees are more valuable than ants. Ladies and gentlemen, we are fortunate in having Henry Onstott, who has debated before us many times, to open the question. Mr. Onstott—*(Applause.* COLONEL *takes a seat.* HENRY *goes to table, adjusts his spectacles, looks at book and papers.)*

HENRY: Mr. Chairman: The subject for debate has been given. I shall not go into a definition of terms as I believe it is sufficiently understood that the bee, in general, is a member of the super family Apoidea—*(Looking at* ABE) and the ant is only a hymenopterous member of the family formicoidea. *(Low murmurs from the crowd)* I am happy to have for my task the defense of the bee. Not that it is the more easy to defend, but it is my heartfelt conviction that the bee is the more useful animal.

WOODSMAN: Jist what I told you, Luke!

HENRY: Hence can I argue from genuine conviction; hence is my argument won already! (*Applause.*)

JIM ONSTOTT (*standing up*): 'Ray, 'ray for Henry!

DENNY (*jumping up*): 'Ray for Abe!

CLARY GROVE BOYS: 'Ray for Abe!

DAVID (*standing up*): Order, please. (*All sit down.*)

HENRY (*raising hands for quiet*): Let these interruptions cease (*all quiet*), please. I wish to base my argument on three main points. Nature has given the bee one primal function—to pollinate the flower. See his busy body fluttering from flower to flower, collecting nectar and pollen, and aiding the plant to propagate. (*Taking a few steps*) What would the world be without flowers; hence, without bees; hence, without a second generation; hence, barrenness—(*Returns to table*) barrenness everywhere? The material value of this function of the bee is alone enormous. The apple crop pollinated solely by bees—(*A few steps*) in—in—(*Back to table to refer to his book*. CLARY GROVE BOYS *laugh*) Asbury County, Maine, was 1,740 ten years ago. Need I go further into this? Need I? (*Opening his arms out.*)

WOODSMAN: Need he? (BERT *laughs*. CLARY GROVE BOYS *laugh*.)

DAVID: Order please!

VOICES: Shhhhhh!

HENRY: Which brings me to my second main point. Ladies and gentlemen, do you realize that the bee is the sole maker of honey? What—(*A few steps*) would this vile world be without honey? (*Hands behind him, slowly to table*) The Bible speaks of it. Witnesseth:—"And he turned aside to see the carcass of the lion; and behold, there was a swarm of bees and honey in it." The value of the honey crop in Sudsburyshire for the year 1823 was £85 3s. 8. Can—may I ask, can the ant produce anything of similar value? Can my opponent measure his ant up to my bee in these, or in any other respects? (*Loud applause*) And yet, I have one more point.

WOODSMAN: Sharpen 'er, Henry! (CLARY GROVE BOYS *laugh*.)

HENRY: The lessons which the bee teaches us are inestimable. Hour on hour he labors to store away for the winter. The blizzard is on him, but his honey is in the comb. Let us go and do likewise. Let us emulate his social structure—his queen—his mason bees—his workers who store his honey. Each bee has his work, each bee *does* his work. Let us study his life. Let us go to him and learn. Ladies and gentlemen, no matter who you be, or whom; or where you be; or of what intelligence—it must appear to you that the bee is much more valuable than the ant. First, he fertilizes. Second, he gives honey. Third, he shows how we should live. Can there be any doubt in your minds? (*Applause.*)

JIM ONSTOTT: No, be dads!

LADIES: No!

CLARY GLOVE BOYS: Shut up!

DAVID: Order!

HENRY: No. I hereby challenge the negative to fetch forward a single main

point he can stand upon—unimpeached! Ladies and gentlemen, the positive—rests! (*He takes book to his seat amidst applause.*)

DAVID (*going to table*): Now I am happy to introduce a young man who
needs no introduction. Abe Lincoln, (*Applause; louder from* DENNY *and*
CLARY GROVE BOYS) who will uphold the negative. (*He sits.*)

DENNY: Hooray!

ABE (*going slowly to table*): Thankee, David. Ladies and gentlemen, I've
done most of my public speakin' on stumps for th' benefit of God's green
forests and Tom Lincoln's 'tato rows. So I probably won't show up very
bright agin' an eloquent, polished speaker like th' honorable *positive*.
(*To* HENRY) I should like to add my praises to theirs though, Henry, for
the able manner in which you handled them bees without gettin' stung!
(*Laughter*) Now—one of th' subjects that appears to be botherin' this
Forum Club is whether bees are more valuable than ants. It wouldn't take
me long to point out a few important functions of the ant if I was a
mind to. It is well known that he has moderate intelligence and lives in
just as ordered a society as the bee. His commerce and trade abound. I've
not got any books to prove it, but I maintain an ant can lift many times
its own weight, and could, if he was a mind to, outrun, outwrastle, and
outargue Henry and me both! (*Laughter and applause.*)

DENNY: 'Ray for th' ants!

MATTY SPARROW: Gimme th' bees!

CLARY GROVE BOYS: Yeah? You be still! 'Ray for Abe!

DAVID: Order, please! (*All quiet.*)

ABE: But more important than all these—ants are known to have better sense,
and more of it, than to stand arg'yin' on such snivelin' subjects as we are.
Ants ain't *agin'* bees. Both of them are valuable, and have their God-
given purposes, folks. Mr. Speaker, it don't worry me a continental which
is more valuable s'long as each keeps into its proper place. Now, if
Henry's bees was to get into your bonnets, or my ants was to git into
your britches, that would be a subject for discussion an' immediate action.
(*Loud laughter*) I'm sorry, but I can't imbibe of the same high seriousness
for this subject as my opponent. It seems to me that the subject for debate
b'fore this Forum ought to be alive—subjects for action, useful for living.
The things we hear, the decisions we arrive at, ought to be helpful to us.
The Lord knows there are plenty of problems here with us folks in
Illinoy. (*Loud applause.*)

HENRY (*jumping up*): Mr. Speaker, the gentleman is beside the point of this
debate!

DAVID (*standing*): Abe, will you please keep to the subject?

JIM ONSTOTT (*jumping up*): Put 'im out!

BERT: Set down, Onstott!

DAVID: Order, order!

HOHEIMER: Give Henry th' nacherilization proceedin's! (HENRY *returns to
seat.*)

MATTY SPARROW (*standing, turns to* CLARY GROVE BOYS): What you boys
need is a good horsewhuppin'.

CLARY: You ain't big enough to do it.

MATTY SPARROW: You'd think they was brung up in a barn.

BONES (*making a face at her*): Aw, you ladies dry up! (MATTY *starts for* BONES; *is stopped by* MRS. TAYLOR. CLARY GROVE BOYS *laugh.*)

CLARY GROVE BOYS: Go on, Abe!

ABE (*motioning for silence*): You fellers hold your 'taters, now. (*All quiet down—sit*) I'll fetch th' subject back t' ants or bust a hame-string. (*Crossing to left of table*) Folks, I've had some long talks with several ants along th' Sangamon River. (BERT *laughs.* CLARY GROVE BOYS *laugh*) Do you know what they told me? Well—they said if they was us, they would do something about those bends in the river that keep the *Talisman* from comin' up from St. Louis—that keep New Salem from sending its goods to a market in Saint Louis and New Orleans. We've got the land, the pastures, the crops—all we need is a market to sell in, an outlet. We could raise our crops and the broad river would carry them to market and fetch us back sugar and iron, and furniture—(*Low murmurs*) things we cain't raise nor otherwise get. Ladies and gentlemen, what I propose to you tonight is—that—

JIM ONSTOTT (*leaping up*): Objections! (*The* CLARY GROVE BOYS *let up a yell.*)

HOHEIMER (*standing up*): Let Abe go on!

WOODSMAN: Good boy!

DAVID (*jumping up*): Order! Order, please! (*All quiet.*)

ABE: If there seems to be no connection betwixt what I have to say and th' subject under discussion—

ARMSTRONG (*yelling*): Go to 'er, Abe!

MATTY SPARROW: Put those boys out!

CLARY: You an' who else?

DAVE VANCE: Let Abe give his proposition!

CLARY GROVE BOYS: Let's have it! Go on, Abe!

ARMSTRONG: Everyone shut their mouths!

ABE (*holding out hands for silence*): Ladies and gentlemen—(*Crowd quiets*) I'll set down as soon as you let me say what I come here to say. And th' upshot of my whole speech here t'night is—that, by my own initiative, and through the offices of my kind friends, I want to take this opportunity, hereby and forthwith, to announce myself as candidate for Sangamon County to the Legislature of the State of Illinois. (ANN *slowly stands. Gasps of surprise from crowd*) I do wish to announce my platform as one of local reform and "Internal Developments," as the politicians say. I am especially interested in the development of waterways; and the natural resources of Sangamon County, and its marketing! I am—ladies and gentlemen, further—*done*, I reckon! (*Slow crescendo of excitement culminating in applause and general pandemonium.*)*

---

* Copies of this play, in individual paper-covered acting editions, are available from Samuel French, Inc., 25 W. 45th St., New York, N.Y. or 7623 Sunset Blvd., Hollywood, Calif. or in Canada Samuel French (Canada), Ltd., 26 Grenville St., Toronto, Canada.

THE TIME OF YOUR LIFE*

✺ WILLIAM SAROYAN (1908–   )

"*William Saroyan's touching and robust fantasia of life, love, lust, liberty and the pursuit of happiness in a waterfront barroom in San Francisco projects its intangible values across the footlights with clarity and warmth.*"[1] *This play, though it lacks a clearly defined plot, is filled with alive, unique and likable characters. One in particular, Kit Carson, is an extravagant braggart who can unfold one exaggerated tale after another. In the following episode, the oral interpreter has the opportunity to project through voluble speech a few of Kit's far-soaring and vigorous thoughts.*

> *An old man who looks as if he might have been Kit Carson at one time walks in importantly, moves about, and finally stands at Joe's table.*

KIT CARSON
Murphy's the name. Just an old trapper. Mind if I sit down?

JOE
Be delighted. What'll you drink?

KIT CARSON
(*Sitting down*)
Beer. Same as I've been drinking. And thanks.

JOE
(*To* NICK)
Glass of beer, Nick.
> NICK *brings the beer to the table,* KIT CARSON *swallows it in one swig, wipes his big white mustache with the back of his right hand.*

KIT CARSON
(*Moving in*)
I don't suppose you ever fell in love with a midget weighing thirty-nine pounds?

JOE
(*Studying the man*)
Can't say I have, but have another beer.

---

* From *The Time of Your Life*, by William Saroyan. Harcourt, Brace & Co., Copyright 1939. Reprinted by permission of William Saroyan. Copyright renewed 1966 by William Saroyan.
1 *Theatre Arts*, December 1939, p. 871.

KIT CARSON
> (*Intimately*)
Thanks, thanks. Down in Gallup, twenty years ago. Fellow by the name of Rufus Jenkins came to town with six white horses and two black ones. Said he wanted a man to break the horses for him because his left leg was wood and he couldn't do it. Had a meeting at Parker's Mercantile Store and finally came to blows, me and Henry Walpal. Bashed his head with a brass cuspidor and ran away to Mexico, but he didn't die.
Couldn't speak a word. Took up with a cattle-breeder named Diego, educated in California. Spoke the language better than you and me. Said, Your job, Murph, is to feed them prize bulls. I said, Fine, what'll I feed them? He said, Hay, lettuce, salt, beer, and aspirin.
Came to blows two days later over an accordion he claimed I stole. I had *borrowed* it. During the fight I busted it over his head; ruined one of the finest accordions I ever saw. Grabbed a horse and rode back across the border. Texas. Got to talking with a fellow who looked honest. Turned out to be a Ranger who was looking for me.

JOE
Yeah, You were saying, a thirty-nine pound midget.

KIT CARSON
Will I ever forget that lady? Will I ever get over that amazon of small proportions?

JOE
Will you?

KIT CARSON
If I live to be sixty.

JOE
Sixty? You look more than sixty now.

KIT CARSON
That's trouble showing in my face. Trouble and complications. I was fifty-eight three months ago.

JOE
That accounts for it, then. Go ahead, tell me more.

KIT CARSON
Told the Texas Ranger my name was Rothstein, mining engineer from Pennsylvania, looking for something worth while. Mentioned two places in Houston. Nearly lost an eye early one morning, going down the stairs. Ran into a six-footer with an iron-claw where his right hand was supposed to be. Said, You broke up my home. Told him I was a stranger in Houston. The girls gathered at the top of the stairs to see a fight. Seven of them. Six feet and an iron claw. That's bad on the nerves. Kicked him in the mouth when he swung for my head with the claw. Would have lost an eye except for quick thinking. He rolled into the gutter and pulled

a gun. Fired seven times. I was back upstairs. Left the place an hour later, dressed in silk and feathers, with a hat swung around over my face. Saw him standing on the corner, waiting. Said, Care for a wiggle? Said he didn't. I went on down the street and left town. I don't suppose you ever had to put a dress on to save your skin, did you?

JOE

No, and I never fell in love with a midget weighing thirty-nine pounds. Have another beer?

KIT CARSON

Thanks.
(*Swallows glass of beer*)
Ever try to herd cattle on a bicycle?

JOE

No. I never got around to that.

KIT CARSON

Left Houston wtih sixty cents in my pocket, gift of a girl named Lucinda. Walked fourteen miles in fourteen hours. Big house with barb-wire all around, and big dogs. One thing I never could get around. Walked past the gate, anyway, from hunger and thirst. Dogs jumped up and came for me. Walked right into them, growing older every second. Went up to the door and knocked. Big negress opened the door, closed it quick. Said, On your way, white trash.

Knocked again. Said, On your way. Again. On your way. Again. This time the old man himself opened the door, ninety, if he was a day. Sawed-off shotgun, too.

Said, I ain't looking for trouble, Father. I'm hungry and thirsty, name's Cavanaugh.

Took me in and made mint juleps for the two of us.

Said, Living here alone, Father?

Said, Drink and ask no questions. Maybe I am and maybe I ain't. You saw the lady. Draw your own conclusions.

I'd heard of that, but didn't wink out of tact. If I told you that old Southern gentleman was my grandfather, you wouldn't believe me, would you?

JOE

I might.

KIT CARSON

Well, it so happens he wasn't. Would have been romantic if he had been, though.

JOE

Where did you herd cattle on a bicycle?

KIT CARSON

Toledo, Ohio, 1918.

JOE

Toledo, Ohio? They don't herd cattle in Toledo.

KIT CARSON

They don't anymore. They did in 1918. One fellow did, leastaways. Book-keeper named Sam Gold. Straight from the East Side, New York. Sombrero, lariats, Bull Durham, two head of cattle and two bicycles. Called his place The Gold Bar Ranch, two acres, just outside the city limits.

That was the year of the War, you'll remember.

JOE

Yeah, I remember, but how about herding them two cows on a bicycle? How'd you do it?

KIT CARSON

Easiest thing in the world. Rode no hands. Had to, otherwise couldn't lasso the cows. Worked for Sam Gold till the cows ran away. Bicycles scared them. They went into Toledo. Never saw hide nor hair of them again. Advertised in every paper, but never got them back. Broke his heart. Sold both bikes and returned to New York.

Took four aces from a deck of red cards and walked to town. Poker. Fellow in the game named Chuck Collins, liked to gamble. Told him with a smile I didn't suppose he'd care to bet a hundred dollars I wouldn't hold four aces the next hand. Called it. My cards were red on the blank side. The other cards were blue. Plumb forgot all about it. Showed him four aces. Ace of spades, ace of clubs, ace of diamonds, ace of hearts. I'll remember them four cards if I live to be sixty. Would have been killed on the spot except for the hurricane that year.

JOE

Hurricane?

KIT CARSON

You haven't forgotten the Toledo hurricane of 1918, have you?

JOE

No. There was no hurricane in Toledo in 1918, or any other year.

KIT CARSON

For the love of God, then what do you suppose that commotion was? And how come I came to in Chicago, dream-walking down State Street?

JOE

I guess they scared you.

KIT CARSON

No, that wasn't it. You go back to the papers of November 1918, and I think you'll find there was a hurricane in Toledo. I remember sitting on the roof of a two-story house, floating northwest.

JOE

(*Seriously*)

Northwest?

KIT CARSON

Now, son, don't tell me *you* don't believe me, either?

JOE

(*Pause. Very seriously, energetically and sharply*)

Of course I believe you. Living is an art. It's not bookkeeping. It takes a lot of rehearsing for a man to get to be himself.

KIT CARSON

(*Thoughtfully, smiling, and amazed*)

You're the first man I've ever met who believes me.

MOONY'S KID DON'T CRY*

✒ TENNESSEE WILLIAMS (1914–)

Moony's Kid Don't Cry *was one of Tennessee Williams' first plays and was given a place in* The Best One-Act Plays *of 1940, edited by Margaret Mayorga. In this play one senses the emotions of loneliness, anger and despair that are present in the personages of Moony and his wife Jane. These deep-souled feelings are roused by the Depression, the burden of a new baby and the intense desire to get away from the mechanized and ordinary routine of life. They are, in addition, augmented by the torturous dichotomy that exists between the value systems held by Moony and his wife.*

There is in this moving play the sensitive characters, the sweep of lines, the projection of symbolism and the physical action which will require thoughtful consideration on the part of the interpreter. The play is reprinted in its entirety and might also serve to challenge the interpreter's skill and adeptness in the cutting and arrangement of material.

MOONY'S KID DON'T CRY

SCENE: *Kitchen of a cheap three-room flat in the industrial section of a large American city.*

Stove and sink are eloquent of slovenly housekeeping. A wash line, stretched across one corner of the room, is hung with diapers and blue work shirts. Above the stove is nailed a placard, KEEP SMILING. *The kitchen table supports a small artificial Christmas tree.*

By far the most striking and attractive article in the room is a brand new hobbyhorse that stands stage center. There is something very gallant, almost exciting, about this new toy. It is chestnut brown with a long flowing mane of fine golden silk, glittering painted eyes, distended nostrils and scarlet upcurled lips. It looks like the very spirit of unlimited freedom and fearless assault.

As the curtain opens, the stage is dark except for a faint bluish light through the window and door panes. Off stage, in the next room, are heard smothered groans and creaking bedsprings.

JANE. [*Off stage.*] Quit that floppin' around. It keeps me awake.

MOONY. Think I'm gettin' any sleep, do you?

[*Sound: more rattling.*]

JANE. Quiet! You'll wake the kid up.

MOONY. The kid, the kid! What's more important, him sleepin' or me? Who brings home the pay check, me or the kid?

[*Pause.*]

JANE. I'll get up an' fix you a cup a hot milk. That'll quiet you down maybe.

[MOONY *grumbles incoherently.* JANE *pads softly into the kitchen. She is amazingly slight, like a tiny mandarin, enveloped in the ruins of a once gorgeously flowered Japanese silk kimono. As she prepares the hot milk for* MOONY, *she pads about the kitchen in a pair of men's felt bedroom slippers which she has a hard time keeping on her small feet. She squeezes the kimono tight about her chest and shivers. Coughs once or twice. Glances irritably at the alarm clock on window sill which says nearly four o'clock in the morning.* JANE *is still young, but her pretty, small-featured face has a yellowish, unhealthy look. Her temples and nostrils are greased with Vick's Vap-o-Rub and her dark hair is tousled.*]

MOONY. [*Off stage.*] I'm gettin' up, Jane.

JANE. [*Strident whisper.*] What for? I'll bring yer milk in. [*Sound: scraping of furniture and heavy footsteps.*] That's it, be sure you wake the kid up—clumsy ox! [MOONY *appears in the doorway, a strongly built young workingman about twenty-five years old. He blinks his eyes and scowls irritably as he draws on his flannel shirt and stuffs it under the belt of his corduroy pants.*] It's that beer-drinkin'. Makes gas on yer stomach an' keeps yuh from sleepin'.

MOONY. Aw, I had two glasses right after dinner.

JANE. Two a them twenty-six ounces!—Quit that trampin' around, for Christ's sake! Can't you set still a minute?

MOONY. Naw, I feel like I got to be movin'.

JANE. Maybe you got high blood pressure.

MOONY. Naw, I got a wild hair. This place's give me the jitters. You know it's too damn close in here. Can't take more'n six steps in any direction without comin' smack up against another wall. [*Half grinning.*] I'd like to pick up my ax and swing into this wall—Bet I could smash clean through it in a couple of licks!

JANE. Moony! Why didn't I marry an ape an' go live in the zoo?

MOONY. I don't know.

[JANE *pours the steaming milk into a blue cup.*]

JANE. Set down an' drink that. Know what time it is? Four o'clock in the morning!

MOONY. Four o'clock, huh? [*He continues to move restlessly about.*] Yeah. Soon ole fact'ry whistle be blowin'. Come on, you sonovaguns! Git to work!—Ole Dutchman be standin' there with his hands on his little pot-belly, watchin' 'em punch in their cards. "Hi, dere, Moony," he says,

"late agin, huh? Vot you tink dis iss maybe, an afdernoon tea?" That's his
joke. You know a Dutchman always has one joke that he keeps pluggin'
at. An' that's his. Ev'ry morning the same damn thing—

JANE. Yeah? Well—

MOONY. "Ha, ha, Moony," he says, "you been out star-gazin' las' night!
How many vas dere, Moony? How many stars vas dere out las' night? Ha,
ha, *ha!*" [*Strides over to the window— flings it up.*]

JANE. Put that back down! I ain't got a stitch a clothes on under this.

MOONY. I'll say to him, "Sure, I seen 'em las' night. But not like they was
in Ontario, not by a long shot, Mister!" Grease-bubbles! That's what they
look most like from here. Why, up in the North woods at night—

JANE. [*Impatiently.*] The North woods! Put that thing down!

MOONY. Okay. [*Obeys.*]

JANE. Here. Drink yer milk. You act like a crazy man, honest to Jesus
you do!

MOONY. Okay. Would that give the Dutchman a laugh!

JANE. What would? You better be careful.

MOONY. He'll go all over the plant—tell the boys what Moony said this
morning—Said he'd seen the stars las' night but not like they was in Ontario
when he was choppin' down the big timber.

JANE. Yes, you'll give him a swell impression with talk of that kind. I'm
dog-tired. [*Pours herself some of the steaming milk.*]

MOONY. Ever seen the St. Lawrence River?

JANE. Naw, I've seen wet diapers, that's all, for so long that—

MOONY. That's what I'll ask the Dutchman. I'll ask him if he's ever seen
the St. Lawrence River.

JANE. [*Glancing at him suspiciously.*] What would you ask him that for?

MOONY. She's big. See? She's nearly as big and blue as the sky is, an' the
way she flows is straight north. You ever heard of that, Jane? A river that
flowed straight north?

JANE. [*Indifferently, as she sips her hot milk.*] No.

MOONY. Only river *I* ever known of that flowed north!

JANE. Emma says a drop of paregoric would keep his bowels from
runnin' off like that. I think I'll try it next time.

MOONY. We was talkin' about it one day an' Spook says it's because the
earth is curved down that way toward the Arctic Circle! [*Grins.*]

JANE. What?

MOONY. He said that's why she flows north—

JANE. Who cares?

MOONY. Naw, the Dutchman don't neither. That's why I tell him. Makes
it funny, see? I'll tell him she's big, damn big, an' they call her the Lake of
a Thousand Islands!

JANE. He'll say you're crazy. He'll tell you to go an' jump in it!

MOONY. Sure he will. That's what makes it funny. I'll tell him she's big
an' blue as the sky is with firs an' pines an' tamaracks on both sides of her
fillin' the whole God beautiful air with—the smell of—Hot milk, huh?

Wouldn't that give the Dutchman a laugh? Hot milk at four o'clock in the mornin'! He'd go all over the plant an' tell the boys that Moony must have his liddle hot milk at night when he goes bye-bye with the Sandman!

JANE. Louise Krause's husband commenced to sayin' such things an' they called out the ambulance squad. Right now he's in a strait jacket in the psycopathic ward an' when Louise went up to see him he didn't remember who she was even! De-menshuh *pre*-cox they called it! [MOONY *seizes cup and dashes milk to floor.*] Moony!—What d'yuh think yuh're doin', yuh big lug? Sloppin' good milk on the floor!

MOONY. Hot milk, huh?

JANE. Oh, dear Christ! You an' your kid, what a mess you both are! No wonder they all make fun of you down at the plant. The way that you act there's only one word for it—crazy! [MOONY *snorts indignantly.*] Yes, crazy! Crazy is the only word for your actions!

MOONY. Crazy, huh? Sure them apes think I'm nuts. I'll tell you why, it's because I got some original ideas about some things.

JANE. Original, yeah, you're so stinkin' original it ain't even funny! Believe me if I'd—a-known—

MOONY. I look at things diff'runt [*Struggling for self-justification.*] that's all. Other guys—you know how it is—they don't care. They eat, they drink, they sleep with their women. What the hell do they care? The sun keeps risin' and Saturday night they get paid!—Okay, okay, okay! Some day they kick off. What of it? They got kids to grow up an' take their places. Work in the plant. Eat, drink, sleep with their women—an' get paid Saturday night! But me—[*He laughs bitterly.*] My God, Jane, I want something more than just that!

JANE. What more do you want, you poor fool? There *ain't* nothing more than just that—Of course if you was rich and could afford a big house and a couple of limoozines—

MOONY. [*Disgustedly.*] Aw, you—you don't even get what I'm aimin' at, Jane! [*He sinks wearily on the checkered linoleum and winds arms about knees.*] You never could get it. It's something that ain't contagious.

JANE. Well, I'm glad for that. I'd rather have smallpox.

MOONY. I found a guy once that did. An old duck up on the river. He got his back hurt, couldn't work, was waitin' to be shipped home—We got drunk one night an' I spilled how I felt about things. He said, "Sure. You ain't satisfied. Me neither. We want somethin' more than what life ever gives to us, kid!"

JANE. It gives you what you can get.

MOONY. Oh, I dunno. I look at my hands sometimes. I look an' I look at 'em; God, but they look so damn funny!

JANE. You look at your hands! Such crap!

MOONY. They're so kind of empty an' useless! You get what I mean? I feel like I oughta be doin' somethin' with these two han's of mine besides what I'm doin' now—runnin' bolts through an everlastin' chain!

JANE. Here's something. [*Flings him a dishrag.*] Try holdin' this for a change in them wonderful hands—Mop that milk up off the floor!

MOONY. [*Idly twisting the cloth.*] An' then sometimes I think it ain't my han's that're empty. It's somethin' else inside me that is.

JANE. Yeh, it's probably yer brain. Will you get that milk swabbed up?

MOONY. It's already swabbed! [*Rises and stretches.*] Moony's a free agent. He don't give a damn what anyone thinks. Live an' die, says Moony, that's all there is to it! [*He tosses the wet rag back to the sink.*]

JANE. [*Straightening things in a lifeless, ineffectual way.*] Believe me, if I'd a-known you was gonna turn out this way, I'd a-kept my old job. I'd a-said to Mr. O'Connor, "Sure thing! Go ahead an' get me that chinchilla coat!"

MOONY. Sure you would. I know it, sweetheart.

JANE. [*Beginning to sniffle.*] What's the good of a girl trying to keep herself straight? The way things turn out, a good proposition like Mr. O'Connor could offer would be the best thing. But no! I had such delusions about cha! You talked so swell! You made such a lovely impression that time we first met!

MOONY. Lots of water's run under the bridge since then.

JANE. Yeah.

MOONY. When was that, Jane? How long ago was it?

JANE. Ten months; an' it seems ten years!

MOONY. Ten months. And how old's the kid? One month? Exactly one month?

JANE. [*Furiously.*] You've got a nerve to say that! As if it was me that insisted, that couldn't wait even until we'd—

MOONY. Naw, it wasn't your fault. It was nature got hold of us both that night, Jane. Yuh remember? The Paradise dance hall down on the water front, huh? My first night in town after six months up in the woods. You had on a red silk dress. Yuh remember? Cut down sorta low in front. Hah, you was real pretty then—your hair frizzed up in the back in a thousan' or so little curls that I could just barely poke my littlest finger through!

JANE. [*Falling under a nostalgic spell.*] Yeah. [*Her face softens.*] I useter have it done ev'ry Satiddy night. Mamie said she never seen hair that could take such a curl!

MOONY. [*With sly cruelty.*] Yeh, that's how it was—them curls—an' the red silk dress—it was nature got hold of us both that night, huh, Jane?

JANE. [*Suspecting an innuendo.*] What d'yuh mean by that?

MOONY. The way you pressed up against me when we was dancin'—that was nature, wasn't it, Jane? And when they played "Roses of Picardy" an' the lights was turned out—we was dancin' real slow—we was almost standin' still—your breath was so warm on my neck, so warm—you had on a kind of perfume—

JANE. Perfume? Oh, yes. Narcissus perfume! Mr. O'Connor give it to me for my birthday.

MOONY. Yeah, narcissus, that's it—narcissus! An' what was it, Jane, you whispered in my ear?

JANE. [*Indignantly.*] ME whispered? It was YOU that whispered, not ME!

MOONY. Was it? Maybe it was. You didn't have to say nothin', the way that you danced was enough!—Anyhow I got hooked.

JANE. [*Furiously.*] Hooked! Hooked?! You dare to say such a thing!

MOONY. Yes, I was hooked all right. Narcissus perfume, little curls, an' a low cut dress. Makin' me think that holdin' you in my arms an' waltzin' aroun' a two-bit arch-acher was better'n holdin' an ax in my two han's up in the North woods an' choppin' down big trees!

JANE. [*Choking.*] You—you—! [*Covers her face.*]

MOONY. [*A little less harshly.*] Aw, well, I don't mean that I'm—sorry about it—exactly. . . .

JANE. [*Brokenly.*] How didja mean it, I'd liketa know, then?

MOONY. [*Pacing about the kitchen.*] Oh, I dunno, I dunno! [*Suddenly stops and catches* JANE *in his arms.*] People say things, things happen! What does it mean? I dunno. Seems to me like a crazy man, deaf, dumb, and blind, could have put together a better kind of a world than this is! [*He kisses* JANE's *bare shoulder where the kimono has slipped down a little.*] Let's get out of it, honey!

JANE. [*Sniffling.*] Out of it? What d'yuh mean?

MOONY. [*Violently.*] Chuck it all; the whole damn thing—that's what!

JANE. You mean—[*She backs away from him, frightened.*] *Kill* ourselves?

MOONY. [*Laughing impatiently.*] Well, no—no! I don't wanta DIE! I wanta LIVE!—What I mean is, get out of this place, this lousy town—smoke, whistles, plants, factories, buildin's, buildin's, buildin's!—You get caught in 'em, you never can find your way out!—So break away quick while you can!—Get out where it's clean an' there's space to swing an ax in! An' some time to swing it! Oh, God, Jane, don't you see—see—SEE?

JANE. Yes. You mean hop a freight train. [*Laughs mockingly.*]

MOONY. Sure, that's it if you want to! Tell the Dutchman good-by—

JANE. [*Hysterically.*] Me with the baby an' my infection of the breast— you with your ax! We'll spend Christmas in a boxcar, won't we, Moony?

MOONY. You bet!—Me with my ax, we'll chop a way through this world!

JANE. [*Laughing.*] What a joke—what a lovely SCREAM that is!

MOONY. A joke, huh? Who said a joke?

JANE. Moony, Moony, my great big wonderful man! He'll cut a way [*Chokes with laughter.*]—through this world!

MOONY. [*Getting sore.*] Make fun of me, huh?

JANE. Moony they call him! Down at the plant it's Moony this, Moony that! All of them makin' fun of my man, laughin' at him right to his face, and he's so damn dumb he don't know it! They got your number, they have! The Dutchman's got your number. You're just a star-gazer! You oughta put up your tent an' tell fortunes! Oh, you damn fool! If it wasn't so funny I could cry, I could cry! You with your ax! We'll spend Christmas in a boxcar! You'll chop a way through the world! Ha, ha! You with your ax? What a SCREAM!—Couldn't even chop down a kid's Christmas tree—I hadda buy one at the dime store! An' that horse—[*She gets breathless and hoarse from laughter.*] That's the best one! Brings home a five-dollar hobbyhorse when we ain't even got money enough to pay the hospital bill!

MOONY. I lied to you, Jane. I paid ten-fifty for that little horse.

JANE. [*Aghast.*] Ten-fifty? You—you— No, it's not possible—even you couldn't—

MOONY. It was worth more than that!

JANE. Worth more? More? Worth—[*She is breathless.*]

MOONY. Sure it was!

JANE. Buys a ten-fifty hobbyhorse for a month-old baby—They lock people up for doin' less than that!

MOONY. Aw, he'll grow up to it, Jane. [*He is a little abashed.*] I had one o' these things when I was a kid.

JANE. You musta got thrown off it an' landed on your head!

MOONY. Naw, Dad got drunk one Saturday night, an' bought me one at a junk shop. Mother, she felt like you did, when he come home with it. But me, I was nuts about it. Him an' me, both, we got on the horse—him in back, me in front—an' sang "Ride a Cock-horse to Banbury Cross."

JANE. Oh, my God! Now I know where you got it. He was a lunatic, too!

MOONY. Naw, he was smart. He run out on us.

JANE. Run out on your mother, he did? Well, it's not surprising!

MOONY. I never heard of him since.

JANE. Well—he probably got what was comin' to him.

MOONY. [*With quick rage.*] Better than what I got!

JANE. What you got?

MOONY. A skinny yellow cat—that's what I got!

JANE. [*Gasping.*] Oh—! God oughta strike you down dead for sayin' a thing like that!

MOONY. Yeah? I say it again—a yellow cat—a skinny yellow cat!

[JANE *strikes him across face.* MOONY *becomes like a mad animal. Roars and lunges forward—clutches* JANE *by throat. They grapple fiercely for several moments. Then* JANE *collapses in his arms.*]

JANE. [*Weakly.*] Lemme go—please—for God's sake!

MOONY. [*Disgustedly.*] Ahhh—ye're too soft! [*He flings her away from him. She falls against interior door, and hangs onto knob and edge of sink for support.* MOONY *hitches his belt undecidedly. He can't look at* JANE's *dazed face. He is ashamed, but still defiant.*] I'm leavin' you now—get that? I'm checkin' out. You can tell the Dutchman to give you my pay—owes me three days—time an' a ha'f for Saturday—[*Gives his belt final hitch, and moves over to peg where his lumberman's jacket is hanging. He gives* JANE *a swift furtive glance as he puts on the jacket. Says: "Hmmm!"—Stoops down to pick up his ax, feels the blade with a gingerly pride. Takes awkward practice swing. Eyes glow triumphantly to life. He looks again at* JANE *like an escaped animal at a cage. She does not move. She stares at him with hurt animal eyes.* MOONY *spits on his fingers, runs them along the ax blade again. Hoarsely.*] Pretty sharp, still. Good ole ax—hmmm! [*He starts toward the outer door.*] Maybe I'll—see you sometime—Jane. [*Fumbles with latch.*]. So long. [*He jerks door open. Stands on threshold.*] Hmmm. Feel that wind. Good an' clear tonight. A touch of frost in the air. An' them stars. Millions of 'em, huh? Quantity production, everythin' on a big scale—that's God! Millions of stars—millions of people. Only He knew what to do with the stars. Stuck 'em up there in the sky to look pretty. But people—down here in the mud. Ugh! Too many of 'em, God! They must have run away with you, I guess. Crawlin' over each other, snatchin' and tearin', livin' an' dyin' till the earth's just a big soup of dead bodies! How did that happen? Gosh, it's sure funny! Oh, well, what's the use? A man's gotta live his own life. Cut his own ways through the woods somehow—

[*The cold air sweeping into the room brings* JANE *out of her stupefaction. She slides to the floor and crawls toward* MOONY *like a half-crushed animal.*]

JANE. Moony! [*Hoarsely.*] You wouldn't walk out on me, honey? Me with the baby and my infection of the breast, and no money or nothing?

[MOONY *turns toward her a tortured face. Snatches at his pockets and flings a few coins on the floor.*]

MOONY. Four bits! Tobacco money! Now you got the whole works—so good-by!

JANE. Wait! [*She clutches his arm and her fury makes her inescapable.*] There's something you got to take with you! Your property, Moony—you might as well take it along!

MOONY. I got all I want.

JANE. No, you ain't. There's something else that goes with you. You just wait here for a second. I'll wrap it up for you—[*Goes quickly door upstage.*]

MOONY. What the hell are you—[*He hesitates at the door.*] [JANE *quickly reappears with the baby in her arms.*]

JANE. Here! Here's your kid, Moony! Take him with you. Sure. Go along, now, the *two* of you! [*Shoves baby into* MOONY's *unwilling arms.*] Me, I can't be bothered with no brats. I got to go back to work. O'Connor will give me my old job back. Sure he will. You two can go an' hop a freight an' spend Christmas in a boxcar. Maybe you'll find your old man—You'll have a swell time singin'—"Ride a Cock-horse" together! [*She laughs wildly and runs out of the room.*]

[MOONY *gingerly holds the baby. Looks helplessly down at its face. Frowns. Swears under his breath—Finally slams the door shut.*

MOONY. Another one of her lousy tricks! [*Baby starts crying.*] SHUT UP! [*Then more softly.*] Moony's kid don't cry! [*He smiles slightly and rocks the baby in his arms.* Naw, Moony's kid don't cry. Grows up an' swings a big ax like his Daddy. Cuts his own way through the woods. [*He walks away from the door, completely absorbed now in the baby, and apparently forgetting that he ever had any intention of going away.*] Lookit the hobbyhorse! [*Stands above the new toy.*] Santie Claus bought it for Moony's Kid. Ten-fifty it cost! See? How shiny it is? Nice, huh? What are you cryin' for? Daddy ain't goin' nowhere. Naw!—Daddy was only—foolin'. . . .

SLOW CURTAIN

TOO MANY THUMBS*

❧ Robert H. Hivnor (1915–   )

TOO MANY THUMBS is a three-act satire which takes place in the combined office and laboratory of an unnamed university. The animal psychologist, Assistant Professor Arthur P. Smith, and the professor of comparative religion, Professor G. E. Macklebee, are interested in a recently acquired young, brilliant male chimpanzee. The assistant professor is interested in the animal's mind, and the professor in his soul. The chimpanzee, which they have named Too Many Thumbs, is, as you might expect, the subject of a number of experiments.

Previous to the episode reprinted here—which is the closing of Act I—we learn that Psyche, a female chimpanzee, has been a subject of the experiments. She has not been able to put the blocks together correctly in order to reach for the bananas. It seems she would rather lie on her back and balance the blocks on her feet. And when she does succeed in building a tower of blocks under the bananas, she kicks it over and flip flops with glee. For ten months she has fumbled around with assistant professor Smith's academic future and in so doing has caused him to postpone his wedding. Psyche has lived alone almost a year, and Smith thinks that "isolation stupefies chimpanzees as well as human beings" so he decides that she needs a male chimpanzee as a "boy friend." The assistant professor gives considerable thought to this because this new procedure might change the factors of the problem and might invalidate the whole experiment. However, Smith decides to get the new chimp. He goes to the cage of Psyche and announces his decision, "Wake up, lazybones! You're going to have a mate. And no civilized city slicker, either, no over-educated zoo product, but a real one hundred percent wild chimpanzee fresh from darkest Africa."

Too Many Thumbs arrives and is put into the cage with Psyche, who is somewhat afraid. Too Many Thumbs is indifferent to Psyche and so assistant professor Smith and his laboratory assistant, Johnson, pull him out of the cage to check his teeth, measure his head, examine his throat and take his blood pressure. After this examination, they put him into the cage with Psyche again and leave the room. The assistant professor feels quite sure that ". . . there might be an article in the caps of those molars."

Too Many Thumbs stands in the center of the cage and sniffs intelligently. He sees Psyche and says:

TOO MANY THUMBS. Hm. A chimpanzee about ten years old. Female. I'd say she weighed about sixty pounds. (*He goes to her pen and knocks loudly*

on the door. When she doesn't answer) Hello. Hello. (*Impatiently*)
Come on out, for heaven's sake.
(*Silence.*)
TOO MANY THUMBS. I won't hurt you. I'm as afraid of you as you are of me.
Where are you from? You—if you will pardon the expression—smell like
a lowland ape. Where are you from . . . ah, what did you say your name
was?
PSYCHE (*a high voice from within*). Psyche.
TOO MANY THUMBS (*to himself*). What a name. (*Calling out*) And where
are you from, Psyche? Nigeria? The Congo?
PSYCHE (*sticking her head out of the door of her pen*). I was born in the
Cleveland zoo.
TOO MANY THUMBS. Oh, a North American, eh? (*Aside*) She's no beauty,
is she!
PSYCHE (*aside*). Dear me, he's rather young.
TOO MANY THUMBS. Come on down and be friendly. (*He extends his hand
up to her.*)
PSYCHE. You don't know how glad I am to see a hand with some real
fingernails on it.
TOO MANY THUMBS. Come on. Don't be scared. If fate ever threw two
persons together, she's thrown us.
(*She laughs and climbs down with exaggerated grace.*)
PSYCHE. Well.
(*They embrace and sit side by side on their haunches, chimpanzee style.*)
TOO MANY THUMBS. Well.
(*She giggles.*)
PSYCHE. What's your name? I told you mine.
TOO MANY THUMBS (*proudly*). Too Many Thumbs.
PSYCHE (*fondly*). Too Many Thumbs.
TOO MANY THUMBS. (*He always refers to himself with wonder and great
pride.*) I'm from the jungle, but I was born in a cave in the mountains.
PSYCHE. A sure-enough, real wild, rough and tumble jungle ape. Let me
look at you.
TOO MANY THUMBS. Three months ago I was making nests out of leaves,
resting on the great living breast of the jungle. Home! Home! Will I
never see you again?
PSYCHE. Tell me about the jungle. (*Sentimentally*) The Fatherland!
TOO MANY THUMBS. Some other time. For the moment shall we say that the
mind walks barefoot in the jungle and that nothing, not even god, is
strange. Here everything is strange.
PSYCHE. I guess you can get used to everything . . . except monotony.
TOO MANY THUMBS. What's it all mean, Psyche? At first I thought I had
died and that those baby-faced creatures were ghosts, apes that had
passed over, but I felt one and he was as warm as you are. What's it all
mean? I don't mean just being jerked out of the jungle and thrown in
this place, but the whole business. What does life mean?

PSYCHE. Well, I've given up trying to figure things out. I just live from day to day.

TOO MANY THUMBS. Never give up. The mind will know because it wills to know and it will know what it wills.

PSYCHE. My! You look so young and you go on like an old man. How old are you, if I may be so inquisitive?

TOO MANY THUMBS. Four or five or six.

PSYCHE. Hm. Now I forget just when mountain chimpanzees grow up.

TOO MANY THUMBS (*rather excited about himself*). I'm as strong as a gorilla.

PSYCHE. But do you have the voice of the fully-developed male?

TOO MANY THUMBS (*in his most masculine manner*). Fully developed! Who knows if I'm fully developed? Physically, there is a time when you can say, "I am a man," and that time has been with me. (*Psyche sighs.*)

TOO MANY THUMBS. But mentally it's not so easy. What kind of an experience would prove that the brain has arrived at maturity?

PSYCHE. Goodness! I didn't mean to start you off. Never you mind. You just hold me tight and tell me some more about the jungle.

TOO MANY THUMBS. The whole world's a jungle.

PSYCHE. Too Many Thumbs, you grow on one. Sometimes I think you're handsome. The underhang of your jaw, those beautiful arms, which almost reach to the ground . . . but I see that you're shy. (*Making advances*) Don't be bashful, Too Many Thumbs.

TOO MANY THUMBS. Someday I'll snap you up by the nape of the neck with my teeth and sling you up in the tallest tree.

PSYCHE (*coyly*). Ah, ha! Then maybe you have known a woman in that jungle of yours.

TOO MANY THUMBS. Known? Yes. Just three moons ago four of us river boys were going along the ground when we came upon a little female. She recoils feminine-like and extends all four hands in fear. We grabbed her and tore her limb from limb.

PSYCHE (*withdrawing her arm from around his neck*). Oh.

TOO MANY THUMBS. Psyche, why do those bananas grow upside down?

PSYCHE. That's not a tree. That's a test.

TOO MANY THUMBS. They smell like bananas.

PSYCHE. They're real, all right, but they're bait. The idea is that I want bananas. I race about fitting those blocks into some old platform. Then I stand on it and reach the bananas. And then for some reason the people in there jump all over themselves.

TOO MANY THUMBS. It's been a long time since I had any fresh fruit.

PSYCHE. Oh, you mustn't take one. Besides the blue block is gone.

TOO MANY THUMBS. Huh?

PSYCHE. They want to be here when I finally get bored enough to do the trick, so they take away the blue block and put it out there. You can't reach without it. Oh, they're crafty.

TOO MANY THUMBS. Why don't you do it and get it over with?

PSYCHE. They'd just give me another problem to do and this is one of the pleasantest ones I've had. Believe me, honey, I've been through hell. Once—I get the shivers and shakes when I think of it—once they never fed me without ringing a bell. A high bell for sweet, a low one for the sour. It helped me pucker for awhile. But then they started to bring them together.

TOO MANY THUMBS. Yeh, well . . .

PSYCHE. My mouth didn't know which way to pucker. I began to go crazy and walk around on my hind legs like this. (*She mimics a man walking. Then seriously*) I tell you, that's why I think they're gods; only creatures with a bit of the fiend in them could think up such tricks.

TOO MANY THUMBS. Poor Psyche. Still, I think it's the right thing to take the tests as they come. Fate is fate.

PSYCHE. Well, I'd do their old tests if they gave me a kind word once in a while.

(*Enter Smith from east. He smiles when he sees Too Many Thumbs and Psyche holding hands.*)

SMITH. Lovey-dovey already, eh?

TOO MANY THUMBS (*chuckling*). Isn't he sick lookin'? What's wrong with him? Snake bite?

PSYCHE. You may be referring to the ruler of the universe.

TOO MANY THUMBS (*laughing*). Oh, Psyche! Ho, ho, ho, ho.

PSYCHE. You think you're so smart. They know a thing or two. (*Smith goes to the office door and knocks on it softly.*)

SMITH. Jenny! Jenny!

TOO MANY THUMBS. Forgive my skepticism, but I have my own ideas about the ruler of the universe and he doesn't fit.

JENNY (*opening the door*). What is it?

SMITH. Look. They're holding hands.

JENNY. How cute!

SMITH. Maybe the problem won't be solved but something's going to happen.

JENNY. Oh, I hope it won't be long.

(*Smith and Jenny embrace and kiss.*)

PSYCHE (*a hoarse whisper to Too Many Thumbs*). To be a god and take into your arms a goddess. (*Upon reflection, to herself*) Or, to be a chimpanzee and take into your arms a chimpanzee.

TOO MANY THUMBS. I guess he likes her, but I couldn't stand all that bare skin.

PSYCHE (*to herself*). Love . . . I wonder how *they* do it.

(*Enter Johnson with a file. Jenny and Smith separate.*)

JOHNSON. I have the file.

SMITH. Oh, yes. I'll call you if anything happens, Jenny.

JENNY. 'Bye.

(*She goes into office.*)

TOO MANY THUMBS (*to Psyche*). No, I simply can't believe they are related in any way to the divine.

SMITH. Now did you check these figures? Sometimes these field parties get off the beam.

JOHNSON. They're all right. I checked and double-checked.

SMITH (*nodding to Too Many Thumbs*). Get him out here. I hope he isn't a freak of some kind.

(*Johnson goes into the cage.*)

PSYCHE (*to Too Many Thumbs*). They're animals, I suppose.

TOO MANY THUMBS. They're not gods.

(*Too Many Thumbs is interrupted by Johnson taking him out of the cage and lifting him onto the desk. Smith plops the head measuring device on his head again.*)

SMITH. Both of us could be wrong. (*Reading device*) No. We have an extraordinary animal on our hands, Johnson.

JOHNSON. Maybe he has some disease. Hydrocephalus or something like that.

SMITH. I thought of that but there's no other symptom. Bring in the block test.

(*Johnson produces a large rack with irregular holes in it, together with the blocks that fit into it. He puts this in front of Too Many Thumbs and Smith peels an orange and divides it into sections.*)

PSYCHE (*shaking her head*). The shapes test. Poor Too Many Thumbs!

JOHNSON. Try your oversize cerebellum on that.

TOO MANY THUMBS. Ah, an orange.

(*Too Many Thumbs reaches for it but the professor withdraws it. Then Johnson puts several of the blocks in place and Smith gives him a section of the orange.*)

JOHNSON. Ym, yum.

TOO MANY THUMBS. I get it. You have to work for it. (*Sighs*) Life is the same all over the world.

(*Too Many Thumbs places all the blocks in position with amazing rapidity.*)

JOHNSON. Forty seconds!

SMITH. Incredible. It took Psyche over five minutes. (*He gives Too Many Thumbs his reward, a slice of orange.*)

TOO MANY THUMBS (*smacking lips*). Smsptchm.

PSYCHE (*calling to Too Many Thumbs*). Take your time on those tests, silly. They'll just make you do it again.

(*Smith holds up another piece of orange after Johnson has removed the blocks.*)

TOO MANY THUMBS. Again.

PSYCHE. You'll see. If the gods want anything, it's repetition. Again and again and again.

(*Too Many Thumbs blithely begins to replace the blocks when Johnson rings an enormous handbell in his ear. Too Many Thumbs clasps his hands to his ears in surprise. Psyche squeals with laughter.*)

PSYCHE. You'll see.

(*But Too Many Thumbs resolutely finishes his task and grabs his slice of orange from the hand of Smith.*)

TOO MANY THUMBS (*eating*). Life is full of obstacles . . . but nothing will stop me from doing what fate causes me to do.

PSYCHE. He'll wake up at midnight with that bell ringing in his ears.

JOHNSON (*looking up from his notebook*). I got it.

(*The blocks are dumped out of the tray again and Smith holds up another piece of orange.*)

TOO MANY THUMBS. Again? (*Psyche laughs.*) Well, those are nice oranges. Oh, give it here. Fate can be fun.

(*Too Many Thumbs touches one of the blocks and sparks fly out of his fingers—the block has been charged with electricity. Too Many Thumbs screams and Psyche squeals with laughter.*)

JOHNSON. That was a darn good reaction, wasn't it, Doc?

SMITH. We are dealing here with an excellent nervous system. (*He holds up two orange slices.*)

JOHNSON. More, Too Many Thumbs?

(*Too Many Thumbs looks longingly at the oranges and moves to get them but inhibits himself and a look of anxiety passes over his face.*)

PSYCHE (*mimicking Too Many Thumbs*). Those are very nice oranges. (*She laughs.*)

TOO MANY THUMBS (*soberly*). Between my eyes and that orange there's a kind of shadow.

PSYCHE. You'll learn. You'll see that they're really gods and one hundred percent for gods and that it's best not to have anything to do with them. Oranges, candy, chewing gum, strawberry sundaes! I've had them all, to my regret. The only thing is to live in one's own world, forego the baits of the gods and live like a chimpanzee.

TOO MANY THUMBS. I can't agree with you . . . woman.

PSYCHE. Wait till you get the ice water, the flypaper, the castor oil.

TOO MANY THUMBS. There must be some meaning connected with these orange and bananas and ice cream sundaes. Why all this trouble to tempt me upward? I will aspire. Pain or no pain, I will eat an orange.

PSYCHE. You'll learn.

SMITH. Johnson, not a word of this to anyone. We have an astounding animal on our hands.

JOHNSON. Maybe there's a book in him.

SMITH. No doubt about it. Now one thing, be careful about leaving that blue block in there. I thought it would be months before he could possibly concentrate on that problem, but now I'm not so sure. (*To Too Many Thumbs, giving him a pat on the head*) All right for now, Too Many Thumbs.

(*Johnson escorts Too Many Thumbs back into the cage and takes out the blue block.*)

PSYCHE (*to Johnson as he takes out the blue block*). Don't worry, Four-eyes, those bananas can turn brown before I get 'em. Bucket carrier. Stealer of my substance.

SMITH. Johnson, you see what we lab people are up against. These expedition men have his measurements all wrong. Now the only thing we can depend on is records. If they are wrong, where are we? (*Johnson is attentive and nodding sagely as they both walk off east.*) Errors like this have been accumulating since time began.

(*Too Many Thumbs cowers despondently by the wall, brooding. The men snap the light out as they go out and it is darker.*)

PSYCHE. Poor boy.

(*She goes over and puts her arm around him, but, lost in thought, he hardly regards her.*)

PSYCHE. Don't eat your heart out like that. I felt the same way the first month I was here. Then I stopped taking life seriously and I've been putting on weight ever since.

TOO MANY THUMBS. Is it possible that this world was not made for chimpanzees? This time, this space, and this consciousness—were they not designed for the destiny of our race? Those pale people . . .

PSYCHE. Devils.

TOO MANY THUMBS. They're not ghosts of chimpanzees . . . yet they have something to do with death. Perhaps they make it . . .

PSYCHE. Don't bother your little head about it, Too Many Thumbs. Why, your heart is going pitter-pat. Don't be so excited!

TOO MANY THUMBS. There couldn't be any race greater than chimpanzees, could there?

PSYCHE. No, no. Calm down, Too Many Thumbs.

TOO MANY THUMBS. This is no dream, no made-up world. And the reasons why we are tested are real. I must think that.

PSYCHE. Forget about them. If you want something nicer, put your head close to mine.

TOO MANY THUMBS. I must have faith.

PSYCHE. You're young, but I can whisper something in your ear that will make you old in a second.

TOO MANY THUMBS. Maybe oranges are just oranges, but in the structure of aspiring there is a meaning.

PSYCHE. I have something better than their ole oranges. And you won't have to solve any puzzles. For your little hairy chest *is* the answer. Smooth out that intellectual forehead and think about your lil' Psyche.

(*Psyche kisses him, but Too Many Thumbs pushes her aside, springs up and goes to the colored blocks and begins to construct with them a platform under the gallows.*)

PSYCHE. Look at him. Life's supremest pleasure at his elbow and he wants to climb twelve feet in the air for something to eat.

TOO MANY THUMBS (*muttering as he works fitting the intricately shaped blocks together*). They couldn't be hanging there for nothing.

PSYCHE. Besides, they took the blue block out. Even if you do put all of them in the right place you won't be able to reach 'em.

(*He builds the truncated pyramid and stands upon it hand outstretched, but he wants ten or twelve more inches to reach the fruit.*)

PSYCHE. You see.

TOO MANY THUMBS. I must get them. I must.

PSYCHE. Wait until tomorrow. They'll bring back the block that goes on top.

TOO MANY THUMBS (*straining toward his goal*). I must.

PSYCHE (*pleading*). Forget about it. Come here to me, Too Many Thumbs, I'll help you forget.

TOO MANY THUMBS (*roaring and raging*). Oh, god blast it!

PSYCHE. Too Many Thumbs, can't you see that I'm better'n that ole bunch of bananas!

(*Too Many Thumbs turns and stares at her.*)

PSYCHE. My lips taste better than those things.

(*He descends the pyramid and approaches her with narrowed eyes.*)

PSYCHE. At last. I believe you've got the idea. Well, there's a prize in it. Now come put your head upon my lap and I'll tell you the facts of life. (*As he approaches*) That's right. But don't be so serious.

(*Too Many Thumbs grips her with both hands about the throat.*)

PSYCHE. Too Many Thumbs!!

(*He strangles her. When she is lifeless, Too Many Thumbs peers into her face and grunts with satisfaction. Then he carries her to the pyramid and puts her on top of it. He stands upon her body and with the added height this provides he can now reach his goal. With an exultant cry he takes one of the bananas. Then he sits down upon Psyche and begins peeling it as the curtain comes down.*)

BECKET OR THE HONOR OF GOD*

🐦 JEAN ANOUILH (1910–　)

In his play Becket Or The Honor of God, *Jean Anouilh vividly portrays two men, King Henry II and Thomas Becket.*

As young men, these two were fond companions, sharing a warm fellowship in waging battles, carousing and merrymaking. After some time King Henry decides that, for political reasons, Becket should be made Chancellor of England.

Once Becket is made Chancellor, he completely abandons his former life and espouses supreme allegiance to God, not to the crown. Henry's wrath toward Becket and his religious allegiance forces Becket to flee to France. After a period of time, the political climate between France and England changes, forcing the King of France to ask Becket to leave the country. However, because the King of France is fond of Becket, he persuades Henry to try one last effort at reconciliation.

In this scene we find Becket and King Henry alone in the middle of the bare plain at La Ferté-Bernard, facing each other. Each is mounted on his horse. The wind is sharp, cold and blustering.

KING. You look older, Thomas.

BECKET. You too, Highness. Are you sure you aren't too cold?

KING. I'm frozen stiff. You love it of course! You're in your element, aren't you? And you're barefooted as well!

BECKET. (*Smiling*) That's my latest affectation.

KING. Even with these fur boots on, my chilblains are killing me. Aren't yours, or don't you have any?

BECKET. (*Gently*) Of course.

KING. (*Cackling*) You're offering them up to God, I hope, holy monk?

BECKET. (*Gravely*) I have better things to offer Him.

KING. (*With a sudden cry*) If we start straightaway, we're sure to quarrel! Let's talk about trivial things. You know my son is fourteen? He's come of age.

BECKET. Has he improved at all?

KING. He's a little idiot and sly like his mother. Becket, don't you ever marry!

BECKET. (*Smiling*) The matter has been taken out of my hands. By you, Highness! It was you who had me ordained!

* Reprinted by permission of Coward-McCann, Inc., from *Becket, or The Honor of God*, by Jean Anouilh, translated by Lucienne Hill. © 1960 by Jean Anouilh and Lucienne Hill.

KING. (*With a cry*) Let's not start yet, I tell you! Talk about something else!

BECKET. (*Lightly*) Has your Highness done much hunting lately?

KING. (*Snarling*) Yes, every day! And it doesn't amuse me any more.

BECKET. Have you any new hawks?

KING. (*Furiously*) The most expensive on the market! But they don't fly straight.

BECKET. And your horses?

KING. The Sultan sent me four superb stallions for the tenth anniversary of my reign. But they throw everyone! Nobody has managed to mount one of them, yet!

BECKET. (*Smiling*) I must see what I can do about that some day.

KING. They'll throw you too! And we'll see your buttocks under your robe! At least, I hope so, or everything would be too dismal.

BECKET. (*After a pause*) Do you know what I miss most, Sire? The horses.

KING. And the women?

BECKET. (*Simply*) I've forgotten.

KING. You hypocrite. You turned into a hypocrite when you became a priest. (*Abruptly*) Did you love Gwendolen?

BECKET. I've forgotten her too.

KING. You did love her! That's the only way I can account for it.

BECKET. (*Gravely*) No, my prince, in my soul and conscience, I did not love her.

KING. Then you never loved anything, that's worse! (*Churlishly*) Why are you calling me your prince, like in the old days?

BECKET. (*Gently*) Because you have remained my prince.

KING. (*Crying out*) Then why are you doing me harm?

BECKET. (*Gently*) Let's talk about something else.

KING. Well, what? I'm cold.

BECKET. I always told you, my prince, that one must fight the cold with the cold's own weapons. Strip naked and splash yourself with cold water every morning.

KING. I used to when you were there to force me into it. I never wash now. I stink. I grew a beard at one time. Did you know?

BECKET. (*Smiling*) Yes. I had a hearty laugh over it.

KING. I cut it off because it itched.

He cries out suddenly, like a lost child:

Becket, I'm bored!

BECKET. (*Gravely*) My prince. I do so wish I could help you.

KING. Then what are you waiting for? You can see I'm dying for it!

BECKET. (*Quietly*) I'm waiting for the honor of God and the honor of the King to become one.

KING. You'll wait a long time then!

BECKET. Yes. I'm afraid I will.

A pause. Only the wind is heard.

KING. (*Suddenly*) If we've nothing more to say to each other, we might as well go and get warm!

BECKET. We have everything to say to each other, my prince. The opportunity may not occur again.

KING. Make haste, then. Or there'll be two frozen statues on this plain making their peace in a frozen eternity! I am your King, Becket! And so long as we are on this earth you owe me the first move! I'm prepared to forget a lot of things but not the fact that I am King. You yourself taught me that.

BECKET. (*Gravely*) Never forget it, my prince. Even against God. You have a different task to do. You have to steer the ship.

KING. And you—what do you have to do?

BECKET. Resist you with all my might, when you steer against the wind.

KING. Do you expect the wind to be behind me, Becket? No such luck! That's the fairy-tale navigation! God on the King's side? That's never happened yet! Yes, once in a century, at the time of the Crusades, when all Christendom shouts "It's God's will!" And even then! You know as well as I do what private greeds a Crusade covers up, in nine cases out of ten. The rest of the time, it's a head-on wind. And there must be somebody to keep the watch!

BECKET. And somebody else to cope with the absurd wind—and with God. The tasks have been shared out, once and for all. The pity of it is that it should have been between us two, my prince—who were friends.

KING. (*Crossly*) The King of France—I still don't know what he hopes to gain by it—preached at me for three whole days for me to make my peace with you. What good would it do you to provoke me beyond endurance?

BECKET. None.

KING. You know that I am the King, and that I must act like a King! What do you expect of me? Are you hoping I'll weaken?

BECKET. No. That would prostrate me.

KING. Do you hope to conquer me by force then?

BECKET. You are the strong one.

KING. To win me round?

BECKET. No. Not that either. It is not for me to win you round. I have only to say no to you.

KING. But you must be logical, Becket!

BECKET. No. That isn't necessary, my Liege. We must only do—absurdly—what we have been given to do—right to the end.

KING. Yet I know you well enough, God knows. Ten years we spent together, little Saxon! At the hunt, at the whorehouse, at war; carousing all night long the two of us; in the same girl's bed, sometimes . . . and at work in the Council Chamber too. Absurdly. That word isn't like you.

BECKET. Perhaps. I am no longer like myself.

KING. (*Derisively*) Have you been touched by grace?

BECKET.   (*Gravely*) Not by the one you think. I am not worthy of it.

KING.   Did you feel the Saxon in you coming out, despite Papa's good collaborator's sentiments?

BECKET.   No. Not that either.

KING.   What then?

BECKET.   I felt for the first time that I was being entrusted with something, that's all—there in that empty cathedral, somewhere in France, that day when you ordered me to take up this burden. I was a man without honor. And suddenly I found it—one I never imagined would ever become mine—the honor of God. A frail, incomprehensible honor, vulnerable as a boy-King fleeing from danger.

KING.   (*Roughly*) Suppose we talked a little more precisely, Becket, with words I understand? Otherwise we'll be here all night. I'm cold. And the others are waiting for us on the fringe of this plain.

BECKET.   I am being precise.

KING.   I'm an idiot then! Talk to me like an idiot! That's an order. Will you lift the excommunication which you pronounced on William of Aynsford and others of my liegemen?

BECKET.   No, Sire, because that is the only weapon I have to defend this child, who was given, naked, into my care.

KING.   Will you agree to the twelve proposals which my Bishops have accepted in your absence at Northampton, and notably to forego the much-abused protection of Saxon clerics who get themselves tonsured to escape land bondage?

BECKET.   No, Sire. My role is to defend my sheep. And they are my sheep.
      A pause.
Nor will I concede that the Bishops should forego the right to appoint priests in their own dioceses, nor that churchmen should be subject to any but the Church's jurisdiction. These are my duties as a pastor—which it is not for me to relinquish. But I shall agree to the nine other articles in a spirit of peace, and because I know that you must remain King—in all save the honor of God.
      A pause

KING.   (*Coldly*) Very well. I will help you defend your God, since that is your new vocation, in memory of the companion you once were to me—in all save the honor of the Realm. You may come back to England, Thomas.

BECKET.   Thank you, my prince. I meant to go back in any case and give myself up to your power, for on this earth, you are my King. And in all that concerns this earth, I owe you obedience.
      A pause

KING.   (*Ill at ease*) Well, let's go back now. We've finished. I'm cold.

BECKET.   (*Dully*) I feel cold too, now.
      Another pause. They look at each other. The wind howls.

KING.   (*Suddenly*) You never loved me, did you, Becket?

BECKET.   In so far as I was capable of love, yes, my prince, I did.

KING. Did you start to love God?
  He cries out:
You mule! Can't you ever answer a simple question?
BECKET. (*Quietly*) I started to love the honor of God.
KING. (*Somberly*) Come back to England. I give you my royal peace.
May you find yours. And may you not discover you were wrong about
yourself. This is the last time I shall come begging to you.
  He cries out:
I should never have seen you again! It hurts too much.
  His whole body is suddenly shaken by a sob.
BECKET. (*Goes nearer to him; moved*) My prince—
KING. (*Yelling*) No! No pity! It's dirty. Stand away from me! Go back
to England! It's too cold out here!
  BECKET *turns his horse and moves nearer to the* KING.
BECKET. (*Gravely*) Farewell, my prince. Will you give me the kiss of
peace?
KING. No! I can't bear to come near you! I can't bear to look at you!
Later! Later! When it doesn't hurt any more!
BECKET. I shall set sail tomorrow. Farewell, my prince. I know I shall
never see you again.
KING. (*His face twisted with hatred*) How dare you say that to me after
I gave you my royal word? Do you take me for a traitor?
  BECKET *looks at him gravely for a second longer, with a sort of pity
  in his eyes. Then he slowly turns his horse and rides away. The
  wind howls.*
KING. Thomas!
  But BECKET *has not heard. The* KING *does not call a second time. He
  spurs his horse and gallops off in the other direction. The lights
  fade. The wind howls.*

A RAISIN IN THE SUN*

✍ LORRAINE HANSBERRY (1930–1965)

Lorraine Hansberry's drama A Raisin in the Sun *is basically about a dream that Lena Younger (Mama) has of a "house with a patch of dirt," a dream that Walter Lee Younger (Brother) has of owning a liquor store and becoming wealthy, a dream that Beneatha Younger (Sister) has of becoming a physician.*

The story takes place in the Southside of Chicago where Mama, recently widowed, has received $10,000 from her husband's insurance. It is this money that provides the incentive for the fulfillment of their cherished dreams.

Throughout the play there are many excellent scenes that will test your interpretative skill as a reader. Perhaps one of the most demanding is the one reprinted here, which is challenging to the oral interpreter because it demands an awareness of environmental influence upon speech. There is Ruth, tired and disappointed, whose speech indicates that she is well on her way to becoming a "settled woman"; Beneatha, intense and energetic, who speaks with a Southside Chicago influence; and Mama, full body and strong, whose speech "is as careless as her carriage is precise."

At this particular moment in Scene I, Ruth has sent her son Travis off to school. Walter and Beneatha have been "picking" at each other and talking about the money that is coming tomorrow. Then Walter goes off to his work as a chauffeur. Mama makes her appearance and shows concern over the fussing that has gone on between her two children, Walter and Beneatha. Mama is also troubled over the condition of Ruth, her daughter-in-law. The subject of money is brought up and evokes the following spirited discussion:

MAMA (*Thoughtfully, and suddenly very far away*)   Ten thousand dollars—

RUTH   Sure is wonderful.

MAMA   Ten thousand dollars.

RUTH   You know what you should do, Miss Lena? You should take yourself a trip somewhere. To Europe or South America or someplace—

MAMA (*Throwing up her hands at the thought*)   Oh, child!

RUTH   I'm serious. Just pack up and leave! Go on away and enjoy yourself

---

some. Forget about the family and have yourself a ball for once in your
life—

MAMA (*Drily*) You sound like I'm just about ready to die. Who'd go
with me? What I look like wandering 'round Europe by myself?

RUTH Shoot—these here rich white women do it all the time. They don't
think nothing of packing up they suitcases and piling on one of them big
steamships and—swoosh!—they gone, child.

MAMA Something always told me I wasn't no rich white woman.

RUTH Well—what are you going to do with it then?

MAMA I ain't rightly decided. (*Thinking. She speaks now with emphasis*)
Some of it got to be put away for Beneatha and her schoolin'—and ain't
nothing going to touch that part of it. Nothing. (*She waits several
seconds, trying to make up her mind about something, and looks at* RUTH
a little tentatively before going on) Been thinking that we maybe could
meet the notes on a little old two-story somewhere, with a yard where
Travis could play in the summertime, if we use part of the insurance for
a down payment and everybody kind of pitch in. I could maybe take
on a little day work again, few days a week—

RUTH (*Studying her mother-in-law furtively and concentrating on her ironing, anxious to encourage without seeming to*) Well, Lord knows, we've
put enough rent into this here rat trap to pay for four houses by now . . .

MAMA (*Looking up at the words "rat trap" and then looking around and
leaning back and sighing—in a suddenly reflective mood—*) "Rat trap"—
yes, that's all it is. (*Smiling*) I remember just as well the day me and
Big Walter moved in here. Hadn't been married but two weeks and
wasn't planning on living here no more than a year. (*She shakes her
head at the dissolved dream*) We was going to set away, little by little,
don't you know, and buy a little place out in Morgan Park. We had even
picked out the house. (*Chuckling a little*) Looks right dumpy today. But
Lord, child, you should know all the dreams I had 'bout buying that
house and fixing it up and making me a little garden in the back—(*She
waits and stops smiling*) And didn't none of it happen.
      (*Dropping her hands in a futile gesture*)

RUTH (*Keeps her head down, ironing*) Yes, life can be a barrel of dis-
appointments, sometimes.

MAMA Honey, Big Walter would come in here some nights back then
and slump down on that couch there and just look at the rug, and look
at me and look at the rug and then back at me—and I'd know he was
down then . . . really down. (*After a second very long and thoughtful
pause; she is seeing back to times that only she can see*) And then, Lord,
when I lost that baby—little Claude—I almost thought I was going to lose

Big Walter too. Oh, that man grieved hisself! He was one man to love his children.

RUTH Ain't nothin' can tear at you like losin' your baby.

MAMA I guess that's how come that man finally worked hisself to death like he done. Like he was fighting his own war with this here world that took his baby from him.

RUTH He sure was a fine man, all right. I always liked Mr. Younger.

MAMA Crazy 'bout his children! God knows there was plenty wrong with Walter Younger—hard-headed, mean, kind of wild with women—plenty wrong with him. But he sure loved his children. Always wanted them to have something—be something. That's where Brother gets all these notions, I reckon. Big Walter used to say, he'd get right wet in the eyes sometimes, lean his head back with the water standing in his eyes and say, "Seem like God didn't see fit to give the black man nothing but dreams—but He did give us children to make them dreams seem worth while." (*She smiles*) He could talk like that, don't you know.

RUTH Yes, he sure could. He was a good man, Mr. Younger.

MAMA Yes, a fine man—just couldn't never catch up with his dreams, that's all.
(BENEATHA *comes in, brushing her hair and looking up to the ceiling, where the sound of a vacuum cleaner has started up*)

BENEATHA What could be so dirty on that woman's rugs that she has to vacuum them every single day?

RUTH I wish certain young women 'round here who I could name would take inspiration about certain rugs in a certain apartment I could also mention.

BENEATHA (*Shrugging*) How much cleaning can a house need, for Christ's sakes.

MAMA (*Not liking the Lord's name used thus*) Bennie!

RUTH Just listen to her—just listen!

BENEATHA Oh, God!

MAMA If you use the Lord's name just one more time—

BENEATHA (*A bit of a whine*) Oh, Mama—

RUTH Fresh—just fresh as salt, this girl!

BENEATHA (*Drily*) Well—if the salt loses its savor—

MAMA Now that will do. I just ain't going to have you 'round here reciting the scriptures in vain—you hear me?

BENEATHA How did I manage to get on everybody's wrong side by just walking into a room?

RUTH If you weren't so fresh—

BENEATHA Ruth, I'm twenty years old.

MAMA What time you be home from school today?

BENEATHA Kind of late. (*With enthusiasm*) Madeline is going to start my guitar lessons today.
        (MAMA *and* RUTH *look up with the same expression*)

MAMA Your *what* kind of lessons?

BENEATHA Guitar.

RUTH Oh, Father!

MAMA How come you done taken it in your mind to learn to play the guitar?

BENEATHA I just want to, that's all.

MAMA (*Smiling*) Lord, child, don't you know what to do with yourself? How long it going to be before you get tired of this now—like you got tired of that little play-acting group you joined last year? (*Looking at* RUTH) And what was it the year before that?

RUTH The horseback-riding club for which she bought that fifty-five-dollar riding habit that's been hanging in the closet ever since!

MAMA (*To* BENEATHA) Why you got to flit so from one thing to another, baby?

BENEATHA (*Sharply*) I just want to learn to play the guitar. Is there anything wrong with that?

MAMA Ain't nobody trying to stop you. I just wonders sometimes why you has to flit so from one thing to another all the time. You ain't never done nothing with all that camera equipment you brought home—

BENEATHA I don't flit! I—I experiment with different forms of expression—

RUTH Like riding a horse?

BENEATHA —People have to express themselves one way or another.

MAMA What is it you want to express?

BENEATHA (*Angrily*) Me! (MAMA *and* RUTH *look at each other and burst into raucous laughter*) Don't worry—I don't expect you to understand.

MAMA (*To change the subject*) Who you going out with tomorrow night?

BENEATHA (*With displeasure*) George Murchison again.

MAMA (*Pleased*) Oh—you getting a little sweet on him?

RUTH You ask me, this child ain't sweet on nobody but herself—(*Under-breath*) Express herself!
(*They laugh*)

BENEATHA Oh—I like George all right, Mama. I mean I like him enough to go out with him and stuff, but—

RUTH (*For devilment*) What does *and stuff* mean?

BENEATHA Mind your own business.

MAMA Stop picking at her now, Ruth. (*A thoughtful pause, and then a suspicious sudden look at her daughter as she turns in her chair for emphasis*) What *does* it mean?

BENEATHA (*Wearily*) Oh, I just mean I couldn't ever really be serious about George. He's—he's so shallow.

RUTH Shallow—what do you mean he's shallow? He's *Rich!*

MAMA Hush, Ruth.

BENEATHA I know he's rich. He knows he's rich, too.

RUTH Well—what other qualities a man got to have to satisfy you, little girl?

BENEATHA You wouldn't even begin to understand. Anybody who married Walter could not possibly understand.

MAMA (*Outraged*) What kind of way is that to talk about your brother?

BENEATHA Brother is a flip—let's face it.

MAMA (*To* RUTH, *helplessly*) What's a flip?

RUTH (*Glad to add kindling*) She's saying he's crazy.

BENEATHA Not crazy. Brother isn't really crazy yet—he—he's an elaborate neurotic.

MAMA Hush your mouth!

BENEATHA As for George. Well. George looks good—he's got a beautiful car and he takes me to nice places and, as my sister-in-law says, he is probably the richest boy I will ever get to know and I even like him sometimes—but if the Youngers are sitting around waiting to see if their little Bennie is going to tie up the family with the Murchisons, they are wasting their time.

RUTH You mean you wouldn't marry George Murchison if he asked you someday? That pretty, rich thing? Honey, I knew you was odd—

BENEATHA Nó I would not marry him if all I felt for him was what I feel now. Besides, George's family wouldn't really like it.

MAMA Why not?

BENEATHA Oh, Mama—the Murchisons are honest-to-God-real-*live*-rich colored people, and the only people in the world who are more snobbish than rich white people are rich colored people. I thought everybody knew that. I've met Mrs. Murchison. She's a scene!

MAMA You must not dislike people 'cause they well off, honey.

BENEATHA Why not? It makes just as much sense as disliking people 'cause they are poor, and lots of people do that.

RUTH (*A wisdom-of-the-ages manner. To* MAMA) Well, she'll get over some of this—

BENEATHA Get over it? What are you talking about, Ruth? Listen, I'm going to be a doctor. I'm not worried about who I'm going to marry yet—if I ever get married.

MAMA *and* RUTH *If!*

MAMA Now, Bennie—

BENEATHA Oh, I probably will . . . but first I'm going to be a doctor, and George, for one, still thinks that's pretty funny. I couldn't be bothered with that. I am going to be a doctor and everybody around here better understand that!

MAMA (*Kindly*) 'Course you going to be a doctor, honey, God willing.

BENEATHA (*Drily*) God hasn't got a thing to do with it.

MAMA Beneatha—that just wasn't necessary.

BENEATHA Well—neither is God. I get sick of hearing about God.

MAMA Beneatha!

BENEATHA I mean it! I'm just tired of hearing about God all the time. What has He got to do with anything? Does he pay tuition?

MAMA You 'bout to get your fresh little jaw slapped!

RUTH That's just what she needs, all right!

BENEATHA Why? Why can't I say what I want to around here, like everybody else?

MAMA It don't sound nice for a young girl to say things like that—you wasn't brought up that way. Me and your father went to trouble to get you and Brother to church every Sunday.

BENEATHA Mama, you don't understand. It's all a matter of ideas, and God is just one idea I don't accept. It's not important. I am not going out and be immoral or commit crimes because I don't believe in God. I don't even think about it. It's just that I get tired of Him getting credit for all the things the human race achieves through its own stubborn effort. There simply is no blasted God—there is only man and it is he who makes miracles!

(MAMA *absorbs this speech, studies her daughter and rises slowly and crosses to* BENEATHA *and slaps her powerfully across the face. After, there is only silence and the daughter drops her eyes from her mother's face, and* MAMA *is very tall before her*)

MAMA Now—you say after me, in my mother's house there is still God. (*There is a long pause and* BENEATHA *stares at the floor wordlessly.* MAMA *repeats the phrase with precision and cool emotion*) In my mother's house there is still God.

BENEATHA In my mother's house there is still God.
(*A long pause*)

MAMA (*Walking away from* BENEATHA, *too disturbed for triumphant posture. Stopping and turning back to her daughter*) There are some ideas we ain't going to have in this house. Not long as I am at the head of this family.

BENEATHA Yes, ma'am.
(MAMA *walks out of the room*)

RUTH (*Almost gently, with profound understanding*) You think you a woman, Bennie—but you still a little girl. What you did was childish—so you got treated like a child.

BENEATHA I see. (*Quietly*) I also see that everybody thinks it's all right for Mama to be a tyrant. But all the tyranny in the world will never put a God in the heavens!
(*She picks up her books and goes out*)

RUTH (*Goes to* MAMA's *door*) She said she was sorry.

MAMA (*Coming out, going to her plant*) They frightens me, Ruth. My children.

RUTH You got good children, Lena. They just a little off sometimes—but they're good.

MAMA No—there's something come down between me and them that don't let us understand each other and I don't know what it is. One done almost lost his mind thinking 'bout money all the time and the other done commence to talk about things I can't seem to understand in no form or fashion. What is it that's changing, Ruth?

RUTH (*Soothingly, older than her years*) Now . . . you taking it all too seriously. You just got strong-willed children and it takes a strong woman like you to keep 'em in hand.

MAMA (*Looking at her plant and sprinkling a little water on it*) They spirited all right, my children. Got to admit they got spirit—Bennie and Walter. Like this little old plant that ain't never had enough sunshine or nothing—and look at it . . .
(*She has her back to* RUTH, *who has had to stop ironing and lean against something and put the back of her hand to her forehead*)

RUTH (*Trying to keep* MAMA *from noticing*) You . . . sure . . . loves that little old thing, don't you? . . .

MAMA Well, I always wanted me a garden like I used to see sometimes at the back of the houses down home. This plant is close as I ever got to having one. (*She looks out of the window as she replaces the plant*) Lord, ain't nothing as dreary as the view from this window on a dreary day, is there? Why ain't you singing this morning, Ruth? Sing that "No Ways Tired." That song always lifts me up so—(*She turns at last to see that* RUTH *has slipped quietly into a chair, in a state of semiconsciousness*) Ruth! Ruth honey—what's the matter with you . . . Ruth!

Curtain

THE ROYAL HUNT OF THE SUN*

PETER SHAFFER (1926–)

In Peter Shaffer's theatrical recipe, he mixes together some history and allegory, adds a theme of gold and ruin, liberal dashes of conflict, pinches of irony, symbolism, philosophy and religion. Into this he sifts and stirs two defiant and spirited characters: Pizarro, the Sixteenth Century leader of Spanish adventurers, and Atahuallpa, king of the Incas. From Mr. Shaffer's recipe evolves one of the most magic, dramatic and nutritious pièces de résistance of the Twentieth Century theater–The Royal Hunt of the Sun.

Its distinctive and tangy flavor is dispelled through Martin, now an old soldier, who recalls his earlier expeditions with Pizarro and how the latter and his men conquered the Incas, their leader, the sovereign Atahuallpa, and put him to death.

Act II, Sections XI and XII (presented below), unfold the irony whereby the prisoner Atahuallpa is victorious over the conqueror Pizarro. For it is the spiritual quality of Atahuallpa that captivates Pizarro and from which Pizarro seeks comfort and peace. The interpreter's success in getting a favorable response to these sections lies in his understanding of the irreligious, steely Pizarro and the faithful, aristocratic Atahuallpa, in the reader's ability to keep the emotionally packed situation under control and in maintaining the directness of the dialogue along with the narrative quality of Old Martin.

As the section opens we find Pizarro roped to his prisoner, Atahuallpa. Only three are present–Pizarro, Atahuallpa and Young Martin. Atahuallpa is the first to speak:

XI

ATAHUALLPA. It is no matter. They cannot kill me.

PIZARRO. Cannot?

ATAHUALLPA. Man who dies cannot kill a God who lives forever.

PIZARRO. I wouldn't bet on it, my lord.

ATAHUALLPA. Only my father can take me from here. And he would not accept me killed by men like you. Men with no word. You may be King in this land, but never God. I am God of the Four Quarters and if you kill me tonight I will rise at dawn when my Father first touches my body with light.

PIZARRO. You believe this?

ATAHUALLPA. All my people know it—it is why they have let me stay with you.

PIZARRO. They knew you could not be harmed . . .

ATAHUALLPA. So.

PIZARRO. Was this the meaning? The meaning of my dream? You were choosing me?

YOUNG MARTIN. My lord, it's just a boast. Beyond any kind of reason.

PIZARRO. Is it?

YOUNG MARTIN. How can a man die, then get up and walk away?

PIZARRO. Let's hear your creed, boy. 'I believe in Jesus Christ, the Son of God, that He suffered under Pontius Pilate, was crucified, dead and buried' . . . and what?

YOUNG MARTIN. Sir?

PIZARRO. What?

YOUNG MARTIN. 'He descended into Hell, and on the third day He rose again from the dead . . .'

PIZARRO. You don't believe it!

YOUNG MARTIN. I do! On my soul! I believe with perfect faith!

PIZARRO. But Christ's to be the only one, is that it? What if it's possible, here in a land beyond all maps and scholars, guarded by mountains up to the sky, that there were true Gods on earth, creators of true peace? Think of it! Gods, free of time.

YOUNG MARTIN. It's impossible, my lord.

PIZARRO. It's the only way to give life meaning! To blast out of time and live forever, *us*, in our own persons. This is the law: die in despair or be a God yourself! . . . Look at him: always so calm as if the teeth of life never bit him . . . or the teeth of death. What if it was really true, Martin? That I've gone God-hunting and caught one. A being who can renew his life over and over?

YOUNG MARTIN. But how can he do that, sir? How could any man?

PIZARRO. By returning over and over again to the source of life—*to the Sun!*

YOUNG MARTIN. No, sir . . .

PIZARRO. Why not? What else is a God but what we know we can't do without? The flowers that worship it, the sunflowers in their soil, are us after night, after cold and lightless days, turning our faces to it, adoring. The sun is the only God I know! We eat you to walk. We drink you to sing. Our reins loosen under you and we laugh. Even I laugh, here!

YOUNG MARTIN. General, you need rest, sir.

Pause.

PIZARRO. Yes. Yes . . . yes. (*Bitterly.*) How clever. He's understood everything I've said to him these awful months—all the secret pain he's heard—and this is his revenge. This futile joke. How he must hate me. (*Tightening the rope.*) Oh, yes, you cunning bastard! Look, Martin—behold, my God. I've got the Sun on a string! I can make it rise: (*He pulls the Inca's arm up*)—or set!

He throws the INCA *to his knees.*

YOUNG MARTIN. General . . .!

PIZARRO. I'll make you set forever! Two can joke as well as one. You want your freedom? All right, you're Free! (*He starts circling round* ATA-HUALLPA.) Walk out of the camp! They may stop you, but what's that to you? You're invulnerable. They'll knock you down but your father the Sun will pick you up again. Go on! Get up! . . . Go on! . . . Get up! . . . Go on! . . . Go on! . . . Go on! . . . Go on! . . . Go on! . . . Go on!

He breaks into a frantic gallop round and round the Inca, the rope at full stretch, ATAHUALLPA *turning with him, somersaulting, then holding him, his teeth bared with the strain, as if breaking a wild horse, until the old man tumbles exhausted to the ground. Silence follows, broken only by deep moaning from the stricken man. Quietly the Inca pulls in the rope. Then at last he speaks.*

ATAHUALLPA. Pizarro. You will die soon and you do not believe in your God. That is why you tremble and keep no word. Believe in me. I will give you a word and fill you with joy. For you I will do a great thing. I will swallow death and spit it out of me.

Pause. This whole scene stays very still.

PIZARRO. (*Whispering.*) You cannot.

ATAHUALLPA. Yes, if my father wills it.

PIZARRO. How if he does not?

ATAHUALLPA. He will. His people still need me. Believe.

PIZARRO. Impossible.

ATAHUALLPA. Believe.

PIZARRO. How? . . . How? . . .

ATAHUALLPA. First you must take my priest power.

PIZARRO. (*Quietly.*) Oh, no! you go or not as you choose, but I take nothing more in this world.

ATAHUALLPA. Take my word. Take my peace. I will put water to your wound, old man. Believe.

A long silence. The lights are now fading round them.

PIZARRO. What must I do?

Enter OLD MARTIN.

OLD MARTIN. How can I speak now and hope to be believed? As night fell like a hand over the eye, and great white stars sprang out over the snow-rim of our world, Atahuallpa confessed Pizarro. He did it in the Inca manner. He took Ichu grass and a stone. Into the Ichu grass the General spoke for an hour or more. None heard what he said save the King, who could not understand it. Then the King struck him on the back with the stone, cast away the grass, and made the signs for purification.

PIZARRO. If any blessing is in me, take it and go. Fly up, my bird, and come to me again.

The INCA *takes a knife from* YOUNG MARTIN *and cuts the rope. Then he walks upstage. All the* OFFICERS *and* MEN *enter. During the following a pole is set up above, in the sun, and* ATAHUALLPA *is hauled up into it.*

XII

OLD MARTIN. The Inca was tried by a court quickly mustered. He was accused of usurping the throne and killing his brother; of idolatry and of having more than one wife. On all these charges he was found—

ESTETE. Guilty.

VALVERDE. Guilty.

DE CANDIA. Guilty.

DIEGO. Guilty.

OLD MARTIN. Sentence to be carried out the same night.

ESTETE. Death by burning.

Lights up above in the sun.

ATAHUALLPA *gives a great cry.*

PIZARRO. No! He must not burn! His body must stay in one piece.

VALVERDE. Let him repent his idolatry and be baptized a Christian. He will receive the customary mercy.

OLD MARTIN. Strangling instead.

PIZARRO. You must do it! Deny your Father! If you don't, you will be burnt to ashes. There will be no flesh left for him to warm alive at dawn.

YOUNG MARTIN *screams and runs from the stage in horror.*

You must do it.

In a gesture of surrender the Inca king kneels.

OLD MARTIN. So it was that Atahuallpa came to Christ.

Enter DE NIZZA, *above, with a bowl of water.*

DE NIZZA. I baptise you Juan de Atahuallpa, in honour of Juan the Baptist, whose sacred day this is.

ESTETE. The twenty-ninth of August, 1533.

VALVERDE. And may Our Lord and His angels receive your soul with joy!

SOLDIERS. Amen!

The Inca suddenly raises his head, tears off his clothes and intones in a great voice:

ATAHUALLPA. INTI! INTI! INTI!

VALVERDE. What does he say?

PIZARRO. (*Intoning also.*) The Sun. The Sun. The Sun.

VALVERDE. *Kill him!*

Soldiers haul ATAHUALLPA *to his feet and hold him to the stake.* RODAS *slips a string over his head and while all the Spaniards recite the Latin Creed below, and great howls of 'Inca!' come from the darkness, the Sovereign King of Peru is garrotted. His screams and struggles subside; his body falls slack. His executioners hand the corpse down to the soldiers below, who carry it to the centre of the stage and drop it at* PIZARRO's *feet. Then all leave save the old man, who stands as if turned to stone. A drum beats. Slowly, in semi-darkness, the stage fills with all the Indians, robed in black and terracotta, wearing the great golden funeral masks of ancient Peru. Grouped round the prone body, they intone a strange Chant of Resur-*

*rection, punctuated by hollow beats on the drums and by long, long
silences in which they turn their immense triangular eyes enquiringly up
to the sky. Finally, after three great cries appear to summon it, the sun
rises. Its rays fall on the body.* ATAHUALLPA *does not move. The masked
men watch in amazement—disbelief—finally, despair. Slowly, with hanging, dejected heads, they shuffle away.* PIZARRO *is left alone with the dead
King. He contemplates him. A silence. Then suddenly he slaps it viciously,
and the body rolls over on its back.*

PIZARRO. Cheat! You've cheated me! Cheat . . .

*For a moment his old body is racked with sobs; then, surprised, he feels
tears on his cheek. He examines them. The sunlight brightens on his head.*
What's this? What is it? In all your life you never made one of these,
I know, and I not till this minute. Look. (*He kneels to show the dead
Inca.*) Ah, no. You have no eyes for me now, Atahuallpa: they are dusty
balls of amber I can tap on. You have no peace for me, Atahuallpa: the
birds still scream in your forest. You have no joy for me, Atahuallpa, my
boy: the only joy is in death. I lived between two hates: I die between
two darks: blind eyes and a blind sky. And yet you saw once. The sky
sees nothing, but you saw. Is there comfort there? The sky knows no
feeling, but we know them, that's sure. Martin's hope, and de Soto's
honour, and your trust—your trust which hunted me: we alone make
these. That's some marvel, yes, some marvel. To sit in a great cold
silence, and sing out sweet with just our own warm breath: that's some
marvel, surely. To make water in a sand world: surely, surely . . . God's
just a name on your nail; and naming begins cries and cruelties. But to
live without hope of after, and make whatever God there is, oh, that's
some immortal business surely . . . I'm tired. Where are you? You're so
cold. I'd warm you if I could. But there's no warming now, not ever
now, not ever now. I'm colding too. There's a snow of death falling all
round us. You can almost see it. It's over, lad, I'm coming after you.
There's nothing but peace to come. We'll be put into the same earth,
father and son in our own land. And that sun will roam uncaught over
his empty pasture.

OLD MARTIN. So fell Peru. We gave her greed, hunger and the Cross: three
gifts for the civilized life. The family groups that sang on the terraces
are gone. In their place slaves shuffle underground and they don't sing
there. Peru is a silent country, frozen in avarice. So fell Spain, gorged
with gold; distended; now dying.

PIZARRO. (*Singing.*) 'Where is her heart, O little finch' . . .

OLD MARTIN. And so fell you, General, my master, whom men called the
Son of His Own Deeds. He was killed later in a quarrel with his partner
who brought up the reinforcements. But to speak truth, he sat down
that morning and never really got up again.

PIZARRO. (*Singing.*) 'Where are her plumes, O little finch' . . .

OLD MARTIN. I'm the only one left now of that company: landowner—slave-
owner—and forty years from any time of hope. It put out a good blos-

som, but it was shaken off rough. After that I reckon the fruit always comes sour, and doesn't sweeten up much with age.

PIZARRO. (*Singing.*) 'She is cut up, O little finch. For stealing grain, O little finch' . . .

OLD MARTIN. General, you did for me, and now I've done for you. And there's no joy in that. Or in anything now. But then there's no joy in the world could match for me what I had when I first went with you across the water to find the gold country. And no pain like losing it. Save you all.

He goes out. PIZARRO *lies beside the body of* ATAHUALLPA *and quietly sings to it.*

PIZARRO. (*Singing.*)

> See, see the fate, O little finch,
> Of robber birds, O little finch.

The sun glares at the audience.

ꜫ Essays

FRANCIS BACON (1561–1626)

OF YOUTH AND AGE

A man that is young in years may be old in hours, if he have lost no time; but that happeneth rarely. Generally, youth is like the first cogitations, not so wise as the second; for there is a youth in thoughts as well as in ages; and yet the invention of young men is more lively than that of old, and imaginations stream into their minds better, and, as it were, more divinely. Natures that have much heat, and great and violent desires and perturbations, are not ripe for action till they have passed the meridian of their years: as it was with Julius Cæsar and Septimius Severus; of the latter of whom it is said, "Juventutem egit erroribus, imo furoribus plenam;"[1] and yet he was the ablest emperor, almost, of all the list; but reposed natures may do well in youth, as it is seen in Augustus Cæsar, Cosmus Duke of Florence, Gaston de Foix,[2] and others. On the other side, heat and vivacity in age is an excellent composition for business. Young men are fitter to invent than to judge, fitter for execution than for counsel, and fitter for new projects than for settled business; for the experience of age, in things that fall within the compass of it, directeth them; but in new things abuseth them. The errors of young men are the ruin of business; but the errors of aged men amount but to this, that more might have been done, or sooner.

Young men, in the conduct and manage of actions, embrace more than they can hold, stir more than they can quiet; fly to the end, without consideration of the means and degrees; pursue some few principles which they have chanced upon absurdly; care not to innovate, which draws unknown inconveniences; use extreme remedies at first; and that, which doubleth all errors, will not acknowledge or retract them, like an unready horse, that will neither stop nor turn. Men of age object too much, consult too long, adventure too little, repent too soon, and seldom drive business home to the full period, but content themselves with a mediocrity of success. Certainly, it is good to compound employments of both; for that will be good for the present, because the virtues of either age may correct the defects of both; and good for succession, that young men may be learners, while men in age are actors; and, lastly, good for externe accidents, because authority followeth old men, and favor and popularity youth; but, for the moral part, perhaps, youth will have the preëminence, as age hath

---

[1] "He passed his youth full of errors, of madness even."–*Spartian. Vit. Sev.*

[2] He was nephew of Louis the Twelfth of France, and commanded the French armies in Italy against the Spaniards. After a brilliant career, he was killed at the battle of Ravenna, in 1512.

for the politic. A certain rabbin, upon the text, "Your young men shall see visions, and your old men shall dream dreams,"[1] inferreth that young men are admitted nearer to God than old, because vision is a clearer revelation than a dream; and, certainly, the more a man drinketh of the world, the more it intoxicateth; and age doth profit rather in the powers of understanding, than in the virtues of the will and affections. There be some have an over-early ripeness in their years, which fadeth betimes; these are, first, such as have brittle wits, the edge whereof is soon turned; such as was Hermogenes[2] the rhetorician, whose books are exceedingly subtle; who afterwards waxed stupid. A second sort is of those that have some natural dispositions, which have better grace in youth than in age; such as is a fluent and luxuriant speech, which becomes youth well, but not age; so Tully saith of Hortensius: "Idem manebat, neque idem decebat."[3] The third is of such as take too high a strain at the first, and are magnanimous more than tract of years can uphold; as was Scipio Africanus, of whom Livy saith, in effect, "Ultima primis cedebant."[4]

OF STUDIES

Studies serve for delight, for ornament, and for ability. Their chief use for delight, is in privateness and retiring; for ornament, is in discourse; and for ability, is in the judgment and disposition of business; for expert men can execute, and perhaps judge of particulars one by one; but the general counsels, and the plots and marshalling of affairs, come best from those that are learned. To spend too much time in studies, is sloth; to use them too much for ornament, is affectation; to make judgment wholly by their rules, is the humor of a scholar. They perfect nature, and are perfected by experience; for natural abilities are like natural plants, that need pruning by study; and studies themselves do give forth directions too much at large, except they be bounded in by experience. Crafty men contemn studies, simple men admire them, and wise men use them; for they teach not their own use; but that is a wisdom without them and above them, won by observation. Read not to contradict and confute, nor to believe and take for granted, nor to find talk and discourse, but to weigh and consider. Some books are to be tasted, others to be swallowed, and some few to be chewed and digested; that is, some books are to be read only in parts; others to be

---

1 Joel ii. 28, quoted Acts ii. 17.
2 He lived in the second century after Christ, and is said to have lost his memory at the age of twenty-five.
3 "He remained the same, but *with the advance of years* was not so becoming."— *Cic. Brut.* 95.
4 "The close was unequal to the beginning." This quotation is not correct; the words are: "Memorabilior prima pars vitæ quam postrema fuit,"—"The first part of his life was more distinguished than the latter."—*Livy* xxxviii. ch. 53.

read, but not curiously;[1] and some few to be read wholly, and with diligence and attention. Some books also may be read by deputy, and extracts made of them by others; but that would be only in the less important arguments and the meaner sort of books; else distilled books are, like common distilled waters, flashy[2] things. Reading maketh a full man; conference a ready man; and writing an exact man; and, therefore, if a man write little, he had need have a great memory; if he confer little, he had need have a present wit; and if he read little, he had need have much cunning, to seem to know that he doth not. Histories make men wise; poets, witty; the mathematics, subtile; natural philosophy, deep; moral, grave; logic and rhetoric, able to contend: "Abeunt studia in mores;"[3] nay, there is no stand or impediment in the wit, but may be wrought out by fit studies. Like as diseases of the body may have appropriate exercises, bowling is good for the stone and reins, shooting for the lungs and breast, gentle walking for the stomach, riding for the head and the like; so, if a man's wit be wandering, let him study the mathematics; for in demonstrations, if his wit be called away never so little, he must begin again; if his wit be not apt to distinguish or find difference, let him study the schoolmen, for they are "Cymini sectores."[4] If he be not apt to beat over matters, and to call up one thing to prove and illustrate another, let him study the lawyers' cases; so every defect of the mind may have a special receipt.

[1] Attentively.
[2] Vapid; without taste or spirit.
[3] "Studies become habits."
[4] "Splitters of cummin-seed"; or, as we now say, "splitters of straws," or "hairs." Butler says of Hudibras:—
"He could distinguish and divide
A hair 'twixt south and southwest side."

SAMUEL BUTLER (1612–1680)

A PROUD MAN

Is a Fool in Fermentation, that swells and boils over like a Porridge-Pot. He sets out his Feathers like an Owl, to swell and seem bigger than he is. He is troubled with a Tumour and Inflammation of Self-Conceit, that renders every Part of him stiff and uneasy. He has given himself Sympathetic Love-Powder, that works upon him to Dotage, and has transformed him into his own Mistress. He is his own Gallant, and makes most passionate Address to his own dear Perfections. He commits Idolatry to himself, and worships his own Image; though there is no Soul living of his Church but himself, yet he believes as the Church believes, and maintains his Faith with the Obstinacy of a *Fanatic*. He is his own Favourite, and advances himself not only above his Merit, but all Mankind; is both *Damon* and *Pythias* to his own dear self, and values his Crony above his soul. He gives Place to no Man but himself, and that with very great Distance to all others, whom he esteems not worthy to approach him. He believes whatsoever he has receives a Value in being his; as a Horse in a Nobleman's Stable will bear a greater Price than in a common Market. He is so proud, that he is as hard to be acquainted with himself as with others; for he is very apt to forget who he is, and knows himself only superficially; therefore he treats himself civilly as a stranger with Ceremony and Compliment, but admits of no Privacy. He strives to look bigger than himself, as well as others, and is no better than his own Parasite and Flatterer. A little Flood will make a shallow Torrent swell above its Banks, and rage, and foam, and yield a roaring Noise, while a deep silent Stream glides quietly on. So a vain-glorious insolent proud Man swells with a little frail Prosperity, grows big and loud, and overflows his Bounds, and when he sinks, leaves Mud and Dirt behind him. His Carriage is as glorious and haughty, as if he were advanced upon Men's Shoulders, or tumbled over their Heads like Knipperdolling. He fancies himself a Colosse, and so he is, for his Head holds no Proportion to his Body, and his foundation is lesser than his upper Stories. We can naturally take no view of our selves, unless we look downwards, to teach us how humble Admirers we ought to be of our own Values. The slighter and less solid his Materials are, the more Room they take up, and make him swell the bigger; as Feathers and Cotton will stuff Cushions better than Things of more close and solid Parts.

THE RUDE MAN

Is an *Ostro-Goth*, or northern *Hun*, that wheresoever he comes, invades and all the World does overrun, without Distinction of Age, Sex, or Quality. He has no Regard to any Thing but his own Humour, and that he expects should pass every where without asking Leave, or being asked wherefore, as if he had a Safe-conduct for his Rudeness. He rolls up himself, like a Hedgehog, in his Prickles, and is as untractable to all that come near him. He is an ill-designed Piece, built after the rustic Order; and all his Parts look too big for their Height. He is so ill contrived, that that which should be the Top in all regular Structures, i. e. Confidence, is his Foundation. He has neither Doctrine nor Discipline in him, like a fanatic Church, but is guided by the very same Spirit, that dipped the Herd of Swine in the Sea. He was not bred but reared, not brought up to Hand, but suffered to run wild, and take after his Kind, as other People of the Pasture do. He takes that Freedom in all Places, as if he were not at Liberty, but had broken loose, and expected to be tied up again. He does not eat but feed, and when he drinks goes to Water. The old *Romans* beat the barbarous Part of the World into Civility; but if he had lived in those Times he had been invincible to all Attempts of that Nature, and harder to be subdued and governed than a Province. He eats his Bread, according to the Curse, with the Sweat of his Brows, and takes as much Pains at a Meal as if he earn'd it; puffs and blows like a Horse that eats Provender, and crams his Throat like a screwed Gun with a Bullet bigger than the Bore. His Tongue runs perpetually over every Thing that comes in its Way, without Regard of what, where, or to whom; and nothing but a greater Rudeness than his own can stand before it; and he uses it to as sloven-by Purposes as a Dog does, that licks his Sores and the Dirt off his Feet. He is the best Instance of the Truth of *Pythagoras's* Doctrine, for his Soul past through all Sorts of brute Beasts before it came to him, and still retains something of the Nature of every one.

JOSEPH ADDISON (1672–1719)
AND SIR RICHARD STEELE (1672–1729)

THE TATLER

No. 163. THURSDAY, APRIL 25, 1710.

Idem inficeto est inficetior rure
Simul poemata attigit; neque idem unquam
Æquè est beatus, ac poema cum scribit:
Tam gaudet in se, tamque se ipse miratur.
Nimirum idem omnes fallimur; neque est quisquam
Quem non in aliqua re videre *Suffenum*
Possis———CATUL. DE SUFFENO.

Will's Coffee-house, April 24.

I yesterday came hither about two hours before the company generally make their appearance, with a design to read over all the newspapers; but upon my sitting down, I was accosted by Ned Softly, who saw me from a corner in the other end of the room, where I found he had been writing something. Mr. Bickerstaffe, (says he) I observe by a late paper of yours, that you and I are just of a humour; for you must know, of all impertinencies, there is nothing which I so much hate as news. I never read a Gazette in my life; and never trouble my head about our armies, whether they win or lose, or in what part of the world they lie encamped. Without giving me time to reply, he drew a paper of verses out of his pocket, telling me, that he had something which would entertain me more agreeably, and that he would desire my judgment upon every line, for that we had time enough before us till the company came in.

Ned Softly is a very pretty poet, and a great admirer of easy lines. Waller is his favourite: and as that admirable writer has the best and worst verses of any among our English poets, Ned Softly has got all the bad ones without book, which he repeats upon occasion, to show his reading, and garnish his conversation. Ned is indeed a true English reader, incapable of relishing the great and masterly strokes of this art; but wonderfully pleased with the little Gothic ornaments of epigrammatical conceits, turns, points, and quibbles, which are so frequent in the most admired of our English poets, and practised by those who want genius and strength to represent, after the manner of the ancients, simplicity in its natural beauty and perfection.

Finding myself unavoidably engaged in such a conversation, I was resolved to turn my pain into a pleasure, and to divert myself as well as I could with so very odd a fellow. 'You must understand, (says Ned) that the sonnet I am going to read to you was written upon a lady, who showed me

284

some verses of her own making, and is, perhaps, the best poet of our age. But you shall hear it.' Upon which he began to read as follows:

'TO MIRA ON HER INCOMPARABLE POEM.

I.

'When dress'd in laurel wreaths you shine,
  And tune your soft melodious notes,
You seem a sister of the Nine,
  Or Phœbus' self in petticoats.

II.

'I fancy, when your song you sing,
  (Your song you sing with so much art)
Your pen was pluck'd from Cupid's wing;
  For ah! it wounds me like his dart.'

'Why, (says I) this is a little nosegay of conceits, a very lump of salt: every verse hath something in it that piques; and then the dart in the last line is certainly as pretty a sting in the tail of an epigram (for so I think your critics call it) as ever entered into the thought of a poet.' 'Dear Mr. Bickerstaffe, (says he) shaking me by the hand, every body knows you to be a judge of these things; and to tell you truly, I read over Roscommon's translation of Horace's Art of Poetry three several times, before I sat down to write the sonnet which I have shown you. But you shall hear it again, and pray observe every line of it, for not one of them shall pass without your approbation.

'When dress'd in laurel wreaths you shine.'

'That is, (says he) when you have your garland on; when you are writing verses.' To which I replied, 'I know your meaning a metaphor!' 'The same,' said he, and went on:

'And tune your soft melodious notes.'

'Pray observe the gliding of that verse; there is scarce a consonant in it: I took care to make it run upon liquids. Give me your opinion of it.' 'Truly, (said I) I think it is as good as the former.' 'I am very glad to hear you say so, (says he:) but mind the next:'

'You seem a sister of the Nine.'

'That is, (says he) you seem a sister of the Muses; for if you look into ancient authors, you will find it was their opinion, that there were nine of them.' 'I remember it very well, (said I;) but pray proceed.'

'Or Phœbus' self in petticoats.'

'Phœbus (says he) was the god of poetry. These little instances, Mr. Bickerstaffe, show a gentleman's reading. Then to take off from the air of learning, which Phœbus and the Muses have given to this first stanza, you may observe, how it falls all of a sudden into the familiar; in petticoats!

'Or Phœbus' self in petticoats.'

Let us now, (says I) enter upon the second stanza. I find the first line is still a continuation of the metaphor.

'I fancy when your song you sing.'

It is very right, (says he;) but pray observe the turn of words in those two lines. I was a whole hour in adjusting of them, and have still a doubt upon me, whether in the second line it should be, 'Your song you sing;' or, 'You sing your song.' You shall hear them both;'

> 'I fancy when your song you sing,
>   (Your song you sing with so much art.)'
>   OR,
> 'I fancy when your song you sing,
>   (You sing your song with so much art.)'

'Truly, (said I) the turn is so natural either way, that you have made me almost giddy with it.' 'Dear sir, (said he, grasping me by the hand,) you have a great deal of patience; but pray what do you think of the next verse? '

'Your pen was pluck'd from Cupid's wing.'

'Think! (says I;) I think you have made Cupid look like a little goose.' 'That was my meaning, (says he) I think the ridicule is well enough hit off. But we now come to the last, which sums up the whole matter.'

'For ah! it wounds me like his dart.'

'Pray how do you like that *ah?* doth it not make a pretty figure in that place? *Ah!* it looks as if I felt the dart, and cried out at being pricked with it.'

'For ah! it wounds me like his dart.'

'My friend Dick Easy (continued he) assured me, he would rather have written that *ah!* than to^a have been the author of the Æneid. He indeed objected, that I made Mira's pen like a quill in one of the lines, and like a dart in the other. But as to that——' 'Oh!as to that, (says I) it is but supposing Cupid to be like a porcupine, and his quills and darts will be the same thing.' He was going to embrace me for the hint; but half a dozen critics coming into the room, whose faces he did not like, he conveyed the sonnet into his pocket, and whispered me in the ear, he would show it me again as soon as his man had written it over fair.

SPECTATOR

No. 387. SATURDAY, MAY 24, 1712.

Quid purè tranquillet.—   HOR. EPIST. i. 18. 102.

What calms the breast, and makes the mind serene.

In my last Saturday's paper I spoke of cheerfulness as it is a moral habit of the mind, and accordingly mentioned such moral motives as are apt to cherish and keep alive this happy temper in the soul of man: I shall now consider cheerfulness in its natural state, and reflect on those motives to it which are indifferent either as to virtue or vice.

Cheerfulness is, in the first place, the best promoter of health. Repinings, and secret murmurs of heart, give imperceptible strokes to those delicate fibres of which the vital parts are composed, and wear out the machine insensibly; not to mention those violent ferments which they stir up in the blood, and those irregular disturbed motions which they raise in the animal spirits. I scarce remember, in my own observation, to have met with any old men, or with such, who, to use our English phrase, wear well, that had not at least a certain indolence in their humour, if not a more than ordinary gayety and cheerfulness of heart. The truth of it is, health and cheerfulness mutually beget each other; with this difference, that we seldom meet with a great degree of health which is not attended with a certain cheerfulness, but very often see cheerfulness where there is no great degree of health.

Cheerfulness bears the same friendly regard to the mind as to the body. It banishes all anxious care and discontent, soothes and composes the passions, and keeps the soul in a perpetual calm. But having already touched on this last consideration, I shall here take notice, that the world in which we are placed is filled with innumerable objects that are proper to raise and keep alive this happy temper of mind.

If we consider the world in its subserviency to man, one would think it was made for our use; but if we consider it in its natural beauty and harmony, one would be apt to conclude it was made for our pleasure. The sun, which is as the great soul of the universe, and produces all the necessaries of life, has a particular influence in cheering the mind of man, and making the heart glad.

Those several living creatures which are made for our service or sustenance, at the same time either fill the woods with their music, furnish us with game, or raise pleasing ideas in us by the delightfulness of their appearance. Fountains, lakes, and rivers, are as refreshing to the imagination as to the soil through which they pass.

There are writers of great distinction, who have made it an argument for Providence, that the whole earth is covered with green, rather than with any other colour, as being such a right mixture of light and shade, that it comforts and strengthens the eye, instead of weakening or grieving it. For this reason, several painters have a green cloth hanging near them, to ease the eye upon, after too great an application to their colouring. A famous modern philosopher accounts for it in the following manner. All colours that are more luminous, overpower and dissipate the animal spirits which are employed in sight; on the contrary, those that are more obscure, do not give the animal spirits a sufficient exercise; whereas the rays that produce in us the idea of green, fall upon the eye in such a due proportion, that they give animal spirits their proper play, and, by keeping up the struggles in a just balance, excite a very pleasing and agreeable sensation. Let the cause be what it will, the effect is certain; for which reason, the poets ascribe to this particular colour the epithet of cheerful.

To consider further this double end in the works of nature, and how they
are at the same time both useful and entertaining, we find that the most
important parts in the vegetable world are those which are the most beautiful. These are the seeds by which the several races of plants are propagated
and continued, and which are always lodged in flowers or blossoms. Nature
seems to hide her principal design, and to be industrious in making the earth
gay and delightful, while she is carrying on her great work, and intent upon
her own preservation. The husbandman, after the same manner, is employed
in laying out the whole country into a kind of garden or landscape, and
making every thing smile about him, whilst in reality he thinks of nothing
but of the harvest, and the increase which is to arise from it.

We may further observe how Providence has taken care to keep up this
cheerfulness in the mind of man, by having formed it after such a manner,
as to make it capable of conceiving delight from several objects which seem
to have very little use in them; as from the wildness of rocks and deserts,
and the like grotesque parts of nature. Those who are versed in philosophy
may still carry this consideration higher, by observing, that if matter had
appeared to us endowed only with those real qualities which it actually
possesses, it would have made but a very joyless and uncomfortable figure;
and why has Providence given it a power of producing in us such imaginary qualities, as tastes and colours, sounds and smells, heat and cold, but
that man, while he is conversant in the lower stations of nature, might have
his mind cheered and delighted with agreeable sensations? In short, the
whole universe is a kind of theatre, filled with objects that either raise in us
pleasure, amusement, or admiration.

The reader's own thoughts will suggest to him the vicissitude of day and
night, the change of seasons, with all that variety of scenes which diversify
the face of nature, and fill the mind with a perpetual succession of beautiful
and pleasing images.

I shall not here mention the several entertainments of art, with the
pleasures of friendship, books, conversation, and other accidental diversions
of life, because I would only take notice of such incitements to a cheerful
temper as offer themselves to persons of all ranks and conditions, and which
may sufficiently show us that Providence did not design this world should
be filled with murmurs and repinings, or that the heart of man should be
involved in gloom and melancholy.

I the more inculcate this cheerfulness of temper as it is a virtue in which
our countrymen are observed to be more deficient than any other nation.
Melancholy is a kind of demon, that haunts our island, and often conveys
herself to us in an easterly wind. A celebrated French novelist, in opposition
to those who begin their romance with the flowery season of the year,
enters on his story thus: 'In the gloomy month of November, when the
people of England hang and drown themselves, a disconsolate lover walked
out into the fields,' &c.

Every one ought to fence against the temper of his climate or constitu-
tion, and frequently to indulge in himself those considerations which may

give him a serenity of mind, and enable him to bear up cheerfully against those little evils and misfortunes which are common to human nature, and which, by a right improvement of them, will produce a satiety of joy, and an uninterrupted happiness.

At the same time that I would engage my reader to consider the world in its most agreeable lights, I must own there are many evils which naturally spring up amidst the entertainments that are provided for us; but these, if rightly considered, should be far from overcasting the mind with sorrow, or destroying that cheerfulness of temper which I have been recommending. This interspersion of evil with good, and pain with pleasure, in the works of nature, is very truly ascribed by Mr. Locke, in his *Essay on Human Understanding*, to a moral reason, in the following words:—

"Beyond all this, we may find another reason why God hath scattered up and down several degrees of pleasure and pain, in all the things that environ and affect us, and blended them together, in almost all that our thoughts and senses have to do with; that we, finding imperfection, dissatisfaction, and want of complete happiness, in all the enjoyments which the creatures can afford us, might be led to seek it in the enjoyment of Him with whom 'there is fulness of joy, and at whose right hand are pleasures for evermore.' "

L

SAMUEL JOHNSON (1709–1784)

THE RAMBLER

NUMB. 188. SATURDAY, *January* 4, 1752.

 —*Si te colo, Sexte, non amabo.*   MART.

The more I honour thee, the less I love.

None of the desires dictated by vanity is more general, or less blameable, than that of being distinguished for the arts of conversation. Other accomplishments may be possessed without opportunity of exerting them, or wanted without danger that the defect can often be remarked; but as no man can live, otherwise than in an hermitage, without hourly pleasure or vexation, from the fondness or neglect of those about him, the faculty of giving pleasure is of continual use. Few are more frequently envied than those who have the power of forcing attention whereever they come, whose entrance is considered as a promise cf felicity, and whose departure is lamented, like the recess of the sun from northern climates, as a privation of all that enlivens fancy, or inspirits gaiety.

It is apparent, that to excellence in this valuable art, some peculiar qualifications are necessary; for every one's experience will inform him, that the pleasure which men are able to give in conversation, holds no stated proportion to their knowledge or their virtue. Many find their way to the tables and the parties of those who never consider them as of the least importance in any other place; we have all, at one time or other, been content to love those whom we could not esteem, and been persuaded to try the dangerous experiment of admitting him for a companion, whom we knew to be too ignorant for a counsellor, and too treacherous for a friend.

I question whether some abatement of character is not necessary to general acceptance. Few spend their time with much satisfaction under the eye of uncontestable superiority; and therefore, among those whose presence is courted at assemblies of jollity, there are seldom found men eminently distinguished for powers or acquisitions. The wit whose vivacity condemns slower tongues to silence, the scholar whose knowledge allows no man to fancy that he instructs him, the critick who suffers no fallacy to pass undetected, and the reasoner who condemns the idle to thought, and the negligent to attention, are generally praised and feared, reverenced and avoided.

He that would please must rarely aim at such excellence as depresses his hearers in their own opinion, or debars them from the hope of contributing reciprocally to the entertainment of the company. Merriment, extorted by sallies of imagination, sprightliness of remark, or quickness of reply, is too often what the Latins call, the Sardinian Laughter, a distortion of the face without gladness of heart.

For this reason, no style of conversation is more extensively acceptable than the narrative. He who has stored his memory with slight anecdotes, private incidents, and personal peculiarities, seldom fails to find his audience favorable. Almost every man listens with eagerness to contemporary history; for almost every man has some real or imaginary connexion with a celebrated character; some desire to advance or oppose a rising name. Vanity often co-operates with curiosity. He that is a hearer in one place, qualifies himself to become a speaker in another; for though he cannot comprehend a series of argument, or transport the volatile spirit of wit without evaporation, he yet thinks himself able to treasure up the various incidents of a story, and pleases his hopes with the information which he shall give to some inferior society.

Narratives are for the most part heard without envy, because they are not supposed to imply any intellectual qualities above the common rate. To be acquainted with facts not yet echoed by plebeian mouths, may happen to one man as well as to another; and to relate them when they are known, has in appearance so little difficulty, that every one concludes himself equal to the task.

But it is not easy, and in some situations of life not possible, to accumulate such a stock of materials as may support the expence of continual narration; and it frequently happens, that they who attempt this method of ingratiating themselves, please only at the first interview; and, for want of new supplies of intelligence, wear out their stories by continual repetition.

There would be, therefore, little hope of obtaining the praise of a good companion, were it not to be gained by more compendious methods; but such is the kindness of mankind to all, except those who aspire to real merit and rational dignity, that every understanding may find some way to excite benevolence; and whoever is not envied may learn the art of procuring love. We are willing to be pleased, but are not willing to admire; we favour the mirth or officiousness that solicits our regard, but oppose the worth of spirit that enforces it.

The first place among those that please, because they desire only to please, is due to the *merry fellow*, whose laugh is loud, and whose voice is strong; who is ready to echo every jest with obstreperous approbation, and countenance every frolick with vociferations of applause. It is not necessary to a merry fellow to have in himself any fund of jocularity, or force of conception; it is sufficient that he always appears in the highest exaltation of gladness, for the greater part of mankind are gay or serious by infection, and follow without resistance the attraction of example.

Next to the merry fellow is the *good-natured man*, a being generally without benevolence, or any other virtue, than such as indolence and insensibility confer. The characteristick of a good-natured man is to bear a joke; to sit unmoved and unaffected amidst noise and turbulence, profaneness and obscenity; to hear every tale without contradiction; to endure insult without reply; and to follow the stream of folly, whatever course it shall happen to take. The good-natured man is commonly the darling of the petty wits, with whom they exercise themselves in the rudiments of raillery; for he never takes advantage of failings, nor disconcerts a puny satirist with unexpected sarcasms; but while the glass continues to circulate, contentedly bears the expence of uninterrupted laughter, and retires rejoicing at his own importance.

The *modest man* is a companion of a yet lower rank, whose only power of giving pleasure is not to interrupt it. The modest man satisfies himself with peaceful silence, which all his companions are candid enough to consider as proceeding not from inability to speak, but willingness to hear.

Many, without being able to attain any general character of excellence, have some single art of entertainment which serves them as a passport through the world. One I have known for fifteen years the darling of a weekly club, because every night, precisely at eleven, he begins his favourite song, and during the vocal performance, by corresponding motions of his hand, chalks out a giant upon the wall. Another has endeared himself to a long succession of acquaintances by sitting among them with his wig reversed; another by contriving to smut the nose of any stranger who was to be initiated in the club; another by purring like a cat, and then pretending to be frighted; and another by yelping like a hound, and calling to the drawers to drive out the dog.

Such are the arts by which cheerfulness is promoted, and sometimes friendship established; arts, which those who despise them should not rigorously blame, except when they are practised at the expence of innocence; for it is always necessary to be loved, but not always necessary to be reverenced.

CHARLES LAMB (1775–1834)

BARBARA S——.*

On the noon of the 14th of November, 1743 or 4, I forget which it was, just as the clock had struck one, Barbara S—, with her accustomed punctuality, ascended the long rambling staircase, with awkward interposed landing-places, which led to the office, or rather a sort of box with a desk in it, whereat sat the then Treasurer of (what few of our readers may remember) the Old Bath Theatre. All over the island it was the custom, and remains so I believe to this day, for the players to receive their weekly stipend on the Saturday. It was not much that Barbara had to claim.

This little maid had just entered her eleventh year; but her important station at the theatre, as it seemed to her, with the benefits which she felt to accrue from her pious application of her small earnings, had given an air of womanhood to her steps and to her behaviour. You would have taken her to have been at least five years older.

Till latterly she had merely been employed in choruses, or where children were wanted to fill up the scene. But the manager, observing a diligence and adroitness in her above her age, had for some few months past intrusted to her the performance of whole parts. You may guess the self-consequence of the promoted Barbara. She had already drawn tears in young Arthur; had rallied Richard with infantine petulance in the Duke of York; and in her turn had rebuked that petulance when she was Prince of Wales. She would have done the elder child in Morton's pathetic after-piece to the life; but as yet the "Children in the Wood" was not.

Long after this little girl was grown an aged woman, I have seen some of these small parts, each making two or three pages at most, copied out in the rudest hand of the then prompter, who doubtless transcribed a little more carefully and fairly for the grown-up tragedy ladies of the establishment. But such as they were, blotted and scrawled, as for a child's use, she kept them all; and in the zenith of her after reputation it was a delightful sight to behold them bound up in costliest Morocco, each single—each small part making a *book*—with fine clasps, gilt-splashed, &c. She had conscientiously kept them as they had been delivered to her; not a blot had been effaced or tampered with. They were precious to her for their affecting remembrancings. They were her principia, her rudiments; the elementary atoms; the little steps by which she pressed forward to perfection. "What," she

* From *The Last Essays of Elia*, by Charles Lamb. Published by E. P. Dutton & Co., Inc. in the Everyman's Library Edition. Reprinted by permission.

would say, "could Indian rubber, or a pumice stone, have done for these darlings?"

I am in no hurry to begin my story—indeed I have little or none to tell—so I will just mention an observation of hers connected with that interesting time.

Not long before she died I had been discoursing with her on the quantity of real present emotion which a great tragic performer experiences during acting. I ventured to think, that though in the first instance such players must have possessed the feelings which they so powerfully called up in others, yet by frequent repetition those feelings must become deadened in great measure, and the performer trust to the memory of past emotion, rather than express a present one. She indignantly repelled the notion, that with a truly great tragedian the operation, by which such effects were produced upon an audience, could ever degrade itself into what was purely mechanical. With much delicacy, avoiding to instance in her *self*-experience, she told me, that so long ago as when she used to play the part of the Little Son to Mrs Porter's Isabella, (I think it was) when that impressive actress has been bending over her in some heart-rending colloquy, she has felt real hot tears come trickling from her, which (to use her powerful expression) have perfectly scalded her back.

I am not quite so sure that it was Mrs Porter; but it was some great actress of that day. The name is indifferent; but the fact of the scalding tears I most distinctly remember . . .

As I was about to say—at the desk of the then treasurer of the old Bath theatre—not Diamond's—presented herself the little Barbara S—.

The parents of Barbara had been in reputable circumstances. The father had practised, I believe, as an apothecary in the town. But his practice, from causes which I feel my own infirmity too sensibly that way to arraign—or perhaps from that pure infelicity which accompanies some people in their walk through life, and which it is impossible to lay at the door of imprudence—was now reduced to nothing. They were in fact in the very teeth of starvation, when the manager, who knew and respected them in better days, took the little Barbara into his company.

At the period I commenced with, her slender earnings were the sole support of the family, including two younger sisters. I must throw a veil over some mortifying circumstances. Enough to say, that her Saturday's pittance was the only chance of a Sunday's (generally their only) meal of meat.

One thing I will only mention, that in some child's part, where in her theatrical character she was to sup off a roast fowl (O joy to Barbara!) some comic actor, who was for the night caterer for this dainty—in the misguided humour of his part, threw over the dish such a quantity of salt (O grief and pain of heart to Barbara!) that when she crammed a portion of it into her mouth, she was obliged sputteringly to reject it; and what with shame of her ill-acted part, and pain of real appetite at missing such a dainty, her little heart sobbed almost to breaking, till a flood of tears, which

the well-fed spectators were totally unable to comprehend, mercifully relieved her.

This was the little starved, meritorious maid, who stood before old
Ravenscroft, the treasurer, for her Saturday's payment.

Ravenscroft was a man, I have heard many old theatrical people beside
herself say, of all men least calculated for a treasurer. He had no head for
accounts, paid away at random, kept scarce any books, and summing up at
the week's end, if he found himself a pound or so deficient, blest himself
that it was no worse.

Now Barbara's weekly stipend was a bare half guinea.—By mistake he
popped into her hand—a whole one.

Barbara tripped away.

She was entirely unconscious at first of the mistake: God knows,
Ravenscroft would never have discovered it.

But when she got down to the first of these uncouth landing-places, she
became sensible of an unusual weight of metal pressing her little hand.

Now mark the dilemma.

She was by nature a good child. From her parents and those about her she
had imbibed no contrary influence. But then they had taught her nothing.
Poor men's smoky cabins are not always porticoes of moral philosophy.
This little maid had no instinct to evil, but then she might be said to have no
fixed principle. She had heard honesty commended, but never dreamed of
its application to herself. She thought of it as something which concerned
grown-up people, men and women. She had never known temptation, or
thought of preparing resistance against it.

Her first impulse was to go back to the old treasurer, and explain to him
his blunder. He was already so confused with age, besides a natural want of
punctuality, that she would have had some difficulty in making him understand it. She saw *that* in an instant. And then it was such a bit of money!
and then the image of a larger allowance of butcher's meat on their table
next day came across her, till her little eyes glistened, and her mouth
moistened. But then Mr Ravenscroft had always been so goodnatured, had
stood her friend behind the scenes, and even recommended her promotion
to some of her little parts. But again the old man was reputed to be worth a
world of money. He was supposed to have fifty pounds a year clear of the
theatre. And then came staring upon her the figures of her little stockingless
and shoeless sisters. And when she looked at her own neat white cotton
stockings, which her situation at the theatre had made it indispensable for
her mother to provide for her, with hard straining and pinching from the
family stock, and thought how glad she should be to cover their poor feet
with the same—and how then they could accompany her to rehearsals,
which they had hitherto been precluded from doing, by reason of their
unfashionable attire,—in these thoughts she reached the second landing-
place—the second, I mean, from the top—for there was still another left to
traverse.

Now virtue support Barbara!

And that never-failing friend did step in—for at that moment a strength not her own, I have heard her say, was revealed to her—a reason above reasoning—and without her own agency, as it seemed (for she never felt her feet to move), she found herself transported back to the individual desk she had just quitted, and her hand in the old hand of Ravenscroft, who in silence took back the refunded treasure, and who had been sitting (good man) insensible to the lapse of minutes, which to her were anxious ages; and from that moment a deep peace fell upon her heart, and she knew the quality of honesty.

A year or two's unrepining application to her profession brightened up the feet, and the prospects, of her little sisters, set the whole family upon their legs again, and released her from the difficulty of discussing moral dogmas upon a landing-place.

I have heard her say, that it was a surprise, not much short of mortification to her, to see the coolness with which the old man pocketed the difference, which had caused her such mortal throes.

This anecdote of herself I had in the year 1800, from the mouth of the late Mrs Crawford,[1] then sixty-seven years of age (she died soon after); and to her struggles upon this childish occasion I have sometimes ventured to think her indebted for that power of rending the heart in the representation of conflicting emotions, for which in after years she was considered as little inferior (if at all so in the part of Lady Randolph) even to Mrs Siddons.

---

[1] The maiden name of this lady was Street, which she changed by successive marriages for those of Dancer, Barry, and Crawford. She was Mrs. Crawford, a third time a widow, when I knew her.

HENRY DAVID THOREAU (1817–1862)

THE FALL OF A PINE,* JOURNAL, DEC. 30. TUESDAY . . .

THE FLIES NOW CRAWL FORTH FROM THE CREVICES ALL COVERED
WITH DUST, DREAMING OF SUMMER, WITHOUT LIFE OR ENERGY
ENOUGH TO CLEAN THEIR WINGS

This afternoon, being on Fair Haven Hill, I heard the sound of a saw, and soon after from the Cliff saw two men sawing down a noble pine beneath, about forty rods off. I resolved to watch it till it fell, the last of a dozen or more which were left when the forest was cut and for fifteen years have waved in solitary majesty over the sprout-land. I saw them like beavers or insects gnawing at the trunk of this noble tree, the diminutive manikins with their cross-cut saw which could scarcely span it. It towered up a hundred feet as I afterward found by measurement, one of the tallest probably in the township and straight as an arrow, but slanting a little toward the hillside, its top seen against the frozen river and the hills of Conantum. I watch closely to see when it begins to move. Now the sawers stop, and with an axe open it a little on the side toward which it leans, that it may break the faster. And now their saw goes again. Now surely it is going; it is inclined one quarter of the quadrant, and, breathless, I expect its crashing fall. But no, I was mistaken; it has not moved an inch; it stands at the same angle as at first. It is fifteen minutes yet to its fall. Still its branches wave in the wind, as if it were destined to stand for a century, and the wind soughs through its needles as of yore; it is still a forest tree, the most majestic tree that waves over Musketaquid. The silvery sheen of the sunlight is reflected from its needles; it still affords an inaccessible crotch for the squirrel's nest; not a lichen has forsaken its mast-like stem, its raking mast,—the hill is the hulk. Now, now's the moment! The manikins at its base are fleeing from their crime. They have dropped the guilty saw and axe. How slowly and majestically it starts! as if it were only swayed by a summer breeze, and would return without a sigh to its location in the air. And now it fans the hillside with its fall, and it lies down to its bed in the valley, from which it is never to rise, as softly as a feather, folding its green mantle about it like a warrior, as if, tired of standing, it embraced the earth with silent joy, returning its elements to the dust again. But hark! there you only saw, but did not hear. There now comes up a deafening crash to these rocks, advertising you that

* From *The Writings of Henry David Thoreau Journal*, edited by Bradford Torrey—III Sept. 16, 1851–April 30, 1852, Volume IX. Houghton Mifflin and Co., Boston and New York, 1906.

even trees do not die without a groan. It rushes to embrace the earth, and mingle its elements with the dust. And now all is still once more and forever, both to eye and ear.

I went down and measured it. It was about four feet in diameter where it was sawed, about one hundred feet long. Before I had reached it the axemen had already half divested it of its branches. Its gracefully spreading top was a perfect wreck on the hillside as if it had been made of glass, and the tender cones of one year's growth upon its summit appealed in vain and too late to the mercy of the chopper. Already he has measured it with his axe, and marked off the mill-logs it will make. And the space it occupied in upper air is vacant for the next two centuries. It is lumber. He has laid waste the air. When the fish hawk in the spring revisits the banks of the Musketaquid, he will circle in vain to find his accustomed perch, and the hen-hawk will mourn for the pines lofty enough to protect her brood. A plant which it has taken two centuries to perfect, rising by slow stages into the heavens, has this afternoon ceased to exist. Its sapling top had expanded to this January thaw as the forerunner of summers to come. Why does not the village bell sound a knell? I hear no knell tolled. I see no procession of mourners in the streets, or the woodland aisles. The squirrel has leaped to another tree; the hawk has circled further off, and has now settled upon a new eyrie, but the woodman is preparing [to] lay his axe at the root of that also.

MARK TWAIN (1835–1910)

HOW TO TELL A STORY*

I do not claim that I can tell a story as it ought to be told. I only claim to know how a story ought to be told, for I have been almost daily in the company of the most expert story-tellers for many years.

There are several kinds of stories, but only one difficult kind—the humorous. I will talk mainly about that one. The humorous story is American, the comic story is English, the witty story is French. The humorous story depends for its effect upon the *manner* of the telling; the comic story and the witty story upon the *matter*.

The humorous story may be spun out to great length, and may wander around as much as it pleases, and arrive nowhere in particular; but the comic and witty stories must be brief and end with a point. The humorous story bubbles gently along, the others burst.

The humorous story is strictly a work of art—high and delicate art—and only an artist can tell it; but no art is necessary in telling the comic and the witty story; anybody can do it. The art of telling a humorous story—understand, I mean by word of mouth, not print—was created in America, and has remained at home.

The humorous story is told gravely; the teller does his best to conceal the fact that he even dimly suspects that there is anything funny about it; but the teller of the comic story tells you beforehand that it is one of the funniest things he has ever heard, then tells it with eager delight, and is the first person to laugh when he gets through. And sometimes, if he has had good success, he is so glad and happy that he will repeat the "nub" of it and glance around from face to face, collecting applause, and then repeat it again. It is a pathetic thing to see.

Very often, of course, the rambling and disjointed humorous story finishes with a nub, point, snapper, or whatever you like to call it. Then the listener must be alert, for in many cases the teller will divert attention from that nub by dropping it in a carefully casual and indifferent way, with the pretense that he does not know it is a nub.

Artemus Ward used that trick a good deal; then when the belated audience presently caught the joke he would look up with innocent surprise, as if wondering what they had found to laugh at. Dan Setchell used it before him, Nye and Riley and others use it to-day.

---

* From *How to Tell a Story and Other Essays,* by Mark Twain. Reprinted by permission of Harper & Row, Publishers.

But the teller of the comic story does not slur the nub; he shouts it at you—every time. And when he prints it, in England, France, Germany, and Italy, he italicizes it, puts some whooping exclamation-points after it, and sometimes explains it in a parenthesis. All of which is very depressing, and makes one want to renounce joking and lead a better life.

Let me set down an instance of the comic method, using an anecdote which has been popular all over the world for twelve or fifteen hundred years. The teller tells it in this way:

THE WOUNDED SOLDIER

In the course of a certain battle a soldier whose leg has been shot off appealed to another soldier who was hurrying by to carry him to the rear, informing him at the same time of the loss which he had sustained; whereupon the generous son of Mars, shouldering the unfortunate, proceeded to carry out his desire. The bullets and cannon-balls were flying in all directions, and presently one of the latter took the wounded man's head off—without, however, his deliverer being aware of it. In no long time he was hailed by an officer, who said:

"Where are you going with that carcass?"

"To the rear, sir—he's lost his leg!"

"His leg, forsooth?" responded the astonished officer, "you mean his head, you booby."

Whereupon the soldier dispossessed himself of his burden, and stood looking down upon it in great perplexity. At length he said:

"It is true, sir, just as you have said." Then after a pause he added, "*But he* TOLD *me* IT WAS HIS LEG!!!!!"

Here the narrator bursts into explosion after explosion of thunderous horse-laughter, repeating that nub from time to time through his gaspings and shriekings and suffocatings.

It takes only a minute and a half to tell that in its comic-story form; and isn't worth the telling, after all. Put into the humorous-story form it takes ten minutes, and is about the funniest thing I have ever listened to—as James Whitcomb Riley tells it.

He tells it in the character of a dull-witted old farmer who has just heard it for the first time, thinks it is unspeakably funny, and is trying to repeat it to a neighbor. But he can't remember it; so he gets all mixed up and wanders helplessly round and round, putting in tedious details that don't belong in the tale and only retard it; taking them out conscientiously and putting in others that are just as useless; making minor mistakes now and then and stopping to correct them and explain how he came to make them; remembering things which he forgot to put in in their proper place and going back to put them in there; stopping his narrative a good while in order to try to recall the name of the soldier that was hurt, and finally remembering that the soldier's name was not mentioned, and remarking placidly that the name is of no real importance, anyway—better, of course, if one knew it, but not essential, after all—and so on, and so on, and so on.

The teller is innocent and happy and pleased with himself, and has to stop every little while to hold himself in and keep from laughing outright; and does hold in, but his body quakes in a jelly-like way with interior chuckles; and at the end of the ten minutes the audience have laughed until they are exhausted, and the tears are running down their faces.

The simplicity and innocence and sincerity and unconsciousness of the old farmer are perfectly simulated, and the result is a performance which is thoroughly charming and delicious. This is art—and fine and beautiful, and only a master can compass it; but a machine could tell the other story.

THE CAPTAIN'S STORY*

There was a good deal of pleasant gossip about old Captain "Hurricane" Jones, of the Pacific Ocean,—peace to his ashes! Two or three of us present had known him; I, particularly well, for I had made four sea-voyages with him. He was a very remarkable man. He was born on a ship; he picked up what little education he had among his shipmates; he began life in the forecastle, and climbed grade by grade to the captaincy. More than fifty years of his sixty-five were spent at sea. He had sailed all oceans, seen all lands, and borrowed a tint from all climates. When a man has been fifty years at sea, he necessarily knows nothing of men, nothing of the world but its surface, nothing of the world's thought, nothing of the world's learning but its A B C, and that blurred and distorted by the unfocused lenses of an untrained mind. Such a man is only a gray and bearded child. That is what old Hurricane Jones was,—simply an innocent, lovable old infant. When his spirit was in repose he was as sweet and gentle as a girl; when his wrath was up he was a hurricane that made his nickname seem tamely descriptive. He was formidable in a fight, for he was of powerful build and dauntless courage. He was frescoed from head to heel with pictures and mottoes tattooed in red and blue India ink. I was with him one voyage when he got his last vacant space tattooed; this vacant space was around his left ankle. During three days he stumped about the ship with his ankle bare and swollen, and this legend gleaming red and angry out from a clouding of India ink: "Virtue is its own R'd." (There was a lack of room.) He was deeply and sincerely pious, and swore like a fish-woman. He considered swearing blameless, because sailors would not understand an order un-

* From *How to Tell a Story and Other Essays*, by Mark Twain. Reprinted by permission of Harper & Row, Publishers.

illumined by it. He was a profound Biblical scholar,—that is, he thought he
was. He believed everything in the Bible, but he had his own methods of
arriving at his beliefs. He was of the "advanced" school of thinkers, and
applied natural laws to the interpretation of all miracles, somewhat on the
plan of the people who make the six days of creation six geological epochs,
and so forth. Without being aware of it, he was a rather severe satire on
modern scientific religionists. Such a man as I have been describing is
rabidly fond of disquisition and argument; one knows that without being
told it.

One trip the captain had a clergyman on board, but did not know he was
a clergyman, since the passenger list did not betray the fact. He took a great
liking to this Rev. Mr. Peters, and talked with him a great deal: told him
yarns, gave him toothsome scraps of personal history, and wove a glittering
streak of profanity through his garrulous fabric that was refreshing to a
spirit weary of the dull neutralities of undecorated speech. One day the
captain said, "Peters, do you ever read the Bible?"

"Well—yes."

"I judge it ain't often, by the way you say it. Now, you tackle it in dead
earnest once, and you'll find it'll pay. Don't you get discouraged, but hang
right on. First, you won't understand it; but by and by things will begin to
clear up, and then you wouldn't lay it down to eat."

"Yes, I have heard that said."

"And it's so, too. There ain't a book that begins with it. It lays over 'em
all, Peters. There's some pretty tough things in it,—there ain't any getting
around that,—but you stick to them and think them out, and when once
you get on the inside everything's plain as day."

"The miracles, too, captain?"

"Yes, sir! the miracles, too. Every one of them. Now, there's that business
with the prophets of Baal; like enough that stumped you?"

"Well, I don't know but—"

"Own up, now; it stumped you. Well, I don't wonder. You hadn't had
any experience in raveling such things out, and naturally it was too many
for you. Would you like to have me explain that thing to you, and show
you how to get at the meat of these matters?"

"Indeed, I would, captain, if you don't mind."

Then the captain proceeded as follows: "I'll do it with pleasure. First, you
see, I read and read, and thought and thought, till I got to understand what
sort of people they were in the old Bible times, and then after that it was
clear and easy. Now, this was the way I put it up, concerning Isaac* and the
prophets of Baal. There was some mighty sharp men amongst the public
characters of that old ancient day, and Isaac was one of them. Isaac had his
failings,—plenty of them, too; it ain't for me to apologize for Isaac; he
played on the prophets of Baal, and like enough he was justifiable, con-
sidering the odds that was against him. No, all I say is, 't wa'n't any miracle,
and that I'll show you so's't you can see it yourself.

"Well, times had been getting rougher and rougher for prophets,—that is, prophets of Isaac's denomination. There were four hundred and fifty prophets of Baal in the community, and only one Presbyterian; that is, if Isaac *was* a Presbyterian, which I reckon he was, but it don't say. Naturally, the prophets of Baal took all the trade. Isaac was pretty low-spirited, I reckon, but he was a good deal of a man, and no doubt he went a-prophesying around, letting on to be doing a land-office business, but 't wa'n't any use; he couldn't run any opposition to amount to anything. By and by things got desperate with him; he sets his head to work and thinks it all out, and then what does he do? Why, he begins to throw out hints that the other parties are this and that and t'other,—nothing very definite, may be, but just kind of undermining their reputation in a quiet way. This made talk, of course, and finally got to the king. The king asked Isaac what he meant by his talk. Says Isaac, 'Oh, nothing particular; only, can they pray down fire from heaven on an altar? It ain't much, maybe, your majesty, only can they *do* it? That's the idea.' So the king was a good deal disturbed, and he went to the prophets of Baal, and they said, pretty airy, that if he had an altar ready, *they* were ready; and they intimated he better get it insured, too.

"So next morning all the children of Israel and their parents and the other people gathered themselves together. Well, here was that great crowd of prophets of Baal packed together on one side, and Isaac walking up and down all alone on the other, putting up his job. When time was called, Isaac let on to be comfortable and indifferent; told the other team to take the first innings. So they went at it, the whole four hundred and fifty, praying around the altar, very hopeful, and doing their level best. They prayed an hour,—two hours,—three hours,—and so on, plumb till noon. It wa'n't any use; they hadn't took a trick. Of course they felt kind of ashamed before all those people, and well they might. Now, what would a magnanimous man do? Keep still, wouldn't he? Of course. What did Isaac do? He graveled the prophets of Baal every way he could think of. Says he, 'You don't speak up loud enough; your god's asleep, like enough, or maybe he's taking a walk; you want to holler, you know,'—or words to that effect; I don't recollect the exact language. Mind, I don't apologize for Isaac; he had his faults.

"Well, the prophets of Baal prayed along the best they knew how all the afternoon, and never raised a spark. At last, about sundown, they were all tuckered out, and they owned up and quit.

"What does Isaac do now? He steps up and says to some friends of his, there, 'Pour four barrels of water on the altar!' Everybody was astonished; for the other side had prayed at it dry, you know, and got whitewashed. They poured it on. Says he, 'Heave on four more barrels.' Then he says, 'Heave on four more.' Twelve barrels, you see, altogether. The water ran all over the altar, and all down the sides, and filled up a trench around it that would hold a couple of hogsheads,—'measures,' it says; I reckon it means about a hogshead. Some of the people were going to put on their things and go, for they allowed he was crazy. They didn't know Isaac. Isaac knelt

---

* This is the captain's own mistake.

down and began to pray: he strung along, and strung along, about the
heathen in distant lands, and about the sister churches, and about the state
and the country at large, and about those that's in authority in the government, and all the usual programme, you know, till everybody had got tired
and gone to thinking about something else, and then, all of a sudden, when
nobody was noticing, he outs with a match and rakes it on the under side of
his leg, and pff! up the whole thing blazes like a house afire! Twelve barrels
of *water? Petroleum*, sir, PETROLEUM! that's what it was!"

"Petroleum, captain?"

"Yes, sir; the country was full of it. Isaac knew all about that. You read
the Bible. Don't you worry about the tough places. They ain't tough when
you come to think them out and throw light on them. There ain't a thing in
the Bible but what is true; all you want is to go prayerfully to work and
cipher out how 't was done."

ROBERT BENCHLEY (1889–1945)

FALL IN!*

It may be because I do not run as fast, or as often, as I used to, but I seem to be way behind on my parades. It must be almost a year since I saw one, and then I was in it myself. I don't mean that I started out marching in it, but I got caught up in it and became confused and had to march several blocks before I could get out. It was horrible.

But in spite of the fact that I haven't been out watching them go by, I know that there have been parades, because I have heard the bands. Nothing makes a man feel older than to hear a band coming up the street and not to have the impulse to rush downstairs and out on to the sidewalk. I guess that this symptom of senility comes on after about twenty-five years of rushing downstairs and out on to the sidewalk only to find that it is the Reuben Lodge of the local Order of Reindeer marching by in brown sack suits and derby hats. After a while, this sort of disappointment makes a cynic of a person.

I think that not only was the last parade I ran after made up of men in brown sack suits and derby hats, but the *band* had on brown sack suits and derby hats as well! That definitely crushed me, and now I wouldn't even take my head out of my hand (where it is most of the time) to look out the window at the finest band music that could pass my house . . . Well, I might just *look*.

The American people, however, are still pretty unswerving in their allegiance to any organization which feels like walking up and down the street to music. And as for the police and city officials, they will go out of their way to help make it a gala occasion.

Our municipalities spend thousands of dollars and tear out great handfuls of hair trying to figure out some way of relieving traffic congestion. They arrest pedestrians who don't hold out their hands when making a left turn, and chase automobilists who go straight ahead when they should go around in a circle. They arrange red lights and green lights and orange-by-southeast and blue-by-southwest lights, with systems of bells which only a Swiss bellringer can understand, and all in an attempt to straighten out the tangle in our streets which modern automotive civilization has brought down upon us.

And yet, let the National Association of Cyclone Underwriters petition

* "Fall In!" by Robert Benchley, from *The Benchley Roundup:* A Selection by Nathaniel Benchley. Copyright 1932 by Robert C. Benchley. Reprinted by permission of Harper & Row, Publishers.

for a permit to march up the main street of the city and throw traffic into a five-hour chaos, and not only do they get their permit but the police get out their riot machine guns and help them to spread confusion. There is a flaw somewhere.

In the old days parading was more simple. If the morning paper announced that the circus or the local cavalry troop was to start their parade at the Fair Grounds at 10 A.M., the entire route, all the way along Main Street, through Elm, up Center and down Walnut, would be cleared by 9:45, and the sidewalks lined with expectant throngs hours before the marshals had arrived at the starting point.

"It said in the paper that they would pass by the City Hall about ten-twenty," was the whisper which ran along the curbing. "That would bring them along here about ten twenty-five." The smaller children would start crying shortly after ten-five, and the older ones would begin darting out into the street and tripping over their balloons by ten-fifteen. One would hardly have believed it possible for children to get so smeared with molasses and popcorn in fifteen minutes. In fact, one would hardly have believed it possible for there to have been so many children, and so unattractive.

"Listen, Norman, mamma'll take you right home this minute if you don't stand up here on the sidewalk. Come *here!*" But Norman, knowing that Mamma wouldn't give up her place on the curbing for anything short of a cash bonus, was never impressed. And neither was Evelyn, Harold, Stanley, or Ralph, Junior. They knew that until that parade had gone by Mamma was as good as planted right there, no matter what they did. So they did it.

Then, as the minutes dragged by and no parade appeared, the parents would join their children in little abortive excursions out into the middle of the street to look in the direction of the Fair Grounds. By this time all traffic had entirely disappeared from Main Street, which meant that Dakin's Fish Market was making its deliveries over another route and that it would be noon before McCann & Stodder got their groceries around.

Every now and again some of the older boys would yell, "Here they come!"—at which children would be yanked in from the gutters and hats would topple off as their owners tried to crane their necks to see. But these false alarms soon ceased to have their effect, especially as someone who lived across the street from the Fair Grounds telephoned down that the parade hadn't even started yet, owing to one of the horses refusing to get up or the man who carried the front end of the drum being unable to get up. When this word had been passed around, everyone sat down on the curbing and waited, the comical ones pretending to go to sleep, the more serious-minded ones finishing what they had brought along to eat.

But no one went home. And no traffic passed through the restricted area. It was probably eleven or eleven-thirty before the band was finally heard in the distance and the excitement, for the eighth consecutive time, reached a fever heat. But it made no difference to anyone how long they waited. In those days, *nothing* made any difference to anyone. And civilization is supposed to progress!

Today a parade is no joke. Next to a big fire, there is probably nothing worse than a parade for jamming things up. There are still a lot of people who will wait on a curbing for hours to see one, but there are also a lot of people who *can't* wait on a curbing for hours. Today there are trains to be caught and dates to be kept, and a man who has to catch a train or keep a date never seems to enter into the parade spirit—not when he is held by the necktie and prevented from crossing the street by a large cop while phalanx after phalanx of strangers wearing red sashes and carrying bamboo canes shuffle past. To have one section of a city's populace lining the streets cheering and another section held in check by the police, fuming, is a state of affairs which tends to civic unrest.

Then there is the question of saluting the colors. In the old days, two flags were enough for one parade, and it was a pleasure, not unaccompanied by a thrill, to doff the hat. But today, when every chapter of an organization representing every state in the Union carries the national banner, the thing loses a little of its impressiveness. It is better just to keep your hat in your hand and perhaps genuflect a little at each passing flag.

Of course, if you are in an office and have work to do, there is an almost irresistible urge to rush to the window and hang out whenever a band is heard. I used to do that myself until I got an office over a radio store. For the first two months, every time I heard the martial strains of *Under the Double Eagle* coming from the street below, I would drop everything and tear to the window. It took me two months to discover that the band music came from the loudspeaker projecting from the store below.

It is too bad that the parade as an institution has lost its glamour. If I were police commissioner I would issue parade permits only to those organizations which wore brilliant red coats or could promise to ride camels. Then they would be worth watching. If they could be induced both to wear red coats and ride camels, I might be induced to march with them.

For, in spite of my aversion to parades in general, I have always had a sneaking feeling that I could cut rather a dashing figure in one myself.

JAMES THURBER (1894–1961)

SNAPSHOT OF A DOG*

I ran across a dim photograph of him the other day, going through some old things. He's been dead twenty-five years. His name was Rex (my two brothers and I named him when we were in our early teens) and he was a bull terrier. "An American bull terrier," we used to say, proudly; none of your English bulls. He had one brindle eye that sometimes made him look like a clown and sometimes reminded you of a politician with derby hat and cigar. The rest of him was white except for a brindle saddle that always seemed to be slipping off and a brindle stocking on a hind leg. Nevertheless, there was a nobility about him. He was big and muscular and beautifully made. He never lost his dignity even when trying to accomplish the extravagant tasks my brothers and myself used to set for him. One of these was the bringing of a ten-foot wooden rail into the yard through the back gate. We would throw it out into the alley and tell him to go get it. Rex was as powerful as a wrestler, and there were not many things that he couldn't manage somehow to get hold of with his great jaws and lift or drag to wherever he wanted to put them, or wherever we wanted them put. He could catch the rail at the balance and lift it clear of the ground and trot with great confidence toward the gate. Of course, since the gate was only four feet wide or so, he couldn't bring the rail in broadside. He found that out when he got a few terrific jolts, but he wouldn't give up. He finally figured out how to do it, by dragging the rail, holding onto one end, growling. He got a great, wagging satisfaction out of his work. We used to bet kids who had never seen Rex in action that he could catch a baseball thrown as high as they could throw it. He almost never let us down. Rex could hold a baseball with ease in his mouth, in one cheek, as if it were a chew of tobacco.

He was a tremendous fighter, but he never started fights. I don't believe he liked to get into them, despite the fact that he came from a line of fighters. He never went for another dog's throat but for one of its ears (that teaches a dog a lesson), and he would get his grip, close his eyes, and hold on. He could hold on for hours. His longest fight lasted from dusk until almost pitch dark, one Sunday. It was fought in East Main Street in Columbus with a large, snarly nondescript that belonged to a big burly man. When Rex finally got his ear grip, the brief whirlwind of snarling turned to screeching. It was frightening to listen to and to watch. The burly man

* Copyright © 1945 James Thurber. From *The Thurber Carnival*, published by Harper & Row. Originally printed in *The New Yorker*.

boldly picked the dogs up somehow and began swinging them around his head, and finally let them fly like a hammer in a hammer throw, but although they landed ten feet away with a great plump, Rex still held on.

The two dogs eventually worked their way to the middle of the car tracks, and after a while two or three streetcars were held up by the fight. A motorman tried to pry Rex's jaws open with a switch rod; somebody lighted a fire and made a torch of a stick and held that to Rex's tail, but he paid no attention. In the end, all the residents and storekeepers in the neighborhood were on hand, shouting this, suggesting that. Rex's joy of battle, when battle was joined, was almost tranquil. He had a kind of pleasant expression during fights, not a vicious one, his eyes closed in what would have seemed to be sleep had it not been for the turmoil of the struggle. The Oak Street Fire Department finally had to be sent for—I don't know why nobody thought of it sooner. Five or six pieces of apparatus arrived, followed by a battalion chief. A hose was attached and a powerful stream of water was turned on the dogs. Rex held on for several moments more while the torrent buffeted him about like a log in a freshet. He was a hundred yards away from where the fight started when he finally let go.

The story of that Homeric fight got all around town, and some of our relatives looked upon the incident as a blot on the family name. They insisted that we get rid of Rex, but we were very happy with him, and nobody could have made us give him up. We would have left town with him first, along any road there was to go. It would have been different, perhaps, if he'd ever started fights, or looked for trouble. But he had a gentle disposition. He never bit a person in the ten strenuous years that he lived, nor ever growled at anyone except prowlers. He killed cats, that is true, but quickly and neatly and without especial malice, the way men kill certain animals. It was the only thing he did that we could never cure him of doing. He never killed, or even chased, a squirrel. I don't know why. He had his own philosophy about such things. He never ran barking after wagons or automobiles. He didn't seem to see the idea in pursuing something you couldn't catch, or something you couldn't do anything with, even if you did catch it. A wagon was one of the things he couldn't tug along with his mighty jaws, and he knew it. Wagons, therefore, were not a part of his world.

Swimming was his favorite recreation. The first time he ever saw a body of water (Alum Creek), he trotted nervously along the steep bank for a while, fell to barking wildly, and finally plunged in from a height of eight feet or more. I shall always remember that shining, virgin dive. Then he swam upstream and back just for the pleasure of it, like a man. It was fun to see him battle upstream against a stiff current, struggling and growling every foot of the way. He had as much fun in the water as any person I have known. You didn't have to throw a stick in the water to get him to go in. Of course, he would bring back a stick to you if you did throw one in. He would even have brought back a piano if you had thrown one in.

That reminds me of the night, way after midnight, when he went a-roving in the light of the moon and brought back a small chest of drawers that he found somewhere—how far from the house nobody ever knew; since it was Rex, it could easily have been half a mile. There were no drawers in the chest when he got it home, and it wasn't a good one—he hadn't taken it out of anybody's house; it was just an old cheap piece that somebody had abandoned on a trash heap. Still, it was something he wanted, probably because it presented a nice problem in transportation. It tested his mettle. We first knew about his achievement when, deep in the night, we heard him trying to get the chest up onto the porch. It sounded as if two or three people were trying to tear the house down. We came downstairs and turned on the porch light. Rex was on the top step trying to pull the thing up, but it had caught somehow and he was just holding his own. I suppose he would have held his own till dawn if we hadn't helped him. The next day we carted the chest miles away and threw it out. If we had thrown it out in a nearby alley, he would have brought it home again, as a small token of his integrity in such matters. After all, he had been taught to carry heavy wooden objects about, and he was proud of his prowess.

I am glad Rex never saw a trained police dog jump. He was just an amateur jumper himself, but the most daring and tenacious I have ever seen. He would take on any fence we pointed out to him. Six feet was easy for him, and he could do eight by making a tremendous leap and hauling himself over finally by his paws, grunting and straining; but he lived and died without knowing that twelve- and sixteen-foot walls were too much for him. Frequently, after letting him try to go over one for a while, we would have to carry him home. He would never have given up trying.

There was in his world no such thing as the impossible. Even death couldn't beat him down. He died, it is true, but only, as one of his admirers said, after "straight-arming the death angel" for more than an hour. Late one afternoon he wandered home, too slowly and too uncertainly to be the Rex that had trotted briskly homeward up our avenue for ten years. I think we all knew when he came through the gate that he was dying. He had apparently taken a terrible beating, probably from the owner of some dog that he had got into a fight with. His head and body were scarred. His heavy collar with the teeth marks of many a battle on it was awry; some of the big brass studs in it were sprung loose from the leather. He licked at our hands and, staggering, fell, but got up again. We could see that he was looking for someone. One of his three masters was not home. He did not get home for an hour. During that hour the bull terrier fought against death as he had fought against the cold, strong current of Alum Creek, as he had fought to climb twelve-foot walls. When the person he was waiting for did come through the gate, whistling, ceasing to whistle, Rex walked a few wabbly paces toward him, touched his hand with his muzzle, and fell down again. This time he didn't get up.

E. B. WHITE (1899–)

QUO VADIMUS?*

A GLIMPSE INTO THE FUTURE—YOU KNOW, LIKE
IN THE SUNDAY TIMES MAGAZINE

A man approaching me in East Thirty-fourth Street, in the thick of noon, had so queer a look in his eye, such a fudgy and fearful expression, I stopped him.

"Quo vadis?" I asked.

"You mean me?" he said, sheepishly.

"Yes, sure. Quo vadis?" I repeated. "Where the hell are you going?"

"I won't tell you, because you wouldn't understand," he replied.

"Well then," I said, "I'll put it this way: quo vadimus? Where are either of us going?"

He seemed stunned. A woman, shopping, bumped lightly against him. At length he spoke, in a clear, low, frightened voice.

"I'll tell you where I'm going. I'm on my way to the Crowbar Building, Forty-first and Park, in Pershing Square, named after General Pershing in the Grand Central zone, zone as in Zonite, because I forgot to tell Miss Cortwright to leave a note for Mr. Josefson when he comes in, telling him he should tell the engraver to vignette the halftone on page forty-three of the salesmen's instruction book that Irwain, Weasey, Weasey & Button are getting out for the Fretherby-Quigley Company, which is to go to all their salesmen on the road."

"What do the salesmen sell?" I said, quietly.

"They sell a new kind of shorthand course, called the Quigley Method of Intensive Speedwriting."

"Very good," I said. "That's just the kind of errand I imagined you to be on. As I understand it, recapitulating, you are on your way to the Crowbar Building, Forty-first and Park, in Pershing Square named after General Pershing, hero of the song, 'Many a cootie came over from France in General Pershing's underpants,' in the Grand Central zone, zone as in Zonite, because you forgot to tell Miss Cortwright to leave a note for Mr. Josefson when he comes in, telling him he should tell the engraver to vignette the halftone on page forty-three of a booklet that Irwain, Weasey, Weasey & Button are getting out for the Fretherby-Quigley Company,

* "Quo Vadimus?" from *Quo Vadimus?* by E. B. White. Copyright 1930, 1958 by E. B. White. Originally appeared in the *New Yorker*, and reprinted by permission of Harper & Row, Publishers.

instructing their salesmen how to approach people to sell the Quigley Method of Intensive Speedwriting, which in turn will enable girls like Miss Cortwright to take Mr. Josefson's dictation when he has to send a memo to the engraver telling him not to forget to vignette a halftone in a booklet telling salesmen how to sell shorthand courses. Is that correct?

"That's where I'm going," said the man.

"Well, aren't you ashamed of yourself!" I cried.

"I don't know whether I am or not," he said, with a slight touch of indignation.

"Listen, my friend," I went on, fixing him with my eye, "all you really want is a decent meal when it comes mealtime, isn't it?"

"And a warm place to sleep when it comes night," he added quickly, almost eagerly.

"Exactly, and a warm place to sleep when it comes night. All right then, don't you think that you, who just want a decent meal when it comes mealtime, and a warm place to sleep when it comes night—don't you think you are pretty far from the main issue if you're on your way to tell a Miss Cortwright to leave a note for a Mr. Josefson telling him to . . ."

He motioned me with his hand to stop. "You needn't go on. Yes, I'm far from the issue, sir," he said. "But I do not know what to do. It must be something about the age—what do they call it, the 'machine' age? This Miss Cortwright . . . I don't know. This Josefson . . . I don't know. Nice people, I suppose. It is all so complex. I just drifted into it."

"Exactly," I said. "And it's getting worse, mind you. I predict a bright future for complexity in this country. Did it ever occur to you that there's no limit to how complicated things can get, on account of one thing always leading to another? Did you ever stop to consider how the Cortwrights lead to the Josefsons, and how the Josefsons lead to the engravers? Paths of glory, leading to the engravers, my man. Did you ever stop to think what might happen if people by accident forgot where the whole thing started?"

The man shook his head, very slightly. His eyes were bright but out of focus. I went on, sternly.

"Only the other evening," I said, "I stopped a man on Broadway who had in his face the same look that I detected in *your* face a moment ago. To him, too, I said: 'Quo vadis?' And he, too, told me a story much like yours. He told me, my friend, that he was on his way to see a Mr. Fitch in the Pari-Mutuel Building, who wanted to get permission to make a talking picture of an airplane towing a glider in which was seated a man listening to a radio which was receiving a dialogue between two men named Amos and Andy who were talking together in order to advertise a toothpaste and the name of the toothpaste was . . ."

"Pepsodent," put in my man.

"Yes, Pepsodent. And that man—all he really wanted, when you came right down to it, was a decent meal when it came mealtime."

"And a warm place to sleep when it came night," added my friend, hurriedly.

"Exactly."

There was a pause in our conversation at this point. Cars passed back and forth in the street. Women shoppers brushed lightly against us—women who were on their way to buy fringes for lampshades, women who were on their way to buy printed silk, women who were on their way to buy the hooks that hold the rods that hold the curtains. Suddenly my friend addressed me.

"Now *you* tell *me* where *you're* going!" he said, sharply.

"Ha, not on your life—you don't catch me that way," I cried. "I'm not telling you where I'm going."

"I suppose you're going fishing," said the man, smirking.

"Smirk again and I'll smack you," I said. "I always smack smirkers."

He smirked. I smacked him.

"Now ask me where I'm going!" I said, holding him by the arm.

"I bet I can guess where you're going. I bet you're a writer, on his way to write something. I know your type. You're going to write a story about 'complexity'—about meeting a man in East Thirty-fourth Street who was on his way to the Crowbar Building in Pershing Square, named after General Pershing in the Grand Central zone, zone as in Zonite, because he forgot to tell Miss Cortwright to leave a note for Mr. Josefson to tell the engraver to vignette the half-tone . . ."

"Don't repeat it," I said, breaking down. "That's exactly where I'm going."

". . . so a person like Miss Cortwright will have something to read, and not understand, when she isn't busy with dictation," he said, finishing up.

"That's it."

"And all you want is a decent meal when it comes mealtime, isn't it?" asked my friend.

"And a warm place to sleep when it comes night," I added quickly, almost eagerly.

"Sure, I know," he said. "Well, vale!"

"Vale, kid!" I replied. And we continued on our lonely and imponderable ways.

ART BUCHWALD (1925-   )

DON'T BE A PAL TO YOUR SON*

PARIS.

There are many different attitudes on how to treat American youth. One we heard comes from Al Capp, the cartoonist father of three, who told us:

"When I was six years old my parents put me in a clean shirt, pointed out the direction of school, and told me not to come back for eight years. They never expected to see my teachers, and the teachers never expected to see my parents. Each one had a function. My parents were supposed to feed and clothe me; my teacher was supposed to teach me how to read and write. Neither group had any effect on the other. The only thing my parents knew about my teacher was that 'she was always picking on me.' Every child's teacher was 'always picking on him.'

"My teachers graded me on arithmetic, English, history, and geography. Since I failed all of them, it was obvious I was going to be a cartoonist. But we were never graded for adjustment, emotional stability, or 'Does he get along with other children?' My parents knew I got along with other children just by virtue of the fact I came home every afternoon with a bloody nose or a black eye.

*   *   *

"In those days we didn't worry about emotional stability. All children were emotionally unstable. They were full of hatreds and frustrations. Wouldn't you be if you were half the size of the rest of the world and didn't have a nickel to your name?

"In my day it wasn't a question of which was the best school to send a kid to, it was which was the nearest one. All schools were good, just as all churches were good, and all teachers were good.

"We never heard of words like adjustment, environment, rejection, and community of children. Sure we were unloved. We took it for granted that it was natural for everyone to hate us. No one paid any attention to us. And we, in turn, didn't pick up our father's shotgun and wipe out the whole family.

"The child today is wise to the adult jargon, and as soon as he thinks his parents are paying any attention to him the monster swells up in him. The child who is held in proper contempt by his family is grateful for anything he gets. All he needs is food and shelter. If he's loved, he becomes drunk with power, flexes his muscles, and takes over.

---

* Reprinted by permission of the author.

314

"Those parents who concern themselves with their children's problems are crazy. The problems of a nine-year-old kid cannot be solved in any way except by becoming ten. The problems of a 16-year-old will only be solved by turning 17."

Mr. Capp believes that the emphasis on teen-agers has been damaging. "Teen-agers are repulsive to everybody except each other. We all know that children pass through various stages of insanity, so why try to understand them?"

"But aren't teen-agers unhappy?"

"Sure they are. Let them stay that way. We've put too much emphasis on security. The teen-agers today have been told they have rights. Why should they have rights?

"In Europe kids have no rights. If they ever asked for any they'd get belted by their fathers. But in America, things have been switched around. Children used to try to please their parents—now the parents try to please the children.

*   *   *

"It is my humble belief that we should give American children something they desperately need and crave for—brutality. We must make them feel neglected, insecure, unwanted, and unloved. In return, we'll get courtesy, obedience, good scholastic records, and fewer parents will be killed. They'll be so eager to be wanted that they'll do everything in the world to please us."

"Is there anything else?"

"Yes, don't be a pal to your son. Be his father. What child needs a 40-year-old man for a friend? And forget about teaching him facts of life. There is nothing that a boy could discuss with his father that he couldn't discuss much more openly with his guttersnipe friends.

"Keep in mind we owe children nothing. We'll supply them food, shelter, and clothing only because we're gambling that some day these subhumans will turn into civilized beings and, possibly, make reasonable, honest citizens."

✒ Index of Authors

DATE DUE

OCT 7 '69			

GAYLORD   PRINTED IN U.S.A.